South End Shout

BOSTON'S FORGOTTEN MUSIC SCENE IN THE JAZZ AGE

By Roger House

With Illustrations by James Fox

LEVER PRESS

Lever Press (leverpress.org) is a publisher of pathbreaking scholarship. Supported by a consortium of higher education institutions focused on, and renowned for, excellence in both research and teaching, our press is grounded on three essential commitments: to be a digitally native press, to be a peer-reviewed, open access press that charges no fees to either authors or their institutions, and to be a press aligned with the liberal arts ethos.

The complete manuscript of this work was subjected to a closed ("double-blind") review process. For more information, please see our Peer Review Commitments and Guidelines at https://www.leverpress.org/peerreview

DOI: https://doi.org/10.3998/mpub.12735924
Print ISBN: 978-1-64315-047-5
Open access ISBN: 978-1-64315-048-2

Library of Congress Control Number: 2022947915

Published in the United States of America by Lever Press, in partnership with Michigan Publishing.

In Memory of
James Green & Gerald Gill
Historians, Mentors, Friends

"Jazz isn't music merely; it is a spirit that can express itself in almost anything. The true spirit of jazz is a joyous revolt from convention, custom, authority, boredom, even sorrow—from everything that would confine the soul of man and hinder its riding free on the air."

—Joel A. Rogers, Jazz at Home

Contents

Member Institution Acknowledgments

Lever Press is a joint venture. This work was made possible by the generous support of Lever Press member libraries from the following institutions:

Amherst College
Berea College
Bowdoin College
Carleton College
Central Washington University
Claremont Graduate University
Claremont McKenna College
Clark Atlanta University
College of Saint Benedict & Saint John's University
The College of Wooster
Davidson College
Denison University
DePauw University
Grinnell College
Hamilton College
Harvey Mudd College
Hollins University
Iowa State University
Keck Graduate Institute
Knox College
Lafayette College
Macalester College
Middlebury College
Morehouse College
Norwich University
Penn State University
Pitzer College
Pomona College
Randolph-Macon College
Rollins College
Santa Clara University
Scripps College
Skidmore College
Smith College
Spelman College
Susquehanna University

Swarthmore College
Trinity University
UCLA Library
Union College
University of Idaho
University of Northern Colorado
University of Puget Sound
University of San Francisco
University of Vermont
Ursinus College
Vassar College
Washington and Lee University
Whitman College
Whittier College
Whitworth University
Willamette University
Williams College

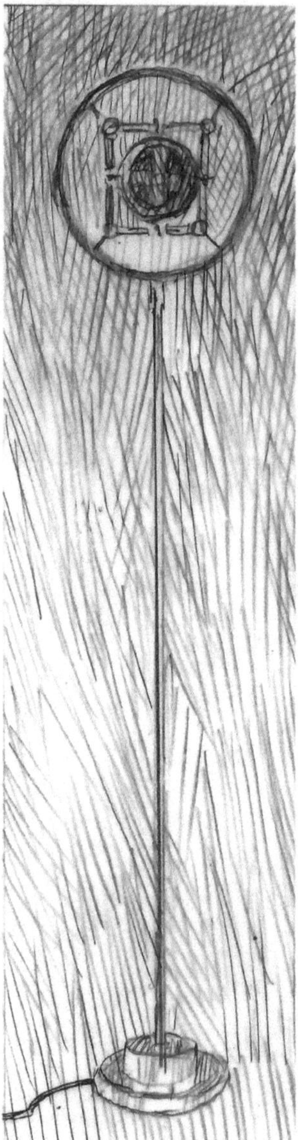

The microphone amplified the voices of South End musicians in the dance halls and ballrooms.

REDISCOVERING A LOST JAZZ SCENE

This book is the story of a forgotten jazz scene that emerged in Boston after the First World War. It was incubated in the city's small Black sector of Frederick Douglass Square, a commercial district located at the intersection of Tremont and Northampton streets. Here, music was created and nurtured in homes, fraternal lodges, supper clubs, dance halls, theaters, and record shops. Among the forms were solo piano, syncopated combos, marching bands, orchestras for society dances, and vinyl recordings of bands near and far. It was supported by a robust union in the social clubs of migrant populations from New York, the South, the West Indies, the Cape Verde Islands, and Canada. Audiences included families with musical traditions, house rent parties, high school bands, music conservatory students, soldiers on leave as well as veterans, Pullman porters on layover, and musicians visiting from out of town. The music entertainment drew a small number of white club owners, musicians, and youths curious about authentic jazz music. Frederick Douglass Square, situated at the crossroads of the South End and Lower Roxbury, was a reference point for the anxieties of music, race, and power associated with jazz culture in Boston.

During the Second World War, the scene expanded from the Tremont Street locus to the stem of Massachusetts Avenue—a corridor to nightclubs, theaters, dance and concert halls, and after-hours joints that supported jazz culture. The music could be heard blaring from establishments at the intersections of Huntington Avenue, Columbus Avenue, and Tremont Street. During the 1940s, jazz musicians generated the shout of big band swing, small combo bebop, and novelty rhythm and blues in rooms large and small. Overall, Boston had an insignificant role in the production of jazz culture; it lacked the nightclub and recording studio infrastructure of Chicago, it lacked the musical theater and radio industry of New York, and it lacked the newsreel and feature film outlet of Los Angeles. However, the idea that jazz culture was restricted to an arch of cities frequented by itinerant bands—New Orleans, Chicago, and New York—has been debunked by a growing body of scholarship on American cultural history. As Detroit jazz historian Lars Bjorn wrote, "It is now recognized that jazz-like music developed simultaneously in many US cities between 1900 and 1920."[1]

The story of the South End jazz scene had been lost in Boston's cultural history. Of course, the city's major contribution was as a birthplace for some key musicians who established their legacies elsewhere—the most talented made careers with orchestras in those more lucrative scenes. Nevertheless, the neighborhoods did offer features that made the city attractive to jazz musicians and drew many people in to study and perform. In recent decades, scholars have probed neglected urban jazz sites in an attempt to recover lost voices in the history. They have examined the modest community scenes for evidence of a deeper understanding of the intersections of African American creativity and influence in popular and theatrical music of the region. This work seeks to add to the program of "correctionist" scholarship in jazz culture history.

It stands on the shoulders of pioneer cultural studies such as "Jazz: A History of the New York Scene," published in 1962 by Sam Charters and Leonard Kunstadt. The research opened a line of scholarly inquiry on the role of jazz in New York City that continues in the recent findings of Travis Jackson. His insights have been influential in conceptualizing ways to define an early jazz scene in Boston. For example, his work explored the role of location in the practice, experimentation, and promotion of music with essential elements such as "groups of participants (musicians, audiences, teachers, venue owners, managers, recording industry personnel, critics, and historians), as well as educational institutions, performance venues, record labels, and publications, which collaborate to present, develop, and comment upon musical events in both recorded and live forms."[2] Michael Heller also shed light on the importance of autonomous spaces for Black music production. His work on loft jazz examined the creative process in Chicago, Pittsburgh, and New York. In researching New York loft jazz of the 1970s, he described the tradition of earlier jazz enclaves in Harlem, noting spaces vital to jazz experimentation during the interwar years: the Clef Club, tenement rent parties, and apartments of musicians where players gathered to practice.[3]

The work also considers the theories over the extent of preservation of West African traditional music principles in the arts of Black Americans. Such observations have been made by Robert Farris Thompson, Samuel Floyd, and Portia Maultsby, among others. Burton Peretti, who chronicled the emergence of jazz scenes in Chicago, Pittsburgh, New York, and other urban communities, argued that the "flowering of jazz in the new Black neighborhoods was a rare triumph of culture and spirit over uncertainty and adversity."[4]

Court Carney examined the tensions of culture, race, and jazz in the interwar decades. He surveyed the symbolism of jazz to a white society anxious over the transformational cycles of industrialization and urbanization. In this climate, race was the most ardent and controversial factor in the acknowledgement of jazz origins and authentic development. Carney asserted that "Issues of race and racism framed much of the debate concerning jazz music as many observers warned of the social implications of accepting cultural forms into white American society."[5]

Such tensions have punctuated the writings on jazz since the earliest days, and the perceptions of Boston writers are little different. The body of work on Boston's jazz history has suffered from a vested interest in elevating the roles of white musicians, establishments, and audiences. In this pursuit, much of the work has spotlighted the activities of the 1950s and later years when the South End jazz scene was in decline as an asset for the Black community. The bias of earlier considerations had the effect of skewing the understanding of Boston's cultural history. The works of "revisionist" white writers spread through their dominant access to mainstream instruments of critical and educative media: newspaper reviews, radio shows, books, and courses at schools of music. Such interpretations have shaped the local culture and negated opposing arguments made by credible authorities in the 1960s, like Gunther Schuller, president of New England Conservatory and cofounder of the Modern Jazz Society. He argued on behalf of recognizing the African American tradition of jazz as both the foundation for modern popular music and as an American "classical" music.

Yet the old views continue to drive the thinking of writers and students today. In such narratives, the Black community role is a backdrop for its service to white stakeholders: musicians were valued for their usefulness as sources of cheap labor, mentors to whites, and entertainers to white audiences. An undue level of attention has been given to white jazz players and institutions that took advantage of the exclusions of race—club owners, booking agents, music schools, youthful voyeurs, and festival organizers. Such bias even found its way into official City Hall records such as the Boston Landmarks Commission's justifications for historical preservation. The 1997 application for the site of Connolly's Bar, once located at 1184 Tremont Street in Lower Roxbury, is one example. This club was opened by Jim Connolly in the 1950s; he and his brother, Stephen, were former owners of the popular Savoy Café in the South End. They sold the Savoy in 1955 and opened separate nightclubs. The report, in describing the historical context and significance of Connolly's Bar, put forward a white-centric narrative.

"Although New Englanders were formally introduced to the sounds of jazz in 1924 at Boston University's Jazz Symposium, this region did not display a true appreciation for this musical genre until the 1940s," the report argues. "Boston's postwar jazz scene is credited to both the musical sensibilities of returning veterans and the avant-garde curriculum by Berklee School of Music." It continues: "Boston's jazz culture crested in the 1950s. At its height, patrons had their pick of venues: Symphony Hall's 'Jazz at the Philharmonic' series; the Metropolitan (now Wang) Theater's big band extravaganzas; the annual 'Globe Jazz Festival' at the Hynes Auditorium; not to mention George Wein's jazz weekend at Fenway Park. The city also boasted more than a dozen jazz clubs."[6]

This description is a snapshot of how cultural gatekeepers have diminished the role of the Black community in fostering a jazz heritage and legacy. The field of study of urban jazz scenes has emerged in part to restore the authority of African American innovation in the formation of the musical culture of modern society. For example, Travis Jackson writes that musicians active in the urban scenes were "involved not only in the exploration of a style, but also in the active defining of that style's parameters through relations with other music, musicians, and audiences." He explains how musicians created pathways to establishing authentic styles of jazz: "The songs, structures, and ways of manipulating them in performance became a mechanism for regulation of group identity and collective memory."[7]

I first began to hear stories of an earlier Boston jazz scene when I lived in Providence, Rhode Island, in the 1980s. I followed Eric Jackson's jazz show, "Eric in the Evening," broadcast on WGBH-FM in Boston. Even more knowledgeable of the past was his father, Sam Jackson, who was known as "Mr. Sam" when he hosted a jazz radio show in Providence in the 1940s. The elder Jackson told colorful stories about the jazz musicians of earlier decades on those occasions when he joined his son in the studio. My curiosity about the music history of the South End and Lower Roxbury deepened in the 1990s when I moved from Providence to Boston to attend graduate school. Back then, the neighborhood was mostly rundown with pockets of gentrification. This was a time when a new population of affluent whites—and a notable gay enclave—fancied themselves as "urban pioneers." They leveraged advantages of race, employment, and finances to qualify for mortgage loans on old rental properties in the district.

By then, only a few relics from the heydays, such as Wally's and Slade's, were still in operation, albeit largely divorced from historical context. Wally's, for instance, was in transition from its roots in the Black community—the old patrons would frequent the club in the afternoon to listen to the jukebox, then give way to white patrons in the evening. This crossover audience commanded attention with spending power and social privilege. Such was the ebb and flow in the 1990s, after which I stopped going on a regular basis. I would return periodically in the 2000s to enjoy the jazz revival campaign of impresario Darryl Settles, a former executive at the Digital Equipment Company who decided to invest in the neighborhood. In 1990, he bought the landmark soul food restaurant Bob the Chef located at Columbus Avenue and Northampton Street. He kept the original menu, changed the name to Bob's Southern Bistro, and introduced live jazz acts. Some years later, he sold the bistro and cofounded the Beehive as a South End restaurant with live jazz for an older white crowd. Settles sold his stake in the Beehive to partners and retook control of his bistro, naming it Darryl's Corner Bar and Kitchen. In addition, he spearheaded the annual Beantown Jazz Festival in 2007, which produced free concerts in the fall to broad acclaim. The event, featuring jazz, blues, and funk acts, drew thousands to the streets and an infusion of cash to the small businesses of the disinvested neighborhood, also becoming a showcase for students at the nearby Berklee College of Music. The African American entrepreneur ultimately turned over control of the event to the college as renovations in the neighborhood made street festivals difficult. Berklee ended the festival in

2019, when the college partnered with the Boston Art and Music Soul Festival (BAMS) to host jazz concerts in Franklin Park.[8]

I began to ponder the music scene of a bygone era. After all, jazz culture has been an instrument for Black Americans to intersect with Anglo-American culture and the cultures of Europe and the Pan-African world. I began to consider questions that would shed light on the importance of this cultural history to the story of jazz and Boston: What were the prominent bands and musicians? How did they nurture a jazz culture in a city known for its sometimes-hostile traditionalism? What was the origin of the Black commercial district of Frederick Douglass Square? How did a fledgling music scene flourish in that area? How did the presence of a strong union chapter for Black musicians enable the rising jazz culture? How did the music culture of the South End hub overlap with the cultural hub of downtown Boston? How did the music of the Harlem stage radiate into the culture of the South End?

In deciding on a title, I thought it appropriate to apply the concept of the ensemble "shout" to the forgotten neighborhood music scene. It refers to the African American style of oral/aural expression in blues and jazz music. One type of shout, for instance, was the way that singers vocalized with the loudness and intensity to be heard over the blare of the orchestra. One of the best-known "shouters" was Jimmy Rushing with the Kansas-territory bands of Walter Page, Bennie Moten, and Count Basie. His bluesy style can be heard on tracks like "Going to Chicago," "Sent for You Yesterday," and "Boogie Woogie." Another type of shout was the convergence of instruments to make a collective statement in one big voice—the definitive ensemble crescendo. Some examples are the Count Basie Orchestra's recordings of "Kansas City Shout" and "I'm Shouting Again."[9] Pianist Teddy Wilson commended the Basie band style as an ensemble that "attacks as one man and starts to swing from the very first note."[10]

Trying to unearth the evidence of the scene in 1920s Boston was a challenge indeed—all the residents and musicians were gone and memories eroded. To reconstruct the era meant sifting through the fragmentary evidence available in primary sources: newspaper articles and advertisements in the *Boston Globe* and Black-owned *Boston Guardian*, transcripts of oral histories conducted with aging musicians and residents, personal accounts of musicians and observers, reports from city agencies like the Landmarks Commission, and recorded songs and film shorts of the society bands during the interwar years. Materials were found on YouTube, uploaded by enthusiasts with a desire to share precious cultural documents. The URLs to a few multimedia primary sources are included in chapter notes; I hope that they will be available for a while.

One of the most valuable publications for gleaning the sentiments of residents was *Lower Roxbury: A Community of Treasures in the City of Boston* by historians Ronald Bailey, Robert Hayden, and Diane Turner. The scholars conducted interviews with elderly residents including a few with memories of the community during the interwar period. This precious booklet is out of print these days, but the transcripts are archived in the Lower Roxbury Black History Project at Northeastern University. Another valuable trove for ascertaining the impressions of musicians was the Oral History Project of Berklee College, which collected the memories of players active in Boston between the 1930s and 1980s. While this project shows bias toward the experiences of white musicians since the 1950s, it also includes a few people with recollections of the earlier decades.

In addition, the Boston Musicians' Association Local 9-535 had conducted interviews with early members of the union and its segregated chapters. Excerpts from some of these recollections were posted on the union website; more importantly, president Pat Hollenbeck was generous enough to provide me with the transcripts of interviews with two of the pioneer members of Local 535, the chapter for Black musicians. Supplementing these interviews with local figures were the conversations between Stanley Dance and members of the Duke Ellington Orchestra as well as other big bands, published in *The World of Duke Ellington* and *The World of Swing: An Oral History of Big Band Jazz*. Finally, several biographical works on musicians active in the South End have provided useful information, such as the chapter on Benny Waters in *Voices of the Jazz Age* by Chip Deffaa and *Rabbit's Blues: The Life and Music of Johnny Hodges* by Con Chapman. Admittedly, the evidence amassed to rediscover a forgotten jazz scene is primarily of a circumstantial and qualitative nature. The accounts include the bias of their writers and the nostalgia of residents; however, the alternative would have been to extend a research process that had already gone on for too long and, in so doing, stifle the dissemination of known information that points to a correction in historical understanding.

The primary research has been placed in the context of secondary sources on Boston cultural history. These publications include the reviews of columnist George Frazier in the *Boston Herald*; *Boston Boy: Growing Up with Jazz and Other Rebellious Passion* by Nat Hentoff; *Myself Among Others: A Life in Music* by George Wein and Nate Chinen; *Boston's Blues* by Art Simas; *Where Hash Rules: The Love Story of Charlie's Sandwich Shoppe in Boston* by G.A. Cuddy; and *The Boston Jazz Chronicles: Faces, Places, and Nightlife 1937-1962* by Richard Vacca. As noted, these works tend to spotlight the interests of white observers to the exclusion of others. In a few instances, writers have taken liberties with the reputations of Black musicians prominent in the South End scene. For example, the historian Eric Hobsbawn, a noted British communist and human rights advocate, assumed the identity of trumpeter Frankie Newton to serve as an interpreter of jazz culture to white youths. Hobsbawn used the name of the jazzman for bylines in the *Nation* and the *New Statesman* seemingly out of fondness.[11]

Finally, I thought it prudent to portray the jazz scene in an unorthodox way. The materials relied on by historians to depict the past—photographs, maps, documents—were in this case either unavailable, peripheral to the subject, or unworthy of reproduction. That being the case, I decided to use an alternative method inspired by an exhibit on art deco design at the Cooper Hewitt Smithsonian Design Museum, *The Jazz Age: American Style in the 1920s*. I also considered the way illustrations were used in the novels of John Dos Passos, the social realist writer of the post-World War I "Lost Generation." His USA Trilogy, a collection of three novels exploring American society during the interwar years, incorporates the drawings of illustrator Reginald Marsh.

I approached an old friend and architectural illustrator, James Fox of Montclair, New Jersey, to create a series of drawings that render the Boston jazz scene. He and I had shared an enjoyment of jazz during our residence in Providence's east side in the early 1980s. I was confident that this highly skilled draftsman could capture the images of sound entertainment in 1920s Boston. The illustrations reference musicians, buildings, and technology for the presentation of music. The images are meant to substantiate the ensemble "shout" of a forgotten era of early jazz music. Finally, this book could not have been completed without the support of Emerson College. My colleagues encouraged a semester leave—and a course reduction under the Judy and Bob Huret Faculty Excellence Award—to conduct research and writing.

I came to enjoy jazz music when growing up in the lower-middle-class neighborhood of East Elmhurst, Queens, New York; it was not the music of my generation but of my parents' and grandparents'. My discovery began in the home when rifling through my parents' record collection. I cannot say that I was a fan of the music—until I had an awakening experience in a grade-school music class. Our regular teacher took a leave of absence toward the end of the term and recruited someone to fill in—that person was the orchestra leader Gil Evans. Why on earth he elected to substitute teach at a predominately Black public school is lost to time; perhaps it was his way of giving back to the community some of the knowledge he had absorbed from African American musical culture. Where our regular teacher had tried to expose us to classical music, he introduced jazz that I could have listened to at home. Still, I was a reluctant student until he pulled me aside one day and said, "Listen to this song and tell me how many instruments you hear." I listened to the music on headphones—something I had never done before—and found myself drawn into the magnetic pull of a melodic guitar riff. I flipped over the album cover to see the face of Wes Montgomery. I stayed after class to finish a few songs and asked if I could listen to it again.

He agreed on the condition that I come to class on time and pay attention. I did, and continued my discovery of Wes Montgomery recordings. As the term grew to a close, I asked if I could borrow the record to play at home. Evans hesitated at first but finally relented. I played that record over and over and began to develop an appreciation for the power of jazz to speak for a culture and to build bridges between cultures. When school ended, I still had the album and would never see Mr. Evans again—or return it. I'd like to think that he would forgive me if he knew the effect it has had.

In closing, I hope that this chronicle of jazz culture in the Black community of Boston might have a similar effect on a reader. Perhaps the stories will spark an interest in jazz among students and a sense of pride in the contributions their community made to the city. In addition, perhaps the stories will help to build a bridge between the cultures. For generations, African American music has been a dynamic but underappreciated generator in the culture of Boston, all the way back to the colonial era when transplanted Africans introduced songs, dance, and music on the waterfront.

The Tremont Theater featured stage shows and silent movies that appealed to white Bostonians like the 1915 film, "The Birth of a Nation." In 1924, it premiered the Harlem revue, In Bamville.

CHAPTER ONE

BEFORE THE JAZZ AGE

Boston's Black Music Culture

The Black community of the Massachusetts Bay Colony took root in the North End in the mid-seventeenth century. The sector was known as "Little Guinea," though likely pronounced as "Ghana" by the transplanted Africans in recognition of the medieval region of origin for many. The waterfront district provided easy access to the maritime needs of seamen, dockworkers, artisans, and servants—such labor enabled by enslaved men and women. Little Guinea, much like the densely populated Black enclaves in other colonial settlements, was a laboratory for cultural creation in a new land. Africans used rituals of song, dance, and prayer to preserve elements of traditional culture—continually refreshed by influxes of newcomers to this emerging seaport in the slave trade—while assimilating the culture of the Yankee maritime. While Little Guinea was hardly a vision of song and dance ritualism like Congo Square in New Orleans, it nonetheless offered a space for music creation.

Some evidence of the efforts of African transplants to preserve principles of cultural continuation can be found in the ceremonies and festivals of the time. Robert Farris Thompson, for example, describes elements of West African philosophy expressed in the arts and culture of transplanted Blacks in the New World. Samuel Floyd investigated the melding of an African American dance and spiritual style from the many ethnic cultures of Africa, and Portia Maultsby explored the preservation of creative principles in the music of African Americans. Of course, such rituals expressed in dance, arts, cuisine, fashions, and music were prevalent in the South, where dense populations of Africans lived in seaport regions of Georgia and the Carolinas. Such factors enabled carnivals like the Jonkonnu (pronounced John Canoe) to take root in North Carolina and Virginia in the early nineteenth century. This festival appears to have spread through ports of call between North Carolina and Jamaica among other West Indian colonies.[1]

The Massachusetts Black population in 1790 was about 5,400 people, and it was a free population since slavery was outlawed by judicial decree in 1783. While this was a small group overseen by a large white majority population, Africans still had space to devise cultural practices to express their sense of common identity. Such was the case for free Black settlements across the colonies of the north as some communities adapted Euro-American holidays and Christian celebrations in ways that reflected African traditions. The New York festival known as "Pinkster" originated as a Dutch colonial ceremony in New York's Hudson River Valley and became a popular annual event in northern Black communities in the eighteenth century. The merriment included parades in costume, the crowning of a festival king, and a cacophony of drums, fiddles, banjos, and "original Congo dance as danced in their native Africa."[2] There were also "Negro election days," a ceremony practiced in seaport communities from New England to the West Indies. Participants selected kings and governors in rituals that resembled the traditions of West African monarchs. In these events, musicians played fiddles as people sang, clapped, and danced; along the way, announcers heralded the virtues of the candidates for ceremonial office. Historian James Horton noted, "The music, the dance, the language, the food, and even the strutting, shaped a common cultural style."[3]

It is unclear whether such activities occurred in Little Guinea, but as a seaport in the international slave trade, it was quite likely a space rife with musical influences of West African transplants and with Anglo-American influences. More research is needed to excavate the musical culture during this colonial era—in particular, evidence of likely chorus music such as men's and women's a cappella groups and religious choirs, as well as the probable songs and dance routines for waterfront work and entertainment such as sea chanteys, folk songs, fiddle music, players of the accordion, percussion spoons, sticks and mallets, and other popular instruments of dock workers, deck hands, and seamen in the colonial period.

Evidence of a desire to sustain an African-centered identity was apparent in the names selected for the social clubs and community organizations. Fraternal lodges were generators of much cultural activity in the Black communities of Boston, New York, and other urban centers as they provided spaces for affirming rituals and events. The best-known society in Boston during the early republic was the African Masonic Lodge. Founded in 1787, this most significant Black collective of shared interest began with thirteen founding members who held a concern in promoting the ideas of self-sufficiency, mutual support, and community development. The African Masons served people in need by supplying firewood in the winter, food to the hungry, cash to members without jobs, and loans to Black merchants.[4]

The pioneer leader was the Methodist minister Prince Hall. Born in Bridgetown, Barbados, circa 1748, Hall was the son of a white English leather worker and a free mixed-race woman of African and French descent. He emigrated to Boston as a young man and found work as a seaman. His ensuing travels fostered an understanding of the common experiences of Africans in the Americas. He served with the Colonial Army during the American Revolution and promoted civil rights in Massachusetts after the war. Such experiences ignited a Pan-African identity and advocacy—in June 1797, he delivered one of the earliest antislavery speeches in the city. Speaking at the Masonic lodge, he pointed to the Haitian insurrection against their colonial enslavers in 1791, commending the uprising for demonstrating the resolve of Black people to be free. (The insurrection played a role in forcing revolutionary France to abolish slavery in 1794, but events would require a war for complete Haitian independence in 1803.) Hall supported a "back to Africa" venture for people seeking to create a new life in the West African colony of Freetown, which had been founded in Sierra Leone by abolitionists as a place for Africans who had remained loyal to their British owners during the American Revolution.[5]

The African Masons were renamed the Prince Hall Masons after his death and continued to serve as a role model for fraternal orders in other seaport communities during the maritime era. Such societies were important for hosting cultural events for a people that enjoyed relative freedom in the state by 1790. Among the other social orders were the Afric-American Female Intelligence Society in 1832, the New England Temperance Society of People of Color in 1835, the Daughters of Zion in 1845, and the Female Benevolent Firm in 1850. In Boston, there was also a chapter of the Grand United Order of Odd Fellows, founded by the Jamaica-born seaman Peter Ogden in New York in 1843. The Odd Fellows hosted the annual Soiree Musicale festival with concerts and a parade in full regalia. In addition to the fraternal orders, the churches of the community sponsored musical events—in fact, it was common for musicians to be members of the same church and fraternal bands. And the African Baptist Church of Boston supported a seven-piece orchestra and choir and provided rehearsal space for musicians.[6]

After more than a century of residence in the North End, Black residents began moving to the West End in the early nineteenth century. The growing population of free people wanted to be closer to jobs at the wharves, streetcar lines, and markets near the waterfront and Scollay Square. The West End, which constituted about 3 percent of the area's population, became the major neighborhood for the estimated 2,000 Africans living there, many of whom had escaped from slave plantations. The Black quarter of the West End rented rooms and stables between Cambridge Street and the north slope of Beacon Hill. Some Black people tried to preserve a sense of African identity in this seaport community in the late decades of the slave trade; outsiders, however, labeled it with the derisive moniker "Nigger Hill." After the Civil War, the community grew with an influx of newcomers from the Northeast and South, and its culture became more secular and recreational. In the West End, as in other urban areas of Black presence, there were groups forming musical clubs, vocal groups, and marching bands for performances in the streets, saloons, and stage. Robert Woods, a Yankee reformer who researched the neighborhood in the early twentieth century, noted, "The West End has ever been the great habitat of the colored race in Boston, and in spite of the exodus of the past few years to the South End, to Cambridgeport and the suburbs at the North, many yet remain."[7]

After the Civil War, many Black communities had access to inexpensive musical instruments used by army bands and marching brass bands to support the troops. The end of the war made these items redundant and available to interested persons. The access to a broad range of orchestra instruments led to the improvement of musical expression beyond its well-developed choral music. By the late nineteenth century, the rise of syncopated instrumental music was noted in the minstrel stage productions, and was an early form of jazz heard in the South End.

The proximity of the Black sector to the helter-skelter of Scollay Square had its benefits and drawbacks. Among the benefits was the network of transit points, theaters, and shops that provided jobs and services for people in the neighborhood, while among the drawbacks was the area's reputation for disorder because of the behavior of sailors and members of transient populations who frequented the saloons, brothels, and burlesque theaters. Woods documents a community comprising law-abiding Black families, show business workers, and numerous residents with backgrounds of petty crimes and vice. The West End location had 88 saloons that primarily served patrons from other areas; these outsiders were those responsible for the brunt of drunk and disorderly behavior, robbery, and prostitution in the back streets and alleys.[8]

The Scollay Square theaters featured traveling minstrel shows for the entertainment of predominately white male audiences. These were the years when white actors wearing blackface makeup dominated the stage, before authentic Black actors were allowed into the industry. This period of the late nineteenth to early twentieth century was a time of hardening rules and beliefs in Jim Crow America. It was also when the distinctive "ragged" beats of syncopated music became notable in Black popular music. Ragtime emerged around the 1890s and was introduced to the minstrel stage by Black stage shows and "coon songs." The theaters in Boston's downtown and South End hosted the Harlem minstrel team of Bert Williams and George Walker and inspired one local composer of such songs: James Vaughn.

Born about 1870, Vaughn attended the Rindge Technical School in Cambridge, where he starred on the football team. His family was part of the movement of Black people from Boston to Cambridgeport after the Civil War. Striving families found a supportive environment in the neighborhood, whose residents included the first Black woman school principal in the state, Maria Louise Baldwin, who lived at 196 Prospect Street.[9] In the 1890s, Vaughn played the piano for theater patrons at a society club and was admired for his renditions of the "Cake Walk" and other syncopated dances, even as critics denounced ragtime as the sounds of illiterate musicians playing waltz music incorrectly.[10] In 1900, Vaughn and Alex Rogers composed the song "Sultan of Zulu," which was commissioned by Williams and Walker and established a long-term relationship with the company. From 1902 to 1909, Vaughn collaborated as a songwriter, music composer, conductor, and musical director for stage productions. Working with Alex Rogers, he composed music for the minstrel songs "It's Hard to Find a King Like Me," "When Sousa Comes to Coontown," "When the Moon Shines," and "Me and de Minstrel Band," among others. Surviving pressings of the minstrel standards of Williams and Walker include "My Little Zulu Baby" in 1901 for Victor Monarch and "Nobody" in 1906 for Columbia.[11]

Vaughn also contributed to the Williams and Walker production of *In Dahomey*, the first all-Black musical comedy to play on Broadway. The creative team included Jesse A. Shipp, Will Marion Cook, and Paul Laurence Dunbar, and the show premiered in February 1903 at the New York Theater, where it ran for fifty-three performances. In Boston, the show was featured at the Globe Theater on Washington Street, a 1,500-seat house in the theater district, and may have attracted special attention because of the local storyline: it featured two befuddled Boston detectives searching for a silver casket meant to be shipped to Africa but gone missing. Among the popular songs were "On Emancipation Day," "My Dahomian Queen," and "When Sousa Comes to Coontown" (lyrics by Alex Rogers and music by James Vaughn and Tom Lemonier).

The September 1908 production of *Bandana Land* was another popular minstrel show to which Vaughn contributed. It played at the Orpheum Theater on Tremont Street—one of the largest theaters in the city at 2,500 seats—with a cast of seventy-five actors and a thirty-piece orchestra as the *Globe* announced "The Orpheum Opens Its Season Tonight with 'Bandana Land.'" Once a setting for high-society gatherings, the Orpheum was serving as a theater for working-class minstrelsy by 1900. Vaughn, along with Cecil Mack, Alex Rogers, Jesse A. Shipp, and Will Marion Cook, composed suggestive odes like "In the Right Church but the Wrong Pew" and "Bon Bon Buddy." The shows attracted a racially diverse following and even included fans among the Yankee Brahmin elites. One *Globe* reviewer wrote that "It is a unique position that

Williams and Walker occupy in Boston—that of being a fad of the society people."[12]

The stigma of minstrel buffoonery burdened the ability of actors and producers to establish an affirming Black theater, according to Hubert Harrison, a Pan-African intellectual of the Harlem Renaissance who wrote and lectured on the intersection of race, culture, and the theater in the Jazz Age. Harrison argues that the Black theater was trapped in the quagmire of minstrel perceptions, and as a result, comedy was the default genre; it took the most creative productions to craft subplots, songs, and music that expressed ideas to affirm the Black experience. While actors like Bert Williams and George Walker were able to become international stars, they were still trapped in a box of demeaning racial perceptions. "Nobody" is one example of a minstrel song that speaks to the experience of such tribulations, composed in 1905 by the Bert Williams songwriting team; it would become an audience favorite.[13] In the song, the character poses a series of challenges and dangers encountered and each time asks who will come to his aid—and the answer is "nobody." The humor builds as the obstacles mount without rescue, such as, "When wintertime comes with its snow and sleet / And me with hunger and cold feet / Who says 'Here's two bits, go and eat'?—Nobody."[14]

Black musicians tried other measures to challenge their marginalization in the musical theaters of Boston. In 1906, for example, community leaders organized a symphony orchestra named the Victorian Concert Orchestra, which operated from about 1913 to 1924 under the direction of violinist, composer, and conductor Clarence Cameron White. White was born in Clarksville, Tennessee in 1880 and studied at Howard University and the Conservatory of Music at Oberlin College. In taking up the violin, he tapped into a tradition of string music beginning with the traditional string bands of West Africa. In 1908, he did advanced study in London under the composer Samuel Coleridge-Taylor before arriving in Boston to open a music studio in 1910. Under his direction, the Victorian Concert Orchestra blended classical elements with spirituals and folk songs; he also used the orchestra to promote the works of other Black composers. One of White's notable compositions was the series of musical inspirations *The Bandanna Sketches*. Each sketch explored a theme of the African American experience: "Chant (Nobody Knows de Trouble I've Seen)," "Negro Dance (Sometimes I Feel Like a Motherless Child)," "Lament (I'm Troubled in Mind)," and "Slave Song (Many Thousand Gone)." He composed the suite *From the Cotton Fields* with the songs "Cabin Song," "On the Bayou," and "Spiritual." His compositions were published by the Carl Fischer Company of New York and performed by acclaimed violinist Fritz Kreisler and Irma Seydel.[15]

The Victorian Concert Orchestra reflected the classical music aspirations of Black professional musicians in a city where the symphony orchestras were closed to them. The audience for the Orchestra performances is undocumented but probably members of the civic and cultural organizations of the Black middle class. Among these were musicians, women's clubs, church groups, fraternal societies, soldiers on leave, and so forth; in addition, there was likely a segment of Yankee society and white musicians that attended the concerts. After a 1928 visit to Haiti, White infused a Pan-African theme in his art song compositions. One such work is the opera *Ouanga* in recognition of the Haitian spiritual practice of vodou, a polytheistic faith that draws on principles of traditional West African religion and elements of Catholicism. The 1931 score chronicles the story of Haiti's first president, the revolutionary leader Jean-Jacques Dessalines. The composition earned White a commendation for Composer of Outstanding Merit by the American Opera Society of Chicago. There apparently survives no recorded legacy for the Victorian Concert Orchestra; however, there are recordings of Clarence Cameron White playing violin solos with symphony orchestras.

In the early twentieth century, Boston began to attract musicians from the society orchestras of Harlem. Among the most notable were the brothers John and James Reese Europe—examples of divergent pathways in a musical family that converged in the South End. The Europe family lived in Washington, DC, and exposed their children to the highbrow musical influences available in the city. John, born about 1875, was the older brother by five years and worked hard to establish a reputation as a pianist. In 1900, he moved to New York City to work as the house pianist at the Little Savoy, a swank club owned by Barron Wilkins on West 35th Street in the Tenderloin district. Set in an old Black quarter of the city, the Little Savoy was touted as "the most important spot where Negro musicians got acquainted with the wealthy New York clientele." James, born in February 1881, studied violin as a teenager, and was advised by the composers Harry Burleigh (the father of spirituals) and Hans Hanke of the Leipzig Conservatory of Music.[16]

By 1900, Black musicians found the music industry of New York City more welcoming than other cities in the Northeast. The musicians' union Local 310 was relatively accepting of the better-trained Black instrumentalists, primarily trained to read classical music and play the popular dances favored by white audiences. On the other hand, the majority of Black musicians trained to play jazz, blues, dance music, and the songs of the minstrel stage were largely shut out of the union and lucrative theater and dance hall venues largely controlled by union contractors. Still, with a large Black community located in the midtown district, musicians found ample work in the dance halls, restaurants, theaters, and summer resort ball rooms.[17] The society bands and theater performers in the New York scene also performed for dances in New England cities such as Hartford, Newport, Salem, and Boston.

Several years after John moved to New York to pursue a career in music, he helped his brother relocate to the city. By 1905, according to Maud Cuney Hare in her pioneer 1936 history *Negro Musicians and Their Music*, they were involved with a small group of about twenty players known as "The Memphis Students." They gathered at the Marshall, a Black-owned café and hotel in Harlem managed by Jimmie Marshall, to talk shop and ways to advance their careers.[18] James Reese Europe was the first president and was hired to direct the music for the minstrel companies of Bert Williams, George Walker, Robert Cole, and J. Rosamond Johnson. By 1910, the brothers were among the cofounders of the New York Clef Club, an organization to promote the occupational interests of as many as 135 musicians. It served the function of a union, hiring hall, and booking agency for Black musicians. John performed in bands and variety shows produced by the club, such as the Marshall Trio ragtime band that included Anthony Tuck on mandolin and William Patrick on vocals. Pianist Eubie Blake, also a member of the Clef Club, recalled John as a great pianist of head arrangements; however, his reluctance to use sheet music made it difficult for other musicians to substitute for him—an issue that would prove to be a challenge during his years in Boston.[19]

In 1910, the Clef Club organized a symphony orchestra under the direction of James Reese Europe. It incorporated early features of the big band section arrangements as well as piano recitations of the minstrel and concert hall compositions of Harry Burleigh, Will Marion Cook, and Will Vodery. The club served the dual purposes of fraternity, labor exchange, hangout for musicians, and concert hall. To an extent, the club addressed the classical music activities of Black professional musicians before the market for jazz was fully developed. As such, the 100-member "symphony" reflected the aspirations and the limits for Black musical opportunity. The orchestra made its debut at the Manhattan Casino in Harlem on May 27, 1910; the performance was part of a larger event and Europe had prepared thirty minutes of music. The audience for the symphony concerts is unclear; however, it is possible to speculate from the use of the venue for other popular Black entertainment events.

The Manhattan Casino was located at 280 West 155th Street, north of the boundaries of early Black Harlem, but accessible by subway. Around 1910, the casino became a popular site for the tournaments of Black church basketball teams. The most prominent churches used the venue as the fans of the teams outgrew their spaces—especially when out-of-town teams or white teams came to play. Among the middle-class audiences for such events were Black fraternal members and Post Office clerks. Churches with basketball teams included St Philip's Episcopal Church, Mother Zion A.M.E. Church, Abyssinian Baptist Church, St. Mark's Methodist Church, and St. Mark's Catholic Church, among others. As such, it is likely that the Clef Club concerts also drew on audience from such institutions. The first symphony concert was considered successful and led to biannual concerts for a while.[20]

In May 1912, the orchestra performed the historic Concert of Negro Music at Carnegie Hall to raise money for the New York Music School Settlement for Colored People. The concert showcased Black folk songs, anthems, ballads, art songs, and syncopated "ragtime" dance music, and was well received by New York society. The success prompted a second concert at Carnegie Hall in February 1913 and a ten-day tour in November to the Academy of Music in Philadelphia; Albaugh Theater in Baltimore; Howard Theater in Washington, DC; City Auditorium in Richmond; and Hampton Institute in Hampton, Virginia. Under James Reese Europe's guidance, the orchestra intermixed folk instruments such as mandolins, banjos, and harp guitars with regular instruments of symphony orchestras such as the trombone and French horn in novel solo and ensemble arrangements.[21] The reception was overall positive: one review of the Howard Theater concert noted a turnout of about 2,000 people and praised the "precision, verity of expression, and technique that made the cultured audience gasp with surprise." However, another reviewer questioned the novelty acts and desired a stronger demonstration of Black mastery of the European classics. In that regard, the reviewer was disappointed in a program that resorted to folk songs and instrumentation rather than traditional classical arrangements: "The music was typical of the light, happy-go-lucky Negro, but there are those among us who are trying to master the classics in music as well as along other lines, and to say that the program satisfied this class would be gainsaying the truth."[22]

Europe was aware of such criticism and countered with an argument on the merits of an orchestra music with roots in the African American culture: "Any white leader of a symphony orchestra would doubtless laugh at the way our Negro Symphony Orchestra is organized," he said, adding, "We have developed a kind of symphony music that, no matter what else you think, is different and distinctive, and that lends itself to the playing of the peculiar compositions of our race."[23]

During the same period, James Reese Europe also established a reputation as the leader of a society ragtime band for ballroom dances and records. In those years, he produced novelty compositions and recordings as the conductor of "Europe's Society Orchestra"—work that probably generated a good deal more income than the symphony concerts. The band comprised musicians from communities in the North and South: Ford Dabney and Leonard Smith, piano; Cricket Smith, cornet; Edgar Campbell and John Russell, clarinet; Tracy Cooper, George Smith, Walter Scott, Allie Ross, James Van Hooten, and William Tyler, violins; Buddy Gilmore and George Jenkins, drums; and five unknown banjo and mandolin players.[24] The band played jaunty dance compositions at upscale nightclubs and dance halls and was among the first Black society orchestras to record for the major labels of Victor, Pathé, and Perfect—and the first to release ragtime songs that sold well.

Europe was in a position to take advantage of innovations in sound recording that enabled the music catalog of "race records." The mass distribution necessitated the marketing brands of ragtime, jazz, gospel, and blues as well as syncopated ballroom dance music.[25] In 1911, for example, clarinetist Wilbur Sweatman recorded "Down Home Rag" as a piano roll issuance. In 1913, Europe arranged a version of "Down Home Rag" as a "turkey trot" for the Victor label; it was considered a pioneer record in the era of social dancing. The tune was distinguished by a frenetic volley of stringed instruments, crashing cymbals, tuba bass, and responsive vocals in the imitation of a turkey holler. Most notably, white audiences in Boston would have recognized the James Reese Europe song arrangements as the music director for the ballroom duo of Irene and Vernon Castle. In 1914, the society band recorded the popular dance tunes "Castle Walk," "Castle House Rag," "Congratulations Waltz (Castles' Lame Duck)," and "You're Here and I'm Here/One Step" by J. D. Kern for the Victor label. His band excluded the banjo and mandolin when recording the foxtrots and waltzes that the Castles used in their studios to teach the popular dances of the day.[26]

By the war years, James Reese Europe had eclipsed his older brother John in the national industry. However, John had established his own reputation in Boston and led a ragtime band at the newly opened Copley Plaza Hotel in Copley Square near the intersection of Huntington Avenue and Dartmouth Street, where railroad tracks separated the affluent Yankee Back Bay from the working-class Black and ethnic South End. For business travelers, the hotel was within walking distance of Back Bay Station and Trinity Station with connections to industrial centers to the south—like Providence, New Haven, and New York—and to the west—like Springfield, Albany, and Buffalo. The hotel hosted ballroom affairs for New Englanders on holiday as well as college dances.

John worked in the hotel as a band member and ragtime pianist during a period when most privately owned Boston accommodations were racially segregated—by custom rather than by law. John was alleged to have had a drinking problem and would binge to the point of incapacitation. When James learned of his brother's episodes, he tried to help out by asking pianist Eubie Blake to go to Boston to cover for the lush. Over time, Blake memorized John's piano routines well enough to replace him on short notice. In 1919, the *New York Sun* reported that John Europe still "plays in a large Boston hotel."[27] Clearly, James Reese Europe was no stranger to the emerging scene in the South End and could rely on his brother's name recognition to pave the way for the debut of his jazz orchestra.

Mechanics Hall hosted the second concert of the James Reese Europe Orchestra in 1919.

CHAPTER TWO

HOW JAMES REESE EUROPE BROUGHT JAZZ TO BOSTON

The James Reese Europe Orchestra brought the spirit of jazz to Boston in the spring of 1919. His collections of musicians melded the styles of marching bands, ragtime syncopation, folk music, and solo improvisations into a modern sound for the postwar era. Europe, who early won regard as the conductor of a society band, organized a martial band that infused the music of war with the rhythms of Black aural expression. Since 1917, when the outfit deployed to France, the Harlem conductor had worked mightily to engage the brass band with audiences in the US and French armies as well as the French public. By 1919, when his band and army unit were demobilized, Europe had won acclaim in the national and international press as the "Jazz King."

His ninety-piece brass band was deployed to France for a fifteen-month engagement as part of the 369th Infantry of the American Expedition Force. Known as the "Harlem Hell Fighters" for their ferocity on the battlefield, the outfit—once disparaged by their own war department—helped France to stop the German advance and to appreciate orchestral jazz. In the chaos of war, the martial band introduced the beauty of syncopated marches and captured the imagination of the public. Indeed, Europe served as an ambassador of jazz, and his accomplishment opened the door to concerts in France for other early jazz bands, such as Will Marion Cook's New York Syncopated Orchestra. Like James Reese Europe's band, Cook's band brought the modern music of the Harlem scene to highbrow European audiences in 1920. Such orchestras helped to gain recognition for jazz as the new sound of a cosmopolitan people—a feat that had eluded a generation of writers and painters in Harlem.

During the war, James Reese Europe was at the forefront of orchestral arrangements that reflected the music of African diasporic cultures. He recruited musicians from British regiment bands in South Africa and the Sudan and Afro-Latin bands in New York. His compositions blended syncopation, novel section arrangements, and folk instrumentation into an early jazz formula with professional standards. His bands innovated a new music that would appeal to the sensibilities of middle-class audiences and forge a precursor to the big band jazz era: "We colored people have our own music that is part of us. It's the product of our souls; it's been created by the suffering and miseries of our race."[1]

As America entered the war in 1917, Europe enlisted as a private in the Fifteenth Regiment of the New York State Guard. The regiment was federalized as the segregated 369th infantry of the national army, and Europe was commissioned as a lieutenant. In France, the band members both fought with the regular infantry and regrouped as an orchestra to lift the spirits of troops going into battle. Europe describes the experience:

> In March, 1918, we went up to the trenches in the Argonne sector, and I was retransferred to my machine-gun company. By the way, I was the first negro officer to command troops in the trenches. I stayed in the trenches from March to July, then they sent me back to the band. We were sent to Paris to play for the Allied conference arranged by General Bliss. We stayed six weeks. After the leader of

the Republican Guard Band heard us play jazz, he asked for some of our music. I showed it to him. He wanted to know how we got our jazz effects. "I don't see that on the paper," he said. "It ain't there," I told him. "You have to train your boys to get that stuff."[2]

The band gave exhibitions of syncopated martial music that created a public sensation in Paris. European audiences, including dignitaries and commanders of the Allied Forces, were impressed by the novel rhythms, arrangements, and instrumentation. Europe explains:

Lots of people think jazz is easy. It's as hard as anything. The French bandmasters thought we had trick instruments. They'd ask to examine our instruments and then cry in surprise: "*Meme que les autres*"—"The same as the others." You see we get those special effects with a roll of the tongue and blowing the instrument about twice as hard as usual. Those were great days in Paris. As I walked around gargling in French, with everyone in the world going crazy over our jazz stuff, I felt like President Wilson must feel over there with everybody around him. We played in all the hospitals in Paris. They all wanted us to stay there forever.[3]

The excitement was reported in the American press as well, such as one review in the *New York Tribune* that called the compositions "worthy of the pen of John Philip Sousa." Europe remarked: "We won France by playing music which was ours and not a pale imitation of others, and if we are to develop in America we must develop along our own lines."[4]

After a fifteen-month deployment, the 369th Infantry returned home to a heroic reception. In February 1919, the orchestra led by Europe was among the units honored in a Broadway ticker-tape parade. He seized the moment to redesign the band as a civilian orchestra for theater and music hall performances. At age thirty-eight, he planned a ten-week tour of venues in cities across the

Northeast and Midwest where soldiers were demobilizing from their army units. The debut concert was held at the Manhattan Opera House in March 1919; among the numbers on the program was "Darktown Strutters' Ball," a minstrel show tune written by Shelton Brooks. The orchestral version featured up-tempo syncopated rhythmic lines accented by comic trombone swoops and novelty sound effects like a slide whistle. At the same time, it indicated the potential for early jazz performance by creating intervals for a cornet solo.[5]

Europe scheduled the tour with selected members of the military band, and Boston was on the itinerary. Preston Sandiford, an aspiring ten-year-old pianist in the South End neighborhood at the time, recalls the excitement: "There was a guy named James Europe. He had been overseas in World War I and had a marching band. It was the first marching band that played swing. He became a terrific popular favorite. When Europe came, he took over Boston by storm."[6] One reason why Europe selected Boston for the tour was the favorable reception his brother's band had found in the Copley Plaza Hotel. Europe would have been aware of the conditions for touring in the city and the amenities for Black travelers. While the city was known for its cold winters and cranky disposition, it was viewed positively by students and tourists. People admired its abolitionist past, open public accommodations, and tolerant cultural institutions—even as they abided by rigid racial customs in commercial and private institutions, the universities, theaters, concert halls, and museums attracted a number of Black students and professionals. More importantly, it drew a steady flow of migrants from the cities and towns of the Northeast and Canada, plantations of the South, and islands of the West Indies. And all this without igniting the violent reactions of working-class whites that menaced Black populations in cities like Tulsa, East St. Louis, Chicago, and other migrant destinations, not to mention towns with army camps that housed Black soldiers.

Bostonians may have been aware of the band through news

articles and sound recordings. In March 1919, the group recorded eighteen sides of ragtime, jazz, and blues for the Pathé and Perfect labels. Among the sides were "St. Louis Blues," "Memphis Blues," and Hesitating Blues" by W. C. Handy; "Darktown Strutters' Ball" by Shelton Brooks; "How Ya Gonna Keep 'Em Down on the Farm" by various writers; "That Moaning Trombone" by T. Bethel; and "Jazz Baby," "Mirandy," "On Patrol in No Man's Land," and "All of No Man's Land is Ours" by Noble Sissle, Eubie Blake, and James Reese Europe. In May, they recorded another six sides for Perfect, including "That's Got 'Em" by Wilbur Sweatman.[7]

Europe also was no doubt aware of the conservative moral standards in the city's entertainment industry—and its association of jazz with negative impressions of race and conduct. Jazz was identified by traditionalists according to the disruptive transformations of war, industrialization, and urbanization. Some related the ragged sounds of syncopation, solo improvisation, and polyrhythmic interplay with the carelessness of mass production and dislocation of urban life. To such authorities, jazz equated to the decline of the old Yankee order and culture.[8] That being said, Boston Yankee and Irish Catholic traditionalists were on alert to stifle cultures stereotyped as "indecent." The New England Watch and Ward Society was one such moral policing service that had been in operation for about forty years when Europe's orchestra hit Boston. Its crusades to outlaw books and plays considered obscene made the phrase "Banned in Boston" a popular term for excessive censorship. The group enabled "Old Yankee" families to maintain social control, often in alliance with reactionary forces in the Catholic community. The society was originally founded as the New England Society for the Suppression of Vice in 1878 as a chapter in a coalition of social leaders to confront the perceived threats of gambling, drugs, prostitution, and bawdy burlesque stage shows.

By 1910, the old Brahmin aristocratic families with names like Lodge, Lowell, Cabot, Peabody, Saltonstall, and Weld constituted the leading dues-paying members of the Society and were instrumental in the passage of a state law against obscenity. Under the law, the Watch and Ward monitors had the power to bypass the police and obtain a court order to investigate sites suspected of illicit activity. Another factor playing into the moral anxieties was the desire to preserve the status of male privilege. The year 1919 was a time of broad challenges to old patriarchal assumptions as Boston suffragettes engaged in a national campaign to pressure Congress for the right to vote. The efforts paid off when Congress sent the Nineteenth Amendment to the Constitution to be ratified by the states. Locally, in addition, such activism carried over in campaigns by women operators with the New England Telephone Company endorsing a labor strike for better conditions.

The Yankee Watch and Ward Society initiatives found supporters among the rival Irish Catholic authorities in city hall, the Suffolk County District Attorney's office, and the Boston Archdiocese of the Catholic Church. Though competitors for power in the city, they had a common cause in policing moral issues such as abortion, birth control, promiscuity, and criticism of the church. Reports on the campaigns against books, magazines, newspapers, musical plays, and cabaret shows subjected the city to ridicule in more wide-open cities like Chicago and New York, yet the campaigns for decency ran deep in the Protestant and Catholic teachings. The most public crusader was the Reverend Jason Franklin Chase, a Methodist Episcopal minister who led the Society from 1902 to 1926 and who once claimed that "a whole high school class of unwedded mothers may be the result of a lascivious book."

Such were the anxieties in Boston when James Reese Europe brought his celebrated orchestra to town in March 1919. Still, traditionalist opposition to jazz music based on questions of quality and respectability was in the early stage of fermentation. The Europe Orchestra, accordingly, was booked to perform at a venue that reflected the ambitions of the professional musicians in the band. They were booked for the Boston Opera House on Huntington Avenue and Opera Place, located on the boundary line of the Black

South End and the Yankee Back Bay. Though past its prime, the old hall still carried an aura of sophistication. Seating 2,750 people, the venue was once known for its advanced stage technology, considered "the best equipped temple of music in America." Here, at the border line of cultural interaction between the races, Europe found a relatively safe space for both groups to enjoy the music of the James Reese Europe Orchestra.[9]

Europe came to Boston on Friday, March 28, and Saturday, March 29, with a sixty-five-piece orchestra. Among the band members were Frank de Broit, Russell Smith, Pops Foster, and Jake Porter on cornets/trumpet; Ward Andrews, Amos Gilliard, Raphael Hernandez, Herb Flemming, trombones; Elige Rijos, Antonio Gonzales, Jesus Hernandez, Arturo Ayala, Pinkhead Parker, reeds; Steve Wright, Herbert Wright, Whitney Viney, Karl Kenny, drums; and Noble Sissle on violin and vocals.[10] In a March 23 announcement, the *Globe* deemed Europe "a leading musician of the colored race" and described the upcoming concerts as an eclectic demonstration of syncopated martial music, spirituals, blues, and jazz-inspired popular tunes. One *Globe* reviewer wrote, "The band is said to be of a quality to compare with the best military bands, but has the advantage of presenting a style of musical entertainment that is all its own, as well as excelling in the exhilarating, characteristically American jazz music."[11]

The orchestra was booked to play four concerts over two days. Tickets cost 50¢ to $1 for the afternoon and 50¢ to $1.50 for the evening. They were sold at the opera house and in the lobby of the Little Building on Tremont and Boylston streets. In the March 27 advertisement in the *Globe*, the Shubert announced "Lieut. James Reese Europe and the Famous 369th Infantry Band" as a "sizzlin', jazzin', raggin', sensation" and as "65 Joy Whooping Jazzers in Khaki."[12] Among the groups that might have appreciated the Boston concert were returning soldiers and sailors, ex-soldiers and sailors, white music enthusiasts, migrants from the Northeast and South, and middle-class Black residents of the city.

The band featured syncopated martial music, spirituals, blues, and jazzed-up popular tunes, including numbers by the full orchestra as well as quartets and choruses. The program lists "St. Louis Blues," "How You Going to Keep Them Down on the Farm" with cornet solos, "Carry Me Back to Old Virginny" by the quartet Four Kings of Harmony, and spirituals by the Southland Singers. The orchestra accompanied pianist Noble Sissle in a rendition of his song "On Patrol in No Man's Land," and staged a percussion demonstration called "Biff Bang Bombardment" by two drummers known as the Percussion Twins. The audience embraced the sounds of ragtime and jazz, and the concert was considered a rousing success. With traditionalist suspicions of racial discord allayed, the ground was set for a return engagement.[13]

During Europe's second Boston concert in May, the city was in the throes of the armistice celebrations. In April, the city had begun preparations to welcome back thousands of New England soldiers and nurses who had served in the war, returning as the major war powers gathered in Versailles to negotiate a treaty. On April 26, 1919, a million New Englanders converged on downtown Boston to welcome home the soldiers of the Twenty-Sixth "Yankee" Division. The soldiers were among the best of the young men in the six New England states sent off to war, drafted from the mills, workshops, shipyards, fisheries, and farms of the region and sent out to face the horrors of mechanized destruction. They were returning to Camp Devens in Ayer, about forty-five miles northwest of Boston. The camp was built atop 1,400 acres of converted swamp and brush taken from the towns of Shirley and Harvard, transformed into 1,400 buildings meant to hold 35,000 troops but overcrowded to hold 40,000 during the war.

Among the troops stationed at Camp Devens were 5,000 Black soldiers who had been mobilized in September 1917. They volunteered to fight for democracy despite their own democratic rights being denied in military camps like Camp Logan in Houston, Texas, where many residents objected to stationing the Black soldiers of the Twenty-Fourth Infantry. Some instigated a confrontation that turned into a melee resulting in the deaths of nineteen people: two soldiers, twelve white police officers, and five white civilians. Despite the dubious circumstances, the army put the Black soldiers on trial in one of the largest court-martials in US history. No such incidents occurred at Devens, and Boston, as the home city of about 28,000 soldiers, was eager to lay out the welcome mat for the entire 250,000-member Yankee Division. The young men of the "Y-D" returned home victorious, though few remained untouched by the realities of industrial war; many were battered in mind and body, and all were anxious about returning to society.[14]

The crowds lined the streets on this cold and rainy afternoon even as concerns over a resurgence of the 1918 flu pandemic loomed large following a reported outbreak among the returning soldiers. Nonetheless, the public came out to hail the parade of soldiers and nurses: "Covered with glory among the bravest of the brave, with their names scrolled over many of the most decisive battlefields of France, the gallant men of the Twenty-Sixth (Yankee) Division are back among the old folks in Boston today."[15] About 20,000 of the soldiers arrived from Camp Devens near Ayer on seven special trains with sixteen cars each. They still wore the uniforms and equipment from the trenches of France, including steel helmets, rifles with fixed bayonets, gas masks, and light packs with a blanket, rolled slicker, filled canteen, and first aid. A caravan of autos transported another 900 wounded men.

The parade took four hours to cover the six-mile route along Beacon, Park, Tremont, and Boylston streets and Commonwealth Avenue. It must have been a curious change of scenery for the "doughboys" with recent memories of the killing fields of Verdun. One *Globe* writer observed, "While they stride through our streets with that superb rhythm of hip and shoulder seen only in marching men; while the crowds thunder hoarse welcome; while the air throbs with the joy of hundreds of thousands of hearts and voices, there are darker memories, graver thoughts which will not be banished from this festival—which no one wishes to banish."[16]

The Yankee Division fought alongside the French Army in some of the fiercest battles of the war. Shipped to France in September 1917, they received basic training in trench warfare tactics such as grenade throwing, machine gun and automatic rifle firing, bayonet sticking, and mortar targeting. In 1918, the division engaged in 210 days of combat with only ten days in a rest zone. They were cited or commended eighteen times by the American and French high commands, including for the prestigious *Croix de Guerre*. Units fought with and without the backing of the French Army. The division was credited with the capture of 3,148 German prisoners, including sixty-one officers, at great cost: the Y-D suffered an estimated 1,730 killed, 3,600 seriously wounded, 2,800 lightly wounded, 3,350 gassed, 285 missing, and 135 taken captive and imprisoned.[17] Many stayed in Boston after demobilization and were primed for entertainment from an orchestra that had distinguished the country in war: "America had heard before of that 'jazz band,' the splendidly trained organization that had won more honors abroad than any other military band," wrote the *Boston Guardian*. "And they knew that Europe had been the father of the band."[18]

On May 9, the James Reese Europe Orchestra arrived in a city anticipating their second concert. This time, the orchestra was booked at the working-class auditorium of Mechanics Hall located on Huntington Avenue and West Newton Street—again along the tracks that divided the South End and Yankee Back Bay. Built in 1881 by the Massachusetts Charitable Mechanics Association, the South End hall could accommodate 8,000 people and was among the largest venues for conventions and events in the city. The return engagement signaled that a local jazz scene was on the rise in Boston. "With rare humor the audience was asked to appreciate a 'highbrow' selection before the band got down to the real business of the evening—jazz," one reviewer writes. "Encore followed encore, and Lieut. Europe, realizing the evening would be long enough to give the audience all the encores it demanded, gave just as many encores as he considered necessary, and then passed on to the next composition."[19]

The audience went wild and showed the depth of potential support for a jazz scene. The triumph of the concert, however, was overshadowed by the tragic aftermath. According to informants, there were tensions between Europe and a young drummer in the orchestra, Herbert Wright, who (like Europe) was a veteran of the war; out of concerns about the drummer's upcoming performance, Europe asked pianist and singer Noble Sissle to make sure Wright was prepared for the show. He was featured in a percussion exhibition with another drummer named Steven Wright; while the men were of no blood relationship, they did share a common family via their childhood in the Jenkins Home for Orphans in Charleston, South Carolina. The two men—who received musical training in the orphanage—were promoted in the orchestra program as the Percussion Twins. Sissle recalled Herbert Wright complaining about the way Europe treated him. He believed that Europe favored Steven, who "never does anything right and he makes mistakes and then Lieutenant Europe looks back in the drummer section and commences to frowning at me."

Sissle encouraged the young drummer to be ready to play that evening; Europe conducted fourteen numbers before leaving the stage for intermission.[20] During the break, Europe and Wright had an argument over his playing. There are conflicting accounts as to what was said between them. One news account states that Europe told Wright to "put more pep in the sticks," to which the drummer took offense. Another account claims that Europe was upset with Wright for walking on and off the stage erratically during the concert. He summoned Wright to his dressing room to speak about the issue, where Wright reportedly got emotionally worked up and staged a temper tantrum, throwing a drum and sticks against the dressing room wall before turning on Europe, who was sitting in a chair.

Charlestown State Prison held drummer Herbert Wright after he was convicted of killing James Reese Europe. During his incarceration, he was permitted to do exhibition jazz drumming for remote radio broadcast.

"Go away from me," said Europe, also recovering from a cold. "I'm a sick man and I don't want to argue with you. Go back on stage." Wright continued to argue, however, and then pulled out a penknife and went after Europe. The conductor used the chair to keep Wright at bay like a lion tamer. Wright held the knife in his balled fist and tried to stab Europe with backhand slashes. Other band members tried to intervene and prevent the knife attack, to no avail. "Herbert Wright hurled himself over the chair. As he came through the air, Jim clasped his body and whirled it away from him," Sissle recalled. "With a backhand blow, he made a wild swing with his knife, brought it down in the direction of Jim Europe's face."[21]

Wright stabbed Europe in the neck before falling down and eventually coming to his senses. Sissle and other band members restrained him and took him out of the room. Sissle returned to find Europe tugging at the collar of his shirt and officer's jacket: "He got the collar unfastened and had taken his white struck-tie from around his neck and a stream of blood spurted from a small wound." At first glance, the wound appeared to be stabilized—Europe was not in great distress and the bleeding was contained. An ambulance took Europe to the emergency room of nearby Boston City Hospital. Sissle recalls Europe saying, "I am going to the hospital, and I will have my wound dressed and I will be at the Commons in the morning, in time to conduct the band. See that the rest of the program is gone through with."[22]

The concert continued under the charge of assistant director Deck Fellowes. The audience was informed that Europe would not return due to an unexpected illness; the program went on as Europe had planned. Meanwhile, a police officer assigned to the concert was informed about the altercation. He, in turn, notified a detective sitting in the audience. Wright was arrested and taken to the police station. Several band members accompanied him in the belief that Europe's condition was good; however, the police and band members were informed by telephone that Europe had taken a turn for the worse. The musicians rushed to the hospital but he passed away at 11:45 p.m., before they could arrive.[23]

Europe is suspected to have died as a result of asphyxiation caused by internal swelling and bleeding from a severed artery that placed fatal pressure on his windpipe. His cold may have complicated his ability to breathe under the circumstances. In addition, there are concerns about the quality of care he received in the emergency room, which was staffed by interns with limited experience and little oversight by senior physicians. Critics also fear that Europe may have been stereotyped as just another jazz musician stabbed at a concert gone awry.[24]

Wright was arrested on a charge of murder, later reduced to manslaughter after two doctors declared him to be suffering from insanity. There is no indication that he suffered an injury in the war; however, many veterans did return home with the undiagnosed mental illness commonly known then as "shell shock," today known as post-traumatic stress disorder (PTSD). The ailment was a diagnosis new to the medical community. It stemmed from the exposure of ordinary people to the extraordinary experiences of mass chaos and killing. Doctors in Britain, France, and the US noted the common symptoms of soldiers impacted by artillery shells, machine gun fire, aerial bombardment, killing of enemy troops, witnessing death, and the like. Many exhibited physical symptoms such as uncontrollable shaking, paralysis, loss of speech, stuttering, dizziness, ringing in the ears, headaches, and feelings of suffocation. Others suffered emotional reactions such as depression, confusion, insomnia, guilt, nightmares, sleepwalking, and overreaction to ordinary noise and incidents.

The methods of diagnosis and treatment for soldiers with war-related mental health injuries were primitive. Many troops who suffered from traumatic stress disorders either declined to acknowledge the problem or to seek treatment out of fear of being labeled unmanly or cowardly. They reentered society and their behavior did not go unnoticed, as depicted in films and stories about damaged ex-soldiers. Many languished at home, others on the streets.[25] During Wright's trial, his defense attorney claimed that whatever psychological problems Wright suffered from were developed during his time at war. He argued that the altercation with Europe was a "culmination of a long series of happenings there." He was sentenced to a term of ten to fifteen years in the Massachusetts State Penitentiary in Charlestown—the current site of Bunker Hill Community College.

In prison, Wright began to put his life back on track with the aid of jazz—he was permitted to resume playing the drums. Why prison officials allowed him access to a drum set and rehearsal space is lost to time, but perhaps the authorities viewed it as therapy for his rehabilitation. No doubt it provided a novel source of entertainment for the prison community and, over time, for Boston radio audiences.[26]

The early 1920s were a time when the few radio stations in cities with growing Black communities occasioned the live broadcast of jazz bands, and the scratchy sound of early Boston radio broadcasts began to leave an imprint of these performances on the musical culture of the city. In Pittsburgh, station KDKA broadcast Lois Deppe and His Serenaders for audiences in 1921. The popular baritone singer managed a dance orchestra with pianist Earl Hines and had recorded songs for the Gennett label: "They were the first African Americans performers ever to appear on radio. The broadcast was played over a loudspeaker on Wylie Avenue and crowds mobbed the street to listen and then stayed to cheer Deppe and Hines when they made it back to the Hill."[27]

Between 1924 and 1927, Boston "radio bugs" were exposed to the drumming exhibitions of Herbert Wright from the Charlestown Prison on station WEEI. Making their debut on the airwaves in 1924, the radio station was located in the Edison Electric Illuminating Company building at 25-39 Boylston Street in Boston. Edison had a portable radio station that used the call letters WTAT to send out to conventions, state fairs, and other locations; this was probably the method used by WEEI to arrange a remote feed of the drumming exhibition from the prison. Wright's jailhouse concert may have been the first live jazz drumming heard on Boston radio; his performance revived the beats and rhythms of the Percussion Twins for new audiences—and no doubt captured the attention of listeners in the Black community.[28]

Wright was released on parole on April 1, 1927, after serving eight years of his sentence. By the mid-1930s, he was married and living in an apartment on Haskins Street near Frederick Douglass Square. He established a reputation as a drumming instructor, and one of his students, Roy Haynes, was the young son of a neighbor. Born in 1925, he lived on Haskins Street in Lower Roxbury when he was briefly tutored by Wright. "My first drum lesson was taken with Herbert Wright," Haynes recalls. "He lived across the street from me so I saw him a lot. He was a short man with medium-brown complexion. I remember his wife too. I knew he was famous and I looked up to him. He was probably my father's age. He was a friend of my father and they use to drink a lot. I had drum lessons with him. He taught me rudimentary stuff; I didn't study that long. I think my father paid him. I was maybe nine or ten years old."[29] Roy would go on to become one of the most renowned drummers in jazz history.

Thus, in ways unforeseen, the James Reese Europe Orchestra set ablaze the embers of the music scene in Boston's Black neighborhoods. His contributions to the culture outlived his tragic demise in the public hospital that spring night. The legacy of his jazz innovations continued to spread in the South End and Lower Roxbury—and in no place more strongly than the fledgling jazz scene of Frederick Douglass Square.

The Graphophone was a tabletop phonograph used to play 78 rpm records. The inexpensive machines were popular with South End record buyers in 1919 and afterwards.

CHAPTER THREE

FREDERICK DOUGLASS SQUARE

Rise of a Black Business District

Frederick Douglass Square was an emerging Black commercial district at the crossroads of the South End and Lower Roxbury. Located at the nexus of Tremont Street, Hammond Street, and Cabot Street, it was a short walk to the Orange Line elevated train station at Washington and Northampton streets. The business district was supported by a predominately working-class population of about 23,500 residents and served as a destination for Black railroad workers and touring musicians in the jazz age. It offered a small version of the dynamic music culture that flowered in the Black sectors of northern cities such as Harlem New York, South Side Chicago, Black Bottom Detroit, and the Hill District of Pittsburgh, among others, during the period of the mass migrations.[1]

Moreover, Frederick Douglass Square was strategically located in the broader sprawl of Black residency that stretched from the old West End sector to a cluster of middle-class homes in the Roxbury Highlands. The boutique size of the city's Black population—13,500 in 1910; 16,350 in 1920; 20,500 in 1930; and 24,000 in 1940—never amounted to more than 2.5 percent of the total population.[2] It may help to explain the absence of violent reactions that erupted in other cities impacted by the migration over the years. During the "Red Summer" of 1919, for example, groups of white thugs both native and immigrant turned on Black neighborhoods in Chicago, East St. Louis, Tulsa, and other cities. No such incidents occurred in Boston, even when law and order broke down in the weeks of the 1919 police strike.

Frederick Douglass Square was a node of commercial activity where Black merchants could hold their own against white competitors. Despite the constraints of limited capital and expertise, the men and women controlled a share of the retail market and provided patrons with a lively service. A sense of the business activity can be gleaned from advertisements in the *Boston Guardian* and the observations of John Daniels, a social worker at the South End Settlement House in the 1900s. Daniels, author of *In Freedom's Birthplace: A Study of the Boston Negroes*, researched the history of Black residences and chronicled the commercial experience. His study noted many Black establishments combining the features of groceries, dry goods, hardware, stationery, tobacco, candy, and general goods. Others provided the multiple services of restaurant, horse-drawn wagon for moving furniture, and real estate agency. He writes, "Negro proprietors offer for sale a range of wares so wide as to enable them to pick up the petty trade of the vicinity."[3]

There were draymen stands (peddlers with horse-drawn wagons), barbershops, shoeshine shops, lunchrooms, laundries, newsstands, and lodging houses. Among the larger specialty businesses was the Eureka Banking Company, which served as real estate business and commercial bank; W. S. Sparrow, a tailor of custom-made clothes for the affluent on Tremont Street; Gilbert C. Harris, the owner of a wig making factory on Washington Street; and Basil F. Hutchins, an undertaker with offices in the South End and Cambridge as well as a livery stable and other properties. The companies anchored a node of small business activity that created a commercial environment where Black consumers could walk into grocery stores, barbershops, and dining rooms with a sense of pride.[4]

In 1920, a visitor to Frederick Douglass Square would have enjoyed staying at the Hotel Melbourne at 805–819 Tremont Street, one of four Black-owned hotels in the neighborhood alongside Young's, the Pitts, and the Carlton. The Melbourne was owned by the family of S. I. Crawford, managing director, and David Crawford, treasurer. "It is the object of new management to cater especially to respectable people," they advertised. "Good music. Good meals. Good order." The reference to "respectable people" may have been a poke at the Upton Hotel, which had been closed by city authorities for disorderly activity, likely related to the use of rooms for prostitution; nonetheless, the Upton was known as a successful lodging house.[5]

Leaving the Melbourne, our visitor would have passed the Bay State Pharmacy at 840 Tremont and noted its promotion by pharmacist William A. Smith as "the House that Service Built." Dr. Smith was the manager and co-owner of the first Black-owned drugstore in Boston, established in 1915, but would soon be joined by another. In the window of Bay State, our visitor might see the beauty products of the Mary E. Moore Manufacturing Company, a Black-owned neighborhood cosmetics maker located at 36 Warwick Street that created "toilet articles for the face, neck, hand, hair and scalp including bleaching cream, cold cream, rouge, shampoo, and complexion powders."[6]

Continuing on Tremont, our visitor could review the selection of dining rooms and restaurants, perhaps considering the Star Lunch, a new restaurant opened by the family of Gomes and Augustus Homans. Then there was the landmark Southern Dining Room of Thomas E. Lucas, who claimed that "Good food and prompt attentive service have made this a most desirable place for discriminating people." There was also Slade's Restaurant at 958 Tremont, where restaurateur Renner Slade supplied his own meat from his chicken farm—the kitchen was noted for its succulent barbecue: "The scent of good chicken dinners waft[ed] down the block and passersby saw Slade's chefs standing at rotisseries in the front window."[7] After a meal, our visitor would pass the offices of professionals like attorney David Crawford at 934 Tremont Street: "Commissioned to accept bail in both criminal and civil cases. Calls answered any hour day or night." Next door, at 957 Tremont, was the office of undertaker and embalmer John O'Brien, who promised "bodies shipped to all parts promptly and efficient service guaranteed." Moving on, they could pick up sheet music, piano rolls, and records at Gamer's Music Store (965 Tremont), or copies of the local Black newsweeklies the *Guardian* and the *Chronicle* at the Community Shop (1021 Tremont): "The Mecca of Magazines and Literature. Anything published ordered on request."[8]

On the way, one might even pass the publisher William Monroe Trotter holding a copy of his eight-page weekly, the *Boston Guardian*. Trotter was a prominent figure in the square with an apartment at 971A Tremont and newspaper office at nearby 977 Tremont. Trotter was a crusading editor with a complicated view on Black solidarity due in part to his mixed racial identity and upper-class sensibilities. While he tended to disavow programs of race nationalism, he still founded a newspaper to cover the community and to print advertisements and supplements on the traveling stage shows of Harlem. George Edward Tynes recalled living above the Trotter apartment at 971A Tremont. As a child, he observed the tall, light-skinned newspaperman as a dashing figure in a long black coat, trademark derby hat, and pockets bulging with papers. He would watch Trotter and his sister, Maude Trotter Stuart, sell copies of the weekly on the streets. He was inspired by the hard-hitting editorials on civil rights issues in the newspaper.[9]

Trotter was one of two Black publishers in the Square, and both were known for their work in promoting the interests of the people. The other was Bill Harrison of the *Boston Chronicle*, with an office on Tremont and Northampton streets. The *Chronicle* was the most widely circulated Black newspaper in New England; it was published by Alfred Haughton and edited by William Harrison. The newspaper was founded by Jamaican immigrants but reported on events in the community and across the Pan-African world.

Kenneth Guscott was born in Boston in 1925 to parents who had emigrated from Jamaica. The family lived in Frederick Douglass Square as early as 1921 and supported the *Chronicle* as part of the West Indian diaspora. Years later, Guscott would work as a "newsie," saying, "We used to sell the *Chronicle*. Every Saturday we would get our little package of *Chronicles* and go out and sell them for 5 cents. We got something like a penny for each sale."[10] Guscott remembered the newspapermen as respected community leaders who used their access to higher education to serve the interests of the race: "Those were the types of leadership people that we had. Bill Harrison and his brother, they had gone to college. They are the ones that inspired us to go to school. They would always impress upon you to get an education."

Continuing on Tremont Street, our visitor could choose from several barbershops and hair salons. There was the Modern Hair Dressing Parlor at 977 Tremont, with "every modern convenience for the care of face and scalp." There was the Douglass Square Barber Shop at 975 Tremont, where owner James Carey employed five barbers and promised "no waiting."[11] From there, our visitor could get a shoeshine at any one of a number of stands. There was the newspaper and shoeshine store on Tremont and Hammond streets where Charles Thomas worked as a boy. Born in March 1919, he was the second generation of his family to live in Boston. One of his grandparents moved from New Jersey to the Black quarter of the West End in the late nineteenth century; the other grandparent emigrated from Britain to Boston. They raised their family in the West End before moving to Frederick Douglass Square. His stepfather owned a shoeshine stand where Thomas worked as a boy. He recalled soliciting customers with the invitation to "Step right up for a quick shine." The stand featured four chairs with brass figurines for your shoes. His ritual included washing shoes clean of dust, applying a coat of shoeshine paste, and buffering with a rag—and he always appreciated a nice tip.[12]

Strolling on Tremont, our visitor could pick up fresh fruit at the Farm Outlet at 1023 Tremont Street. Owner Sturgis Robinson greeted customers at the door in appreciation of the support of the folk in a competitive market. "Before going over to Harrison Ave. or downtown for your fruits and vegetables, come and look us over," he stated. "We know our prices are right and that you need seek no further." Even Trotter had to acknowledge the vitality of a commercial sector independent of white merchant dominance, writing, "The Colored people have come to the conclusion that trading among themselves is wise and are willing to spend money in their own shops when treated right."[13] The neighborhood visitor could even take in a Boston Tigers baseball game. The Tigers were among the best African American teams in New England during the jazz age. The semi-professional team (not part of the Negro Leagues) played in Madison Park, located then at Tremont and Ruggles streets. Touted by regional newspapers as "colored champions of the state," the Tigers were in high demand across New England. "The Tigers will be the first colored team to play on a Mansfield diamond," the Mansfield *News* reported, "and the fact that they always inject plenty of pepper and comedy into their play should go a long way toward attracting a capacity crowd."[14]

Merchants sold the popular tabletop and standing phonographs for households to play the new 78 rpm "race records." The willingness of Blacks to buy the records of their own jazz bands and blues singers had a ripple effect in the retail sector. Households had their choice of inexpensive tabletop record players (known as gramophones or graphophones). The technology used a hand crank to wind the spring that powered the turntable and featured external horns for sound projection. By the early 1920s, the large floor-standing record player known as the "Victrola" became a popular furniture piece of culture in middle-class homes. The evolution of Frederick Douglass Square as a business district was an experiment

The "Victrola" was a large floor-standing record player used as a stylish furniture piece and source of music entertainment in the 1920s.

in economic determination promoted by prominent leaders such as the educator Booker T. Washington and the nationalist Marcus Garvey.

Frederick Douglass Square was dedicated by city officials on February 14, 1917, to mark the 100th birthday of the runaway slave. It was the first such honor the city had ever bestowed on an African American figure. Douglass, whose life spanned the poignant experiences of slavery, freedom, and reinvention as abolitionist writer, newspaper publisher, political orator, and US ambassador to Haiti, was a fitting symbol for the self-made Black community. Douglass actually had little idea of his true date of birth, selecting Valentine's Day as an assumed date on which to celebrate his birthday. He was one of the most influential voices in the Boston antislavery movement until he moved to Rochester, New York, in 1848.

His story of self-determination was well known to Bostonians: he was born Frederick Augustus Washington Bailey on a slave plantation in Talbot County, Maryland, in 1817. In September 1838, he ran away when working in Baltimore, aided by Anna Murray, a free Black woman and member of the Underground Railroad. They lived in Philadelphia and New York City and married that year. They settled in New Bedford, where he worked on the waterfront and learned of the *Liberator*, the abolitionist newspaper of Boston publisher William Lloyd Garrison. In 1841, Douglass attended an antislavery meeting in Nantucket to hear Garrison and revealed his story to the audience. He soon joined figures such as Garrison, Charles Lenox Remond, and William Cooper Nell on the speaking circuit. However, they butted heads in the late 1840s over a number of issues, including his infidelity with a white secretary, Julia Griffith; his decision to publish a competing newspaper to the *Liberator*; and his gradual support of armed resistance to end slavery. Despite the falling out, Douglass remained a beloved figure in the city.[15]

The process for a municipal commemoration of the locale began in January when councilor Walter Ballantyne introduced an order of designation. Ballantyne was born in Hawick, Scotland, in 1855, and achieved notoriety as the first president of the Boston City Council in 1910, when the city shifted from the alderman to the city council system. After one year as president, he served as an at-large councilor until 1918.[16] The order of dedication was endorsed by the city council, and on February 14, mayor James Michael Curley issued a proclamation in observance of Frederick Douglass Day. Celebrations were held in honor of his contributions to American liberty and democracy. Flags were flown on public buildings, and schools used the occasion to teach children about Douglass and the abolitionist movement. There were orations on his role in other areas of national political life by members of the city council and civic leaders. The New England Suffrage League and Massachusetts State Union of Women's Clubs commemorated his pioneer support for women's equality.[17]

The Square was the first dedication of a site to a Black American, but not the first time the city had honored a Black patriot—that legacy went to the ex-slave and seaman Crispus Attucks. Enslaved in Framingham, Attucks ran away in 1750 and found work as a seaman with Boston as home port. He was described as a 6′2″ man of mixed racial heritage with "curl'd hair, his knees nearer together than common." On March 5, 1770, as tensions rose between Britain and the American colony, Attucks was among a crowd of sailors who threw snowballs and rocks at soldiers guarding the Customs House.[18] The forty-seven-year-old Attucks, described as a "stout man with a long cordwood stick," took the lead in confronting Captain Thomas Preston and a contingent of nine soldiers. During the scuffle, Attucks hit a soldier with the stick and the soldiers responded by firing on the crowd. Attucks and four other men were killed in the incident, which would later be branded as the Boston Massacre. Samuel Adams declared Attucks the first martyr in the fight against British colonialism, and the story of Attucks became a cogent symbol of the broader meaning of American freedom in the struggle against the slave interests. In 1851, as the impact of the Fugitive Slave Act was felt in the city, Black abolitionists responded by demanding recognition of their contributions to the country. One Boston campaign sought to preserve the memory of Attucks, proposing that the city establish a monument in his honor, and in 1858, community leaders designated March 5 as "Crispus Attucks Day." In 1888, Boston authorities erected an obelisk in honor of the Boston Massacre and Crispus Attucks, placed in the Boston Common at Tremont and Avery streets.[19]

Decades later, the city again signaled its recognition of Black contributions to the political culture with the designation of Frederick Douglass Square. The dedication took place in a neighborhood that by the 1890s was in decline. Social workers of the South End Settlement House found it "made up of people who have no local attachments and are separated from one another by distinctions and religion." Their impressions are collected in *The City Wilderness* by Robert A. Woods, which includes works by William I. Cole, Fred E. Haynes, Frederick A. Bushee, and Charles D. Underhill. Albert Benedict Wolfe, a Harvard research fellow, wrote a separate study titled *The Lodging House Problem in Boston*, in which he concludes that "It is at once evident that most of these low-paid persons cannot meet even the mere board and room-rent expenses of lodging house life." John Daniels, another research fellow at the South End House, wrote his own history of Blacks in Boston: *In Freedom's Birthplace*.[20]

Their observations helped to account for the history of the early Black experience in the South End area that bordered Chinatown and the Theater District. By 1900, the neighborhood had undergone a transition from an enclave for the households of skilled white labor to a zone of rooming houses for transient workers. The neighborhood lacked any distinctive industry other than the coal and lumber yards on the Albany Street waterfront and the factories that used them. Its chief value was in its proximity to the markets, warehouses, and amusements of the downtown and waterfront. Men and women, writes sociologist Alfred Wolfe, found areas like the South End advantageous for discovering "opportunities for work, and for amusement, excitement, and variety, the attractive force of the unknown, the hypnotic influence of the color and movement and energy of the crowd."[21]

The South End housed the cooks, clerks, waiters, mechanics, tailors, domestics, laborers, craftsmen, and other moderately skilled workers essential to the economy. The residents tended to be single white men and women from locations in New England

and New York, many immigrants from Ireland, Germany, Canada, and "Negroes of the South, who, attracted by wider opportunities than the conservatism of the South will afford them, and by an already extensive colony of their race, came to Boston in the hope of bettering their condition."[22] Neighborhood commerce was geared to meet the needs of a low-wage population of about 35,000 to 40,000 people. One could find "cafes, dining-rooms, laundries, tailor-shops, and drug-stores" along Tremont Street, Washington Street, Columbus Avenue, Dartmouth Street, Shawmut Avenue, and other thoroughfares. A census of local business catering to the lodging population found eighty-seven cafes, sixty-five basement dining-rooms, forty-one saloons, twenty-four liquor stores, seventy-eight laundries, seventy tailor shops, and eleven pool rooms. Larger outlets included furniture and clothing stores with installment plans as well as pawnshops that served as informal banks.[23]

South End real estate had featured low-cost rooms in private homes and tenement buildings run by "widows, thrifty young couples, and people of broken fortunes," wrote Boston sociologist Alfred Wolfe. But then the community housing stock shifted as old family mansions were converted to rooming houses, rear lot tenements, model tenements, apartment houses, and cheap hotels. In 1905, landlords charged lodgers about $2 a week per person for a room.[24] One concern was the economic burden caused by separating the cost of room and board. The old boarding house practice of a widow providing a room and regular meals was a thing of the past. Now, in response, an industry of basement dining rooms sprang up to offer weekly meal plans for the transient lodgers. A typical weekly plan of twenty-one meals (three meals a day) cost $4. A plan of fourteen meals (two a day) was $3. Eating à la carte could be even more expensive. In fact, the combined cost of room and meals could exceed the monthly income of residents.[25]

With the shift to lodging houses, the Black renter had access to housing outside of the decrepit rooms of the West End. People migrated to back-alley rooms near the railroad tracks in the decades after Reconstruction. Wolfe asserted that "many of the older ones were slaves, and are entirely uneducated. Nearly all the Negroes are from the South."[26] The crescent of Black roomers extended from the West End to the South End by the 1900s. A hamlet took root on the streets near the Back Bay Railroad Station and the former Trinity Station near the Trinity Church. Wolfe, a contemporary observer, continued: "The intersection of Dartmouth Street and Columbus Avenue marks the centre of this negro colony. Their choice of this locality is probably due, in part at least, to its proximity to the apartment house, hotel, and private residence districts of the Back Bay."[27]

Within in a few years, the rundown rooming houses in the lower South End became an increasingly mean attraction for prostitutes, pimps, and pickpockets. The Kirkland Street section, once located near the current New England Medical Center train stop, was a downtrodden area noted for cheap rooms, factories, and train tracks to South Station. Wolfe writes, "The Kirkland Street district is visited frequently by the patrol wagon. In fact, this neighborhood is one of the worst in the South End, if not in the whole city."[28] And the poet Robert Lowell wrote that he could open the window in his Back Bay townhouse and "hear the South End / the razor's edge / of Boston's negro culture."[29]

In *Boston's Workers*, authors James N. Green and Hugh Carter Donahue reconsider the interpretations of the Yankee reformers. They note, for example, the cherry-picking of indicators and the bias suggested by titles like *The City Wilderness*. The reformers shed a light on issues of concern to their class interests: poor housing quality, unstable residency, sanitation and disease, crime, idleness, sexual impropriety, and political corruption. In this regard, the reformers promoted the notion of "civilizing the wilderness" much like missionaries in economically and technologically underdeveloped countries. Robert Woods, they wrote, was supportive of the agenda of Yankee reformers such as Theodore Roosevelt,

Woodrow Wilson, and locally, the Boston Democratic mayor in the 1890s, Josiah Quincy IV. Such leaders tried to preserve Yankee power by heading off class conflict and promoting assimilation as a means of social mobility.[30] "The settlement-house professionals were misguided, however, when they sought to 'rehabilitate neighborhood life' according to Yankee values; they ignored the vitality of Boston's ethnic subculture, which provided poor people with meaningful cultural activities," write Green and Donahue, continuing, "They failed to see that working class forms of cooperation existed in the diversity and disorder of South End life."[31]

By the early years of the century, Black workers in skilled trades were able to rent rooms and apartments in the South End and Lower Roxbury. Over time, the class of laborers, waiters, porters, janitors, professionals, and business owners were reported to have amassed about $2.7 million in real estate holdings. By 1910 about 215 families owned 265 parcels with an estimated value of $1.15 million in Boston. Among this group were the parents of the future jazz saxophonists Johnny Hodges and Harry Carney, whose fathers were part of the class of waiters and janitors employed in the hotels near the train stations. In the case of Hodges, according to Con Chapman, the family moved from Cambridgeport to the affordable housing in the district and joined the other "negro waiters, cooks and stewards, barbers, janitors and porters" of the Black middle class. During the war years, such areas of employment laid the foundation for the commercial district of Frederick Douglass Square.[32]

African Americans moved to Frederick Douglass Square in search of better housing in the 1890s. Most were renters priced out of the West End by the wave of Jewish immigrants from Eastern Europe. At first, people rented rooms in the lower South End streets near the Back Bay Railroad Station; from there, people moved deeper into the neighborhood following the street car lines on Tremont Street and the Orange Line El on Washington Street. By 1917, there was a sizeable population of Black renters in the buildings near the transit stops. It was common for families to double up in the rooms of three-decker, townhouse, and tenement buildings. The surge of Black people from the West End was supplemented by migrants from New York and New Jersey as well as the South, who came from the farms and small cities of Virginia, North Carolina, South Carolina, Georgia, and Florida to make a better life.[33]

James E. Guilford Jr. was born on October 7, 1911, to James "Eddie" Guilford and Nancy Bell Haskin Guilford. Both parents were migrants from Virginia, his father from Petersburg and his mother from Lynchburg. They met and married in Boston. The family lived at 28 Sterling Street about the time he was born. James Roberts Davis was born in the city hospital on November 30, 1919, to Mason Davis and Missouri Davis. His father migrated from Dover, Delaware, and his mother from Montgomery, Alabama. The address of their room or apartment in the neighborhood has been lost to time. Ruth Mozell Davis Tinsley, meanwhile, moved to Boston in 1923 at the age of fourteen from Savannah, Georgia. She lived at 23 Holyoke Street with her parents, Calvin Davis of Lake Charles, Louisiana, and Daisy Belle Mitchell of Valdosta, Georgia.[34]

Joining the migrants were emigrants from Nova Scotia and the English-speaking West Indies. George Herbert Tynes was an example of this immigrant experience. He was born on March 16, 1923, to George Edward Tynes and Vivian Cleveland Williams. The couple were former residents of Nova Scotia who had rented a room or apartment on Longwood Avenue for years before his birth. Afterward, the family moved to rooms or apartments on Tremont Street, Kennard Street, Columbus Avenue, and South Huntington Street. Also settling in Boston from Nova Scotia were the parents of Leon Vanward Jacklin Jr. He was born on July 11, 1925, in Massachusetts Memorial Hospital on Harrison Avenue to Leon Vanward Jacklin and Florence Jacklin. The immigrated from Nova Scotia years earlier to escape poverty and rented either rooms or apartments on Charwood Street and later on Oakburn Avenue.[35]

Some residents immigrated to Boston from the islands of the West Indies, primarily Barbados and Jamaica. Mrs. John Leon Vernon Bynoe, who used the name of her husband in the custom of her generation, was born in 1896 in Barbados. John left the country to find work in Canada and Boston around the war years and sent for her in 1920. She made the difficult decision to leave their four children in the care of loved ones and join him to make a home. They brought the children to Boston in 1927 and lived in apartments on Windsor Street and later at 716 Shawmut Avenue. Joseph Leroy Walcott was another example of the Barbados talent pool coming to Boston. Born on January 9, 1897, Walcott immigrated to Boston to be with his two brothers during the war years. They lived in rooms or an apartment at 9 Grenville Place.[36]

Children growing up in the multiethnic South End remembered people getting along. Charles Thomas recalls his family living at 80 Hammond Street in the 1920s, where they rented either a room or apartment from an immigrant landlord: "The people that owned the building and lived underneath of us were Jews, and they had a store on the ground floor. In order to get into our apartment, we had to go on to Sussex Street and that was the entrance to get into their apartment and into our apartment." He noted an interracial family of a white wife and Black husband living on the street: "They didn't seem to have any problems—people throwing stones or rocks into their windows. We were all on good friendly terms."[37]

"I practically knew everybody around me—all the families," explains James Guildford Jr., who lived on Sterling Street as a boy. He recalls, "When I was growing up, this Irish woman who lived right across the street from me where I was born, Mrs. Kane, said there used to be a river running right down through Sterling Street, which was a fact." Leon Vanward Jacklin Jr. expresses the sentiment of grief over a lost time and community: "In those days, I think, it was a sense of everybody being in the same boat and everybody understanding each other."[38] George Adams grew up in the Castle Square section of the South End during this time. His family emigrated from Jamaica and his father worked as a porter for the Pullman Railroad Company out of South Station. The neighborhood consisted of "Irish, Armenian, Jewish, Italian, and Polish along with Blacks," he recalled. "I remember going home from school—changing my clothes and going outdoors to play stickball, marbles, and all the other childhood games with all the different kids in the neighborhood."[39]

At the same time, researchers examining the question of fair employment in the city have discovered a pattern of racial discrimination. By 1920, Black residents were challenged to make a living in a hostile job market. The obstacle of bigotry was pronounced among white employers, employees, and customers alike. "The discrimination in question is very real, and its effects are very plain," observed John Daniels, a research fellow at the South End House. "It shows itself first in a prejudice against Negro applicants for employment." Frederick Bushee, another fellow at the South End House, concluded: "The Negroes in general encounter unusual difficulties in securing employment."[40]

Researchers have concluded that employment discrimination worked in a variety of ways: in the market for personal service jobs, for example, hotels and restaurants preferred to hire white and Asian immigrant workers. Where once cultural traditions protected—and restricted—Black workers in such positions, now they faced the prospect of rapid displacement by foreign workers; for instance, barbers who served white customers were dropped for Italian haircutters, hotel bellboys for Japanese immigrants, and shoeshiners for Greek bootblacks. Female domestics were pushed out by Swedish and German immigrants. Black workers in the skilled trades faced the obstacle of employer responses to the bias of white employees and patrons. When they did hire, retailers tended to favor those Black people with light complexions to avoid drawing attention to skin tones. Such practices could thwart the occupational opportunities of the most hard-working Black residents. "In order to gain promotion he must as a rule do work which is not only equal in quality to that of white employees of the same sort, but better," wrote Daniels. "Even so, his promotion is at best slow and uncertain."[41]

Mostly, job-seekers had to overcome a stereotype of incompetence resulting from deficiencies in skills and work practices, exacerbated by exclusions from occupations. This was especially the case for southern migrants new to the urban job market, the largest segment of the Black workforce. The problem was often one of a mismatch of job skills, time management habits, and other differences in the culture of work on the plantation versus the urban industrial company. Another stereotype was related to the historic low view of Black workers. The vast majority began as slave laborers in agriculture, menial laborers on docks and ships, and domestic service in the colony, though some had developed skilled trades. The native Black population was later joined by southern migrants with similar occupational limitations. As the city industrialized, few people had the training to compete for better jobs and had to work piecemeal to survive. By the 1900s, the situation had improved somewhat as more people had access to better training, yet they still had to contend with the bias of employers, coworkers, and customers: "While admitting that there are many individuals of this race who have exceptional qualifications, they declare that as a class they are unreliable and incompetent."[42]

The employment prospects for Black people improved with the expansion of the Boston economy of the war years. By 1920, Black work participation was primarily in the low-wage service occupations. About two thirds of Black males and three quarters of females worked in positions of personal service. The proportion of those employed in such jobs was far above that of white workers. Among the common jobs for men were waiters, porters, messengers, bootblacks (shoeshiners), hostlers (people who cared for horses), and day laborers. The railroad yards hired Black men to shovel coal, polish trains, and pick up debris on tracks. Among the jobs for women were domestic servants, laundresses, waitresses, dressmakers, nurses, seamstresses, and bookkeepers. The job of cook was among the better paying occupations. The wages of workers could vary from $7 to $12 a week.[43] Thrifty individuals used the small but steady paychecks to good advantage as they moved up from renting rooms to buying houses and the comforts of middle-class life, like musical instruments. Daniels observes, "The Negro people, in considerable degree making a virtue of their necessity, have turned occupations reckoned lowly into the means of substantial economic intrenchment [*sic*]."[44]

Many boys entered the labor force to help the family and hustled for tips shining shoes and delivering newspapers. Kenneth Guscott, for example, remembered performing such duties on the streets of the South End and Lower Roxbury, among other jobs. "Back in those days we had the wood stoves and the coal stoves. Have ice, we would work with the iceman and the coal man on Saturdays. We were young strong bucks then and we would carry the coal and stuff up to the third floor, and he would pay us 2 bucks for the Saturday," he described. "When we were younger, we had a cart and we would go out and sell fruit and vegetables, just like the Italians did. Walking down the street selling that stuff. There are all kinds of things that we used to do." The youthful Benny Waters worked as a busboy and porter cleaning rooms in hotels to make ends meet while taking music classes during the war years. He described, "I worked my way through. I got a job in a restaurant. I got fallen arches by walking on the hard floor, doing that to make a living before I got established in Boston."[45]

In the better-quality settings, the tips in service jobs like waiter, porter, and elevator operator could generate a higher income than could be received in occupations with more social status like clerk and artisan. Wolfe observed that "The percentage of domestic and personal servants is swelled by the great number of negro waiters living about the Back Bay Station." James Guildford Jr. says that his father, James "Eddie" Guildford of Petersburg, Virginia, worked as a waiter at the Woodcock Hotel on the former Dover

Street, now Berkeley Street. In the 1890s, hotel waiters formed the Tremont House Waiters Association, part of the national Colored Waiters Alliance, to improve skills and bargaining power. Porters and waiters in the better hospitality and residence sectors could earn as much as $125 a month. There were an estimated 25–30 luxury hotels, restaurants, supper clubs, and apartment buildings that hired Black people for personal and building services near the South End, such as the Copley Plaza Hotel and the Westminster Hotel.[46]

The most significant indicator for Black economic mobility was the chance to improve trade skills. Black workers gained a foothold in the skilled trades despite objections from white natives and immigrants. In doing so, they heeded the call of Frederick Douglass: his admonishment to "learn trades or starve" emphasized a strategy of academic and industrial preparation for the growth fields of the economy. Supporters of vocational education also stressed the need to educate for the professions and to start businesses to serve markets in the larger society. This strategy was best promoted by educator Booker T. Washington.[47]

George Edward Tynes, for example, emigrated from Nova Scotia in 1909 and did unskilled work in a laundry at first. He later became a chauffeur for a Tufts University professor and then worked in an industrial trade for the Croft Brewing Company on Heath Street. Black people moved into a broader range of skilled trades and developed networks of information on job opportunities in those areas. The family of Pauline Thomas left New Kent County, Virginia, and migrated to Douglass Square circa 1922. They hoped to find "better living conditions and working" and rented a room on Kendall Street and Marble Street. "My mother had a sister who had come here, and her husband was working—he was a longshoreman down on the Northern Pier," she says. "He got my father a job there."[48]

Through better training and education, nearly 25 percent of males and 16 percent of females had entered this sector of the labor market. The jobs commanded good wages and compelled respect for needed abilities—and they were indicators of occupational advancement within the community. Among the positions for men were building janitors, teamsters, barbers, boiler and furnace engineers, and workers in the construction trade. Some also worked as clerks and copyists, salesmen, and high-level messengers for banks and government offices. Among the positions for women were dressmakers, stewardesses, seamstresses, and nurses. During the Jazz Age, Leon Vanward Jacklin, who emigrated to Lower Roxbury from Nova Scotia, worked as a porter and later as a truck driver at the waterfront fish pier. John Milton Corbin moved to the neighborhood from the West Indies and worked as a tailor. Daisy Belle Mitchell Tinsley migrated from Valdosta, Georgia, to Lower Roxbury and was employed as a seamstress.[49]

Janitorial workers were employed by apartment houses, business complexes, and government buildings. They were noted for their hard work, ability, and ambition—many went on to own their own property. As Daniels notes, "The Negro janitors include a larger proportion of property owners than is the case with any other single occupation." Many Black teamsters were employed by the coal companies to make deliveries to business and residential customers. They were known for their hard work, good humor, and kind treatment of the wagon horses. In addition, Black drivers were making inroads as chauffeurs and earning respect for mechanical skill and trustworthiness. In construction, many people worked as carpenters, roofers, plasterers, and wallpaper hangers. Some owned their tools and were self-employed.[50]

The number of Black people in professional fields was miniscule but growing with the influx of middle-class newcomers. An estimated eight percent of the male workers and six percent of females were employed in such fields by the 1910s. Among the trades open to men were shoemakers and realtors; among the professions were doctors, lawyers, dentists, and clergy. Women at this level tended to be owners of small businesses such as dressmakers, lodging houses, and laundries. Among the notable professionals was Philip Allston, who rose from washing bottles to laboratory foreman at a white-owned cosmetics company. The child of former slaves, he was a fair-skinned migrant from North Carolina who came to Boston around 1871 with his mother who worked as a seamstress and hired private tutors for her children. Allston left grammar school to work and help the family. He took night classes in high school and at an art school for thirteen years while working as a bottle washer at the Weeks and Potter Company, a wholesale and retail drug business that later changed its name to the Potter Drug and Chemical Corporation under Warren Potter and George Robert White, the president and noted philanthropist.

After years of working as a bottle washer, Allston was promoted by Warren Potter to head a new laboratory opening on Columbus Avenue. The company supported his training for the position at the Massachusetts College of Pharmacy. As it turned out, Allston was selected to be the foreman of a laboratory staffed by Black technicians. The new laboratory was involved in the production of medicated soaps and the brand named "Cuticura"—which continues to be one of the company's best-known products today.[51]

Many professionals were of biracial heritage, with relatively better access to education and patrons and less biased reactions in the workplace. Some even established client relationships with white and Black patrons, such as attorney Edgar Benjamin, who built a general practice in civil and criminal cases. About two thirds of his clients were white and one third Black. After completing English High School, he studied at Boston University College and then Boston University Law School, where he graduated in 1894. After passing the bar, he was unable to find a job with a law firm and decided to start his own practice. He counseled various companies on legal matters and developed an expertise in the needs of piano manufacturers. He also benefited from the support of a "southern white man" with business connections who referred people to his office. "With the loan of twenty dollars, and a desk and a couple of chairs as an office equipment, I started out, and have remained in the same building but in larger quarters to the present time," he writes, adding, "The Negro asks, insists, and only wants his Manhood Rights."[52]

The shift from agitation to self-improvement through education, industrial training, and small business gained favor in the South End. As Black people gained a foothold in new occupations, some Boston elites known to criticize the strategy of Booker T. Washington as "accommodating" southern reactionary politics had a change of heart. The recognized that his promotion of education for skilled trades and business development were as essential to the development of an oppressed people as political participation. One such person was Boston attorney William A. Lewis. He was part of the vanguard of civil rights activists in the 1890s and was critical of the economic-oriented program identified with Booker T. Washington. A Cambridge native, he attended Harvard Law School in 1893 and became known as a crusader for equal rights. For example, he sued a Cambridge barber for the slight of refusing to cut his hair. The case resulted in an 1895 state civil rights law banning discrimination in public accommodations. Lewis would go on to be appointed to several public offices under the Democratic Party.

In one regard, however, he stepped back from the civil rights radicalism of the Boston political class. That was in the dispute between Monroe Trotter and Booker T. Washington over the best direction to emphasize for Black progress—political participation or economic development. Lewis came to see that both directions were essential to Black development and that such agendas should reinforce one another: it was clear that any program of civil rights was tied to the economic power of the group. As early as 1909, he began to soften his views of the Washington program: "After leaving law school, I was counted as one of the radicals and agitators, but I found so many good people who approved Dr. Washington's course and who were just as sincere in their advocacy of human rights and Negro rights as I myself."[53]

The Frederick Douglass Square commercial district was a model of the Washington program and benefited from the presence of his National Negro Business League, founded in 1900. By the war years, the NNBL boasted chapters in twelve states and 250 cities and towns with a Boston headquarters located at 121 Kendall Street in the Square. The first president was Dr. W. Alexander Johnson, the only Black dermatologist at the time and the cofounder with his wife of a hair product business. The Boston league claimed about 250 businesses, including about 100 in the South End and Lower Roxbury and fifty in predominately white communities. The businesses reportedly hired as many as 1,000 Black employees and 200 white workers.[54]

Besides the family-run business, people with limited access to capital experimented with cooperative neighborhood ventures such as the real estate operation of the Goode Trust Company. It was founded by twenty waiters under Jesse Goode, a former waiter and the company's president. He promoted the idea of waiters depositing small sums of money each week to a real estate investment fund, which grew to become one of the largest Black-owned property management outfits in the city. By 1901, they held in combination about twelve parcels with values of $73,000. Goode went on to cofound Goode, Dunson and Henry, a retail and wholesale grocery store on Shawmut Avenue in the South End. It was a store large enough to compete with white grocers for a share of the white trade while also supplying many smaller Black grocery stores.[55]

Among the institutions in a position to accomplish programs of mutual assistance were the religious organizations. While some old families preferred to attend white churches—and viewed it as a sign of racial equality—the integration of church congregations did create a level of discomfort and tension at times. Moreover, migrants were accustomed to separate worship and saw merit in making their own path in Boston. The Church of God and Saints of Christ was an example of a successful cooperative effort in the

Square. Founded by William Saunders Crowdy, the leader of a cult of Old Testament adherents known as the "Black Israelites," the church was effective in improving the lives of poor southern migrants in the city. William Saunders Crowdy was born into slavery in Maryland in 1847. His mother was a cook on the plantation. Crowdy was exposed to the "ring shout" of old slave culture that drew upon the memories of African tribal spirituality, ancestors, songs, and circle dances, along with Old Testament stories and New Testament teachings. Circa 1863, he ran away from enslavement and took the name of William Saunders Crowdy. He worked as a cook for the Union Army and later bought 100 acres of land in central Oklahoma under a homesteading program.[56]

Crowdy underwent a conversion experience that led him to become an evangelist. The rotund farmer with his white mustache began to preach on the streets of Guthrie, Oklahoma, to the chagrin of friends and neighbors. He established the Church of God and Saints of Christ and took his ministry to Kansas, where he organized three tabernacles in Lawrence, Emporia, and Topeka. He ordained "elders" to lead the chapters and continued to evangelize and open tabernacles in states and cities of the Midwest and Northeast. He also established churches in South Africa and Jamaica. The church services continued the primitive style of expressive worship—the emotional cries, songs, chants, dancing, and preference for Old Testament stories and teachings.

In June 1903, Crowdy founded the Boston Church of God and Saints of Christ. He appointed Elder William H. Plummer as pastor for Boston and spiritual leader for the New England district; Plummer would be ordained as a Bishop in 1909. In 1917, William Crowdy passed away in Boston at the home of Plummer, located at the former 15 Arnold Street in the South End, after a brief illness. By then, Plummer was known as "Grand Father Abraham" to a Boston congregation of about fifty families. Most were poor and illiterate migrants from the South who worked as day laborers for meager wages. Yet by living in a cooperative fashion, they achieved material progress beyond their individual means. The church was located on Shawmut Street and the former Woodbury Street in Lower Roxbury and featured a room for worship, a grocery store, a dry goods shop, and a restaurant.[57]

By 1920, Frederick Douglass Square represented the culmination of the hard work and commercial vision of neighborhood merchants and working-class residents. It hosted a growing Black community of native Bostonians, rural and urban migrants, and Pan-African immigrants. They existed in the dense, multiethnic environment of the Hub of New England. The residents applied their cultural resources with intention—as individuals and community groups—to lay the foundation for a fledgling jazz scene.

HARRY CARNEY

Harry Howell Carney was a young musician living in the South End and Lower Roxbury who mastered the saxophone and clarinet. He became a leading innovator on the baritone sax as a member of the Duke Ellington Orchestra.

CHAPTER FOUR

HOW FREDERICK DOUGLASS SQUARE GAVE BIRTH TO A JAZZ SCENE

Frederick Douglass Square was the incubator of jazz for a generation of fans and aspiring musicians. Here, neighborhood youths embraced the syncopated rhythms of string combos and uniformed marching orchestras in the streets and parks while semiprofessionals formed dance ensembles for the fraternal halls, music stores, and after-hours clubs. As a result, the Square anchored a culture of aural expression that pervaded the neighborhood and forged a soundtrack for everyday life. Over time, the South End and Lower Roxbury jazz scene would seep into the musical culture of mainstream Boston.

It is still possible to flesh out the anatomy of a fledgling music subculture with the fragmentary evidence available. Travis Jackson, in his study of jazz in 1970s New York, described the elements of interactions between musicians, audiences, and spaces vital to the nurturing of a lively scene. From the perspective of musicians, he considered the availability of autonomous spaces for people to connect, rehearse, and hang out, among other factors. For the youths of Frederick Douglass Square, the home was the first autonomous space for the exploration of jazz music. In rooms and apartments, young people listened to records, heard the faint sounds of broadcasts on crystal radio headsets, and practiced sweet tones and slick riffs on accessible instruments.[1]

Take the story of Roy Haynes, born on March 13, 1925, to immigrant parents from Barbados. They lived on Haskins Street in Lower Roxbury, where his parents encouraged an appreciation for Black music sacred and secular. His father was fond of church music and played and sang hymns during the Christmas and Easter holidays: "My father bought a six-room house when I was two years old. We had a cellar and I kept drums down there near the coal furnace. It was great having parents that owned their own home. We had an organ in the house and my father played organ and sang too."[2] As Roy's interest developed, his mother, who did not play, made an effort to provide him with the sheet music of popular songs. She would go to "one of the music stores and buy the music. Whatever the latest song was out." In time, he discovered like-minded neighborhood boys with an interest in jazz band music.[3]

In later years, the friends would pass time listening to his older brother's collection of race records and used them as lessons to understand jazz songs and music. "He knew all the records; he knew everything," Haynes says of his brother, Douglas. "He was the one who had all the records. Billie Holiday, and all of that stuff." As he grew older, he would listen to jazz programs on the radio to stay informed about things: "On the radio stations you heard everything; they used to have something . . . I forget what station, but it was called the 920 Club. This was in the very early forties, and they would be on from afternoon till evening." Douglas worked as a "roadie" for a band and returned with stories that furthered the curiosity of Haynes: "He'd be in New York a lot, and he would always come back and tell me what happened at the Savoy Bar when they would have the bands battle, like Lionel Hampton's band maybe. He knew the people, so I learned a lot through him. In fact, the first drum sticks I picked up were his."[4]

Haynes, as a consequence of this exposure, came to appreciate the musicality in the life around him. On the ethnically mixed street, he recalls hearing the harmonies in the rituals of the day: "Even a funeral, when there would be a Jewish funeral, man they would come outside right in front of my house and they would make sounds like they were chanting." On another occasion, he describes, "We had a Catholic church up on the corner, and the bells were up on the hill, and the bells would toll on the hour. So, when there was a funeral, the bells would go slower. You know that was intriguing to me. To hear that, all of those things."[5] And he came to develop a sense of rhythm from the sound of his own heartbeat: "I always play the beat. I figure everyone should have the beat within them—but a lot of people don't. When you play with someone that has the beat in them, it's easier for you. You can go where you want to go and make the rhythms that you want to make."[6]

Many households encouraged their children to appreciate musical instruments and recordings; it was in such a household that Preston Sandiford matured into one of the most acclaimed figures in the scene. He developed as a pianist, bandleader, and union president, always remembering the early days of encouragement from his immigrant West Indian parents. "I had my first music lesson when I was five, and I played the classics until I was thirteen. My parents sent my sister, who was two years younger than I, and me to the Boston Conservatory. When we got there, the stuff they were teaching us we already knew," he says. "Anyway, we could not afford it because we were a poor family and the school cost $400 a year. So I quit after a year; my sister stayed a little longer. I went to a couple of private teachers after that."[7]

Many of the South End youths credited race records as a tool of jazz exposure. They pledged allegiance to the catalog of blues and jazz recordings and to the phonographs that played them. Youths listened to foxtrots of society bands and theater jazz of orchestras in the homes. They debated the merits on the stoops, street corners, and parks. The neighborhood network of musical youths included Sandiford, Harry Carney, Johnny Hodges, Howard Johnson, Charlie Holmes, and Buster Tolliver. Harry Carney lived on Cunard Street, just a few blocks from the home of Howard Johnson on Shawmut Avenue—in turn, not too far from Johnny Hodges, who lived on Hammond Street.

Hodges was influenced by the early 1920s recordings of Clarence Williams's Blue Five featuring Sidney Bechet on soprano sax on the sides "Wild Cat Blues" and "Kansas City Man Blues." The boys used informal practice with friends to imitate the melodies and develop their skills and knowledge. Charlie Holmes was drawn to the saxophone after seeing an older neighborhood boy blowing a jazz tune at a dance. That boy was Johnny Hodges, and they developed a lifelong friendship. This was after Holmes learned that Howard Johnson played the saxophone and asked a mutual friend to introduce them. Johnson recalls, "So I went to his house on Hammond Street, and he had this little turned-up soprano, one of those shaped like an alto. I played some scales on it, and that was what he wanted to know."[8]

Some families took on the role of preserving musical traditions like in the days of the West African occupational guilds. The family of Walter Johnson worked to perpetuate musical traditions while also encouraging the exploration of melodic lines, rhythms, and harmonies, collecting instruments folk and modern, and pushing the children to experiment with them all. As a result, Walter and his brother Bobby were the first of the children to become professional musicians: Walter on piano and Bobby on banjo. In addition, Bobby played guitar and saxophone; this, in turn, motivated their brother Howard to learn the alto saxophone. Howard Johnson recalled that his father kept "a bunch of instruments around the home—banjos, tipples, mandolins. All us kids used to pick on those things. There were twelve of us, but to my recollection only eight survived. My older brother, Walter Johnson, was quite famous up in Boston, where I was born. He played piano and did all the society work."[9] He continued:

> I got my first saxophone from another brother, Bobby Johnson, who was playing banjo professionally. He was eight years older than me. When he started making some money, he bought himself an alto saxophone, but he couldn't get the knack of it. I used to sneak it out sometimes when he was away. One day he came home and saw me playing it, and I was frightened. I thought my big brother was going to bawl me out, but he didn't. "Keep it," he said. "Take it whenever you want." When he left Boston, he left the saxophone behind, and it became my instrument.[10]

The parents of Charlie Holmes scraped together enough money to buy a piano for their fourteen children to learn the instrument and to practice music—such was their high regard for the culture. The boys' interest was furthered by a kindly teacher who challenged neighborhood children to appreciate instrumental music, whom Holmes recalls only as a "Dr. Holmes" (no relation). He brought together boys to form a band and supplied the instruments if they agreed to take care of them, practice, and play as an ensemble. The doctor was unable to give Holmes the saxophone he wanted, however, and instead assigned him an oboe—one of the most challenging of the reed instruments. He encouraged Holmes to learn it with the promise of a sax at a later date.

"I found a teacher and paid him three dollars for a half-hour lesson," says Holmes. "I was real serious, and I studied this oboe. I tried to make it sound like a saxophone!"[11] The doctor never was able to provide that saxophone, and asked Holmes to make do with the oboe. The boy instead opted to return the instrument and leave the band; in the process, however, he had learned the character of an instrument and to read music and was recruited by the school band—as an oboist! He finally acquired a saxophone in his junior year as a gift from his father, who had squirreled away enough money to buy it. Holmes remembers, "It was a Thursday—I'll never forget—and I knew where kids used to have little dances, with a fellow playing piano. I walked in, took out my horn, and started playing. Everybody was astonished."[12] In similar fashion, the family of Johnny Hodges also instilled an appreciation for music in the home. They encouraged him to study the piano, but he was more interested in "beating up all the pots and pans in the kitchen."[13] Eventually, he took to the saxophone and fell in with a group of boys in the "saxophonist ghetto" of the neighborhood. He credited his boyhood friend Harry Carney as an influence in his understanding of the instrument and development as a reedman; the young Hodges switched from a curved soprano saxophone to a straight one under his encouragement.[14]

The value of a supportive audience to furthering a jazz scene has been noted by Travis Jackson, who writes, "The major function that audience members serve is to provide economic and social support to the musicians."[15] In Frederick Douglass Square, the social clubs and civic groups played a critical role in supporting the dances and musicians. For example, the women's social clubs and auxiliaries in the South End featured dances for soldiers on leave from Camp Devens in Ayer, about 35 miles west of the city. The Soldiers Comfort Unit was created in 1917 to support Black troops at the camp under the direction of two women's clubs in the South End, the League of Women in Community Service at 558 Massachusetts Avenue led by Maria Baldwin, and the Women's Service Center at 464 Massachusetts Avenue led by Mary Patterson Evan Wilson. Baldwin was a highly regarded educator in the city; Wilson, the wife of attorney Butler Wilson. The clubs cosponsored the Comfort Unit in the early years of the war; among their activities was delivering packages of clothing, cards, candy, and cigarettes to the troops. In the South End, they established a hut on a playground for visiting soldiers known as the "Rest House" and organized dances and concerts for them.[16]

On other occasions, the Ladies Auxiliary to Company L, Sixth Massachusetts Guard, sponsored the "Annual May Party and Dance." On Friday, May 23, 1919, for instance, the dance was held at the Bulfinch Street Armory from 8 p.m. to 2 a.m., featuring music by the Leroy Curtis Jazz Band. On Tuesday, June 17, 1919, the Queen Elizabeth Court No. 1 of the Heroines of Jericho (the women's auxiliary to the Masons) sponsored a "Victory Reception and Ball" at Liberty Hall, 2181 Washington Street, with dancing from 9 p.m. to 2 a.m. and music by the Leroy Curtis Orchestra; admission: 50¢. On February 12, 1920, the Soldier's Comfort Unit, directed by Miss Maria L. Baldwin for the benefit of Black soldiers, hosted a "Grand Military Ball" in the William E. Carter Post no. 16 of the American Legion with admission of $1.[17]

Adding to the audiences were the social clubs of West Indian and Cape Verdean immigrants. The events typically featured bands playing calypso and other dance music of the native cultures but also featured jazz bands. The West Indian Cricket Club, for instance, hosted an "After Easter Entertainment" in Ruggles Hall in Lower Roxbury on April 5, 1923, featuring two jazz dance orchestras led by Walter Johnson and Newton Ball, respectively. The Cape Verdean Fraternal League held its monthly dance in Butler Hall at 1095 Tremont Street, on April 4, 1923, and showcased Souza's Keith Circuit Orchestra of New Bedford. The next week, the Jamaica League of Boston held its "Annual Reception and Dance" in Liberty Hall at 2181 Washington Street, Roxbury. Dancing was from 8 p.m. to 2 a.m. with music by Jeffress's Pleasing Orchestra for an admission of 50¢.[18]

Among professional organizations, the events of the Colored Musicians Union Local 535 were most anticipated. On Tuesday, January 20, 1920, for example, they staged the "Fourth Annual Dance and Cabaret" in the elegant convention hall on St. Botolph Street. The hall, located in the South End, was owned by the white Boston Musicians' Association Local 10. Even the Boston Tigers Baseball Club, a semi-professional regional team that played in Madison Park, presented its "Dance and Entertainment" in Ruggles Hall on Wed, May 2, 1923. The dance featured music by Bobby Sawyer and His Hotel Westminster Jazz Orchestra. Dance announcements appealed to members of local fraternity chapters such as Omega Psi Phi, established at Howard University in 1911, and Alpha Phi Alpha, founded at Boston University and Harvard University in 1915.[19]

Fraternal orders were the generators of much cultural activity in urban communities across the country, and Boston was no different. The work of the fraternities of the 1920s were modern extensions of the early mutual aid societies established by free families. By 1919, the substantial influence of fraternal orders was mirrored in communities across the country. These societies established charity funds to assist members and their families during hard times, support social and cultural activities, and shape group identity through organizational structures and rituals.[20] In 1919 Boston, the largest societies were the Odd Fellows, with six lodges and about 600 male members and a women's auxiliary order, the Household of Ruth, with four lodges and 500 members; the Masons, with six lodges and about 450 members and a women's auxiliary, the Heroines of Jericho; and the Order of the Eastern Star. Smaller societies included the Improved Benevolent and Protective Order of Elks of the World, with three lodges and about 250 members; the Colored Knights of Pythias Eastern and Western Hemisphere with four lodges; the Ancient Order of Foresters with its "Courts" rather than lodges; and the Grand United Order of True Reformers with two lodges and about seventy-five members.[21]

The vitality of the jazz scene was enhanced by access to autonomous venues in the neighborhood. In Frederick Douglass Square, the lodges and halls of fraternal societies were critical assets in the presentation of small combo dance bands. Among the notable venues that hosted such affairs was Ruggles Hall, located at the intersection of Tremont Street and Ruggles Street, owned by the Colored Knights of Pythias Temple. "There's a place on Ruggles Street—I think it was called Ruggles Hall," writes Collin Corbin, who resided at 1165 Ruggles Street as a boy. "We used to go up there and dance." Preston Sandiford remembered meeting Duke Ellington in Ruggles Hall. The aspiring pianist recalls, "He was known as Duke Ellington and His Washingtonians. There were only eight men."[22] Two other popular fraternal spaces for staging concerts in the Black community were Liberty Hall at 2181 Washington Street and Butler Hall at 1095 Tremont Street.

On the Huntington Avenue boundary line for the South End and Back Bay were Rivoli Hall at 235 Huntington Avenue and Paul Revere Hall in the Mechanics Hall Building. Jazz radio host Eric Jackson described a jazz room named Berkeley Hall on the edge of the South End and Back Bay—maybe in the Berkeley Building at Boylston and Berkeley streets. He believed that Benny Waters played there with other neighborhood figures around 1921. According to Jackson, the saxophonist "for a time played Saturday afternoon dances at Berkeley Hall with a band led by banjo and guitar player Bobby Johnson. Johnny Hodges was also in that band."[23] Also important to the local scene were performance halls owned by white social clubs in Roxbury willing to rent to Black events. These included the Irish-owned Hibernian Hall and O'Connell Hall on Dudley Street.

Information on the society balls and dances was spread by club members and published in the *Boston Guardian*. At Ruggles Hall, for example, there was a published announcement for the "32nd Anniversary Celebration" dance sponsored by the William C. Nell Lodge no. 3 of the Colored Knights of Pythias on Thursday, May 22, 1919. It featured the Leroy Curtis Jazz Band for an admission of 50¢. Some clubs combined forces to host weeklong festivities where each participating organization took responsibility for planning its own day of events: consider the "Fraternal Nights" at Ruggles Hall in the Knights of Pythias Temple, 5 Ruggles Street, from April 9 to 12, 1923. Monday was the Odd Fellows and Households of Ruth event; Tuesday was the Knights of Pythias Orchestra; Wednesday was the Elks and Daughter Elks of the World. Throughout the week, the Pythians sponsored a "Monster Indoor Circus" with performers, trained animals, and dancing to raise money for their charity fund.[24]

Cornelius "Johnny" Hodges was a young musician in the South End and Lower Roxbury who mastered the alto saxophone. Hodges was known for the beauty of tone and became a legendary soloist in the Duke Ellington Orchestra.

Examples of society dances in other venues include Butler Hall Masonic Temple on Monday, April 2, 1923, at 1095 Tremont Street from 8 p.m. to 2 a.m., admission: 75¢. They also hosted the Rising Sun Lodge's "After Easter Ball" to raise money for a charity fund, which featured music by Ernest Hay's Orchestra.

Finally, there are examples of socials held in spaces that bordered the neighborhood, like the Paul Revere Hall in the Mechanics Building on Huntington Avenue. The Frederick Douglass Court no. 84966 of the Ancient Order of Foresters held its "17th Annual Entertainment" event there on May 22, 1919, from 8 p.m. to 2 a.m. for an admission of $1. The Phyllis Wheatley Temple 22 of the Elks sponsored a "Mid-Night Cabaret and Dance" to raise money for its building fund on Monday, April 9, 1923, at the Dudley Street Opera House, 119 Dudley Street, Roxbury. Dancing was from 8 p.m. to 2 a.m. with music by Walter Johnson's Celebrated Orchestra at an admission of 60¢.[25]

Besides the indoor performance spaces, the fraternal orders also supported parades and conventions with society orchestras and marching bands. By 1920, the larger Black fraternities were able to organize impressive events that gained the notice of state political leaders. For example, the Improved Benevolent Protective Order of Elks staged its 22nd Annual Grand Lodge national convention and demonstrated the appeal of Boston as a destination for the Black middle class. Staged at Faneuil Hall on August 22, 1921, the convention "brought together the most representative and largest number of colored people that, perhaps, has ever gathered in this city."[26] The 10,000 delegates represented the fraternal lodges of many states and were greeted by acting Republican governor Allan Fuller and a liaison to Boston Republican mayor Andrew Peters. Among the local Black civic leaders in attendance were W. Alexander Johnson, president of the Boston Negro Business League; William H. Lewis, a former attorney at the US Department of Justice; the Rev. M. Shaw of the Twelfth Baptist Church; John W. Schenck, a prominent attorney; and many dignitaries of the state lodges. Governor

Fuller welcomed the delegation, saying, "It is very fitting that an organization dedicated to the advancement of brotherhood, truth and justice in the colored race should gather in convention in the historic state of Massachusetts."[27] Fuller described the role of Boston's abolitionists in the antislavery struggle, including Charles Sumner, Wendell Phillips, and William Lloyd Garrison, and concluded by saying, "Massachusetts extends to you her hospitality today. May your stay here be both pleasant and profitable."[28]

That evening, the society held a banquet dinner for 200 delegates at Ruggles Hall followed by an open-air dance and a jazz concert in Frederick Douglass Square. The next day, the 10,000 fraternity members paraded through Boston in full regalia to the accompaniment of twenty-six bands and fifty floats. The marchers passed the State House for review by Governor Fuller, then City Hall for review by Mayor Peters, and proceeded down city streets to end at Frederick Douglass Square. There, fraternal leaders such as Franklin Wright of the Boston lodges and George McMechen, the Elks' Grand Exalted Ruler, stood in review of the procession. The *Boston Globe* reported that the Elks marched from "Commonwealth Avenue and Arlington Street to Beacon, to School, to Washington, to Bromfield, to Tremont, to Boylston, to Park sq, to Columbus av, to Massachusetts av, to Tremont st, to Frederick Douglass Square."[29]

In May 1923, the Massachusetts lodges of the Colored Knights of Pythias and the auxiliary Sisters of the Court of Calanthe held a smaller but no less dramatic spectacle in the city. They staged a variety of events for the 43rd annual "Thanksgiving services" meant to show appreciation for the social work of the lodges. On May 20, 1923, more than 1,000 members from chapters around the state participated in the event. The parade began in Frederick Douglass Square at the intersection of Tremont and Lenox streets and ended in the West End, led by Lieutenant George E. Seamon, a retired officer in the Massachusetts National Guard. Women of the Order of the Court of Calanthe sported white suits and long white capes; the parade featured fraternity members in regalia from lodges with names like Crispus Attucks, Hub City, and Emerald. There was a drill corps and marching band that recruited boys as musician apprentices; the youth, in turn, saw the brass bands as a way to distinguish themselves as up-and-coming musicians. The *Globe* reported that "The parade formed at Douglas [*sic*] square and marched through Tremont street to Camden, to Columbus Av, Park sq, and Charles St, to Charles Street African Methodist Episcopal Church, where the services were held."[30]

The chemistry of the neighborhood jazz scene was further enriched by the access to job information and training. In Frederick Douglass Square, for instance, many young enthusiasts looked to the Harmony Shop as a source for networking before the site was razed in the 1960s for the Douglass Park Apartments. The shop was located on Westfield Street, a former L-shaped strip that linked Tremont Street with Camden and Lenox streets, and was owned by Harry "Bish" Hicks, a pianist and saxophonist and leader of Hicks Famous Jazz Band and Concert Orchestra. The combo played syncopated dance rags with Hicks on piano and sax, D. Clarence Atkins and David Laney both on banjo and trombone, Richard Ward on drums and traps, George Rickson on piano and banjo, and Henry Batchelder, pianist and "tenor jazz comedian."[31] In April 1919, Hicks Famous Jazz Band played at Ruggles Hall for the 13th Anniversary of Eureka Lodge no. 8 of the Knights of Pythias. The next month, the band was featured in a homecoming celebration at Hibernian Hall on Dudley Street, Roxbury. The advertisement informed that "After a very successful tour of the State of Maine during the last four weeks the Hick's [*sic*] first string orchestra will return to their own native Boston and show that they have lost none of their Jazz or Harmony."[32]

In addition to selling records, sheet music, and instruments, the Harmony Shop was a source of information on concerts and jobs. Hicks ran the booking agency Harry Hicks & Co., which recruited bands for college and society dances. The shop also provided rehearsal space and was the site of jam sessions—additional research is needed to determine whether they also recorded songs under a label. Drummer George Latimer remembered, "Every Sunday afternoon all the cats used to bring their instruments and we'd have a jam session, with the door wide open and the crowd in the street around the door getting a load of it."[33] The shop was also a place for referrals to rent parties—known as "house hops"—similar to those enjoyed by migrant families in Harlem and South Side. Some old-time residents of the Square recall such activity in the neighborhood during the jazz age. Collin Corbin, born in Boston in 1921, described the enjoyment of such events: "We use to go to a lot of house parties. Different friends would give a house party and we'd go to them." Johnny Hodges spoke about earning money as a boy by playing piano at neighborhood "house hops" where admission was charged for people to join the dance.[34]

As a result, the Harmony Shop became a gathering place for local musicians, touring jazz bands, and students at the New England Conservatory and Boston Conservatory. Youths could peruse the record bin and sheet music holdings, seek advice from professional players, and maybe even find a mentor in one of the older students from the conservatories. Howard Johnson, for one, became friends with Jerome Don Pasquall, a jazz composer and arranger, and clarinetist and alto saxophonist. Raised in Fulton, Kentucky, Pasquall came to Boston as a seasoned musician to study at the NEC. He was admired for his vast knowledge of music and for his generosity in sharing it with younger enthusiasts. Living in Boston between 1923 and 1927, Pasquall played with local bands as well as with the touring shows of Will Vodery, Noble Sissle, Fletcher Henderson, Jabbo Smith, Tiny Parham, and other Harlem entertainers, and Johnson convinced Pasquall to work with him and Johnny Hodges. In 1927, he was hired to play alto saxophone in the Fletcher Henderson Orchestra in New York City, and became a source of information for South End musicians interested in the jazz scene.

Benny Waters took periodic classes in theory, harmony, solfeggio, and more at the Boston Conservatory. The jazz musicians in Boston took pride in a reputation for their knowledge and ability to read music when many in the field relied on head arrangements. "It was an advantage for me to study, and it was rare, at that age, to study," Waters recalled, adding, "If you know what the other fellow's doing, then you can copy." He took classes for five years and picked up work with the band of banjoist Bobby Johnson. Waters, in turn, mentored Harry Carney and Johnny Hodges, among other young people in the neighborhood.[35]

The amenities of Frederick Douglass Square were an attraction to out-of-town entertainers as well. The arrival of traveling bands added to the legitimacy of the local talent and audience. The sight of brass bands marching down the streets and performing under the pavilion in nearby Madison Park in Lower Roxbury was applauded. The park was a central location for the recreation of residents in the summertime. Located at Tremont and Ruggles streets, the park sheltered residents who sought escape from their sweltering rooms and tenements. Charles Thomas recalled walking to the park with his mother, watching the crowds sauntering about, and sitting in bleachers to watch the Boston Tigers play. He also spoke about listening to brass bands playing popular tunes and ragtime dance music in the pavilion and on the streets. The band he recalled most vividly was the touring Jenkins Orphanage Band from Charleston, South Carolina. The Jenkins marching band, derisively known as "the Pickaninny Band," toured northern cities to raise money for the orphanage.[36]

The orchestra made an annual visit to Frederick Douglass Square, and the tour had become a beloved tradition by the 1920s. The Jenkins boys put on a concert in Madison Park and paraded down Tremont, Shawmut, Hammond, and other streets of the neighborhood. Much anticipated were the antics of the youthful grand marshal, usually one of the smallest boys, holding a baton and strutting along in regalia. Charles Thomas remembered: "They used to come during the summertime because they felt as though if they came here, we would be more sympathetic about giving them funds to keep the school going down there. They used to perform on different streets—they'd play two or three numbers, and the maestro with the minister, he would pass the hat, and they would collect money."[37] As a boy, Ken Guscott recalled the exciting arrival of the orchestra: "The Jenkins Band would come there on a Saturday. Now, the Jenkins Band was a band that came from one of the schools down south. They would come on a bus. They had the Jenkins Band bus. That was a big day when the Jenkins Band came."[38]

The Jenkins Institute has preserved footage of the Orphanage Band performing for a newsreel in 1928. The footage provides a rare glimpse into the style of ragtime bands that were popular forerunners of the jazz orchestras. The newsreel provides an illustration of the type of music that musicians in the South End played about 1919 for the fraternal order parades, school band events, and park concerts under the pavilion. The Jenkins Band, rather than marching for the newsreel camera, stood in two lines with their instruments. The boys in the rear stood while the ones in the front sat and two boys served as conductors and dancers. The uniforms and hats resembled those of Marine cadets, the brass instruments included tubas, trombones, and trumpets, and the drums ranged in size from timpani, bass, tenor, and snare. There were no woodwind instruments apparent. The band started the ragtime march slowly before shifting to an up-tempo syncopated pace. The tubas established a booming bassline and the drums created multiple lines of rhythm. The trumpets blared in a staccato manner, which provided syncopation to the music, and trombone slides rendered a sense of the comedic. The solos were limited to instrument sections trading choruses. [39]

The band was the creation of the Rev. Daniel Jenkins. Born into slavery in the Charleston area, he was orphaned as a boy, and in freedom worked as a migrant laborer to survive. In adulthood, he became a sharecropper and preacher at the small Fourth Baptist Church in Charleston. One way he would supplement his income was by hauling timber from the railroad yard to the lumber mill. In 1891, Jenkins became a leading voice in persuading the church to create an orphanage. He convinced the city council to permit the use of an abandoned warehouse to care for "roaming, thieving wild children." The city approved the request along with a $100 stipend, and the orphanage was founded. Within a year, the service cared for more than 360 boys ranging in age from five to ten years. [40]

Jenkins preached the values of self-reliance, hard work, and personal responsibility. He encouraged the boys to grow their own food and make their own clothes to be self-sufficient. In order to raise funds for a project to buy farmland for the orphanage, he decided to start the brass band, and solicited donations of musical instruments in 1892. It was common for cities to support municipals bands—often extensions of military bands—for marching and ceremonial events; in that spirit, Jenkins received old instruments and uniforms of the Marine cadets at the College of the Citadel. Among the instruments were trumpets, coronets, clarinets, trombones, oboes, tubas, bells, triangles, and drums. With that, the Jenkins Orphanage Band was born.

By 1900, the band had grown to thirty pieces; in later years, they would play at the inaugural ceremonies of presidents Theodore Roosevelt and William Howard Taft and tour cities and towns across the country. By 1920, the band was performing syncopated march music with solo improvisations to the delight of audiences. Some members developed the skills to turn professional and were hired by bandleaders Duke Ellington, Benny Moten, and Count Basie in later years; by coincidence, two boys who became infamous in Boston were the exhibition drummers in the James Reese Europe Orchestra—the drummers Steven Wright and Herbert Wright, billed as the "Percussion Twins." By the late 1920s, Jenkins had achieved his dream of establishing a self-sufficient farm and expanded the orphanage to support five bands and two choral ensembles. The children mentored by the organization remained devoted to its mission long after they left the school. That even included the infamous Herbert Wright, who had settled in the neighborhood after serving his time for the death of James Reese Europe. In the 1930s, Roy Haynes, who grew up as a neighbor to Wright, witnessed his continued loyalty to the band as it marched on Haskins Street. "One time when they came to my street, Herbie Wright was listening to them, and they all got excited and said, 'Herbie's gonna have to get his drum!' They had a snare drum that he could put around his neck," he said, adding, "I'd run and watch from my roof so no one could block my view. Herbert Wright sat in with the band."[41]

Finally, the Richard Earle Pioneer Club was a valued site of the neighborhood jazz scene. It was opened in 1903 by railroad porter Richard Earle to provide accommodations for overnight railroad workers whose route terminated at the Back Bay Station and Trinity Station in Copley Square. The Pioneer Club was located in a three-story red brick building on the former Westfield Street in Frederick Douglass Square, where it offered a welcome and affordable rest spot for the porters, dining car cooks, and waiters laying over in the city. The club provided rooms, beds, meals, and a lounge—few hotels would accept these men, and even if they did, few railway workers could afford to stay in such accommodations. The Pioneer Club, along with the nearby Harmony Shop, were examples of autonomous commercial assets of the jazz scene.

By the 1920s, the Pioneer Club had been bought by two brothers who owned a nearby pharmacy and served as ward bosses for the Democratic Party: Silas "Shag" and Balcom "Bal" Taylor. Under their management, the club became an important generator of jazz and politics in the Black community.[42] The two were migrants from Danville, Virginia, who rose to become licensed pharmacists, civic leaders, and brokers in the rough-and-tumble setting of Boston ward boss politics.

Ruth Mozell Davis Tinsely moved to Boston from Savannah, Georgia, in 1923, and was fourteen years old when her family lived at 23 Holyoke Street in the Square. She recalled being hired by the

Taylor brothers to pass out leaflets on behalf of Democratic Party candidates.[43] Such tactics are how Shag and Bal Taylor were able to organize the South End under Boston mayor James Michael Curley. The Lincoln Pharmacy, located at 922 Tremont Street, was the power base of the brothers and a political center for the community. During Prohibition, they did a bustling trade in whiskey with railroad workers under the auspices of the Prohibition exemptions and the lenient practices of City Hall.

Railroad workers on layover headed to Frederick Douglass Square with their pockets full of tip money. Many partook of the eateries, services, and amusements in the Square—in particular, the back room of the Lincoln Pharmacy, where booze was sold under a legal exemption for dispensaries of medicine.

Railway man George Porter recalled, "A lot of porters used to go to the back room of [Taylor's] drug store on Tremont Street." Ken Guscott, who grew up in the neighborhood, said, "They were allowed to sell half pints of liquor on Saturday and Sunday morning." It was also a stop-off for out-of-town musicians like trumpeter Rex Stewart, who said, "This was a common meeting place for all musicians during those times, principally because Shag sold the best whiskey in town, never mind that we still had Prohibition." The Taylor brothers turned the Pioneer Lounge into an after-hours speakeasy that hired neighborhood musicians; the club hired the George Tynes Orchestra as the featured dance band and as Guscott remembers, "They were allowed to run an after-hours club across the street from where they were."[44]

During the interwar years, the musicians of Frederick Douglass Square had established a culture of jazz authority like their peers in Harlem and South Side Chicago, among others. As they grappled with the new melodic ideas and rhythmic patterns—and even with what to call it—they also looked over their shoulders for the incursion of outside musicians and audiences curious about the development of an authentic jazz scene.

The Little Building, at the intersection of Boylston and Tremont Streets, leased the office of the Charles and Simeon Shribman booking agency.

CHAPTER FIVE

THE COMMERCE OF JAZZ IN BOSTON

The commercial value of Boston's jazz culture during the interwar years has yet to be understood as an engine of enterprise. However, evidence indicates that the economic activity around the music generated a significant number of jobs, income, and wealth—and that most of the benefits went to white participants in the industry. What developed was a protected labor market for musicians, managers, and producers, and exclusive sites of wealth generation for owners of clubs, theaters, and audio equipment factories. In combination, such elites controlled the best jobs and investments while keeping at arm's length the small community of Black practitioners of the craft. The advantages extended to the entire infrastructure of the entertainment industry in the city: from the hotel ballrooms and banquet halls, theaters, dance halls, and supper clubs to the manufacturing and retail sale of records, phonographs, and radio sets. The Black musicians, producers, technicians, and business owners were shut out of the mainstream markets for their culture. They had to contend with the crumbs of neighborhood gigs and business ventures—and even these were sometimes controlled by white overseers.

It was commonplace for entertainment venues in the north to exclude Black people by custom. The exclusionary practices were justified by reasons of racial privilege and private property rights; as such, organizations were able to enact Jim Crow standards on musicians, jobseekers, audiences, merchants, and investors with impunity. Most of the Boston theaters, dance halls, ballrooms, and nightclubs engaged in biased hiring practices for musicians and orchestras. The music industry could be exclusive for arbitrary reasons like the fear of objections from white audiences, unions, and commercial sponsors. When establishments served Black patrons—sometimes on designated days or hours and exceptions for individual cases—the relatively high price of admission and amenities posed a financial barrier to the working-class audience. Still, the systemic methods of Boston were little different from other cities of the Northeast and Midwest—and better than many in the South.

Those venues that featured jazz music would hire white orchestras for the well-paying engagements and Black bands for intermission acts. In general, South End players were paid less, denied royalties, and suffered from high job insecurity. The musicians and managers could face disrespectful treatment from white peers concerned about competition and ready to belittle the value of jazz. When hired by white establishments, they were often the only people of color in the venue, or in the case of the individual musicians, the sole Black player in the orchestra. They had to contend with the stereotypes of minstrelsy—and were sometimes required to wear blackface makeup for theater performances. In the production of jazz for records and radio, Black musicians, composers, and producers were shunned; in the making of audio consumer products, Black technicians and laborers were shunned.[1]

Black bands and players found opportunity in the private parties of affluent families. In the Back Bay, for example, old Brahmin families preferred the South End orchestras for social affairs. Preston "Sandy" Sandiford was one pianist and leader of a society band for such events. The son of immigrants from Barbados, Sandiford was trained in calypso, classical music, popular songs, and swing standards, and studied for a while at the Boston Conservatory—all of which came together for his society orchestra to develop a following among the affluent Yankee families. "I learned to play for parties at this time," he explains. "The Negroes had a lot of Back Bay work." His band was hired to perform for ballroom dance lessons, debutante affairs, and other functions. They played for social gatherings of prestigious Brahmin names like "the Cochorans, the Pickmans, the Searses and all." Prominent families hired the neighborhood musicians for a variety of needs: it could have been for Adeline Cochoran's ballroom dance lessons, or to give music lessons to Sally Sears, Lucy Cochoran, and their friends, or to perform for the seasonal society dances. "So for maybe four or five years, I played their Christmas parties up on Mt. Vernon Street on Beacon Hill. It was a really good deal."[2]

High school dances also provided employment for young musicians. Many of the South End players worked these dances and then the home parties afterward. Charlie Holmes recalls, "After dances, we'd go to them little house-rent parties." Benny Waters was among the few who "played for Sunday afternoon tea parties for the elite of Boston."[3] Meanwhile, pianist Mabel Robinson Simms witnessed the barriers of race and gender in the workplace. Born March 1914 in Cape Charles, Virginia, Simms learned to play piano by ear as a child, saying, "I could read a little, but I play mostly by ear."[4] About 1920, she moved to Boston and found work as a waitress at Slade's dining room in Frederick Douglass Square, where she joined the cadre of young musicians playing house parties: "This woman had a home there on Holyoke Street, and I used to play there on Sunday nights, used to play piano. That's how I started around playin'."[5]

During the Jazz Age, Black bands were largely denied entry to the better-paying nightclubs, theaters, and hotels in Boston. At the same time, the practices were not ironclad, and a few venues hired touring jazz "orchestras"—usually combos of about eight pieces. In 1920, pianist Tom Whaley led the society orchestra at the Hotel

Avery on Washington Street and Avery Street on the edge of the theater district. The hotel served an affluent clientele and hired the bands to perform popular standards—but no "hot jazz." Musicians also found work in the joints that served Black audiences in Bristol County and on Cape Cod. Dean Earl spoke about playing for Cape Verde dances in New Bedford and Osterville, and Preston Sandiford recalls his experience as a sixteen-year-old pianist: "I had a lot of work at in-town cafes and roadhouses on the outskirts of town. It was all very new and interesting for me. I stayed with that for quite a while and did a lot of substituting where a guy with a regular job wanted to take a night or two off."[6] Finally, there were seasonal opportunities for bands and musicians in the circuit of summer yachting clubs, dance halls, and ballrooms across New England. Pianist Earle "Nappy" Howard, in the 1920s, led a band in Hartford and toured the ballrooms that dotted the coast from Connecticut to Maine. He hired the fourteen-year-old Johnny Hodges to fill in and recalls the enthusiastic response of audiences to the rising star blowing a gold soprano sax: "He had all the folks cheering him on."[7]

Boston establishments seeking to hire Black bands did so under the watchful gaze of Local 9, the union for white musicians. Mabel Robinson Simms spoke to the frustration of being excluded from jobs and the broader resentment felt by Black musicians: "There was always a little friction there, as far as I'm concerned. Sometimes, like I said before, Local 9 members would get the good jobs and so forth. That we didn't agree with." She continues, "We did put up a fuss when the shows would come to the theaters. Seemed like only Local 9 members would get the jobs. So we start kicking up a fuss, they'd probably hire maybe one or two 535 members."[8] Pianist Everett G. "Dean" Earl recalled the situation had little changed when he visited Boston in the 1930s. Born in Brooklyn, he toured with a vaudeville act before settling in the city after World War II. "The colored bands did mostly gigs (as opposed to steady work), and there were only one or two clubs," he said.[9]

The marginalized South End musicians faced a capricious work environment. About 1930, Simms learned about the insecurity of musicians unprotected by a union when she was hired as the pianist for the Monterey Club on Columbus Avenue in the South End. The waitress got the job after being recommended by someone who had attended a house party where she played: "They needed a piano player there. I went in my uniform, my white uniform, and that's how I started playin' around. And I worked there, I worked there quite a few years." At the time, she was not a member of Local 535, the union for Black musicians—even if she had been, it is doubtful that the union had the resources to monitor small neighborhood clubs. She described a workplace where the manager used the threat of dismissal to discipline her and other musicians on a regular basis: "Every week I'd get fired for playing too much. Never heard of it before. Then he'd send for me at Monday, every week it happened that way."[10] From his own experiences, Dean Earl cautioned "that a union was really necessary, and especially where there's so much competition and there are so many thieves in the business."[11]

While the Boston establishments relied on white musicians as the interpreters of jazz, some of the musicians sought out Black peers to learn about the principles of swing. In this way, they showed a modicum of respect for Black musical authority—at least until they learned the secrets. "We exchanged men from time to time and worked together," Preston Sandiford said, adding, "The old-timers in the union got me a job right downtown."[12] Writer David Hajdu probed the consequences of race, culture, and economics in American popular music in his article for *Mother Jones* titled "Who's Got the Blues?" In it, he raises the question "How did the blues, a serious form of expression rooted in the hard life of a marginalized people, become a good-time music for moneyed tourists?"[13] This question was relevant to the commerce of jazz in the 1920s as well.

One controversial demonstration of a sense of cultural entitlement was to brand the music. Black players tended to consider the term "jazz" a definition created by critics to impose western artistic standards and control the music. Sandiford, for instance, preferred the musicians' notion of swinging to better describe their experiments with polyrhythmic patterns, uptempo pacing, loud dynamics, solo runs, and ensemble voicing. He found the label "jazz" as used by critics to be an attempt to appropriate Black aural culture: "Jazz to us represented a whole different conception, sounded like a European derivation."[14] This sentiment was shared by other musicians of the era like pianist Teddy Wilson. "It was not jazz musicians but jazz critics who stuck those labels on various currents in jazz," he wrote in his memoir. "I am often very much in doubt about their accuracy."[15] The Chicago musician Eddie Condon—a white jazzman who acknowledged the Black origins—also rejected the label. The banjoist and guitarist made his objections clear in the title of his autobiography: *We Called It Music*. Another example of cultural power was the branding of the polyrhythmic small combo music of Joe Oliver, Louis Armstrong, and other transplanted New Orleans musicians as "Dixieland jazz"—a term that would be widely used by Boston promoters in the early 1940s revivalism. To promoters in the 1920s, the allusion to Old South symbols in the names of songs and bands was appealing to audiences; to Black players, however, the imagery was a frustrating throwback to the days of the Confederacy and minstrelsy and a denial of their urban modernity.

The imbalance of power between the unions had real implications on access to jobs, income, and wealth in the commerce of jazz in Boston. The union members of Local 9 (one chapter of the expanding syndicate of the American Federation of Musicians) conducted business in an elegant neoclassical brick building at 56 St. Botolph Street, the border of the South End and Back Bay. During the Jazz Age, the AFM saw its national membership balloon from 84,000 in 1917 to 146,000 in 1928. The New York City chapter was one of the largest, with about 15,500 members; unlike

Boston, it did not establish separate chapters for white and Black musicians—although it did narrowly define the professionalism of Black musicians and cherry-pick for membership. The AFM protected local jobs from competition with non-union musicians and from those outside of the district. For its services, the union collected annual dues of about $50 and enacted stringent rules for out-of-town musicians, who had to seek "transfers" of their home memberships to play in other locales. People seeking to validate these transfers had to do so through the locals that represented their racial group. Dean Earl explained the process he encountered when he went to the main office of Local 9 to apply for the change while on tour. "I went to deposit a transfer that you're going to be in town for so long," he described. "He [Local 9] says, 'Oh, you people have a union, you go up to Tremont Street.' We didn't even know where Tremont Street was! But I know it was a trumpet player and myself. It was supposed to be a flash act, five dances and a trumpet and a piano player."[16]

The American Federation of Musicians was able to command higher wages and better conditions because of their distinct skills, growth of industry, and enforcement of rules. Players moving to cities with union chapters often had to wait up to six months before they could receive a new union card to work. In Boston, Local 9 represented white musicians working in the live music industry of nightclubs, supper clubs, dance halls, ballrooms, theaters, and concert halls. The symphony and pops hired the musicians they wanted, but those musicians were represented by the union and worked under a contract negotiated by the union. The contracts covered wages and benefits and work conditions. In the larger array of live music work, such as concert halls and theaters, union contractors oversaw the hiring for bands. They also monitored the hiring of orchestras and regulated the ability of non-resident musicians to work in the city. Many of the musicians were mainstays in the theaters and concert hall orchestras but also filled in for jazz combo work. One argument used by Local 9 musicians to justify exclusionary practices was that Black musicians were unable to read music and thus would be unreliable in orchestras. They contended that the experience of jazz soloists and small combo interplay was incompatible with the precision instrument sections of large orchestras.[17]

At the Local 9 headquarters, Monday was when assignments were nailed down for the week, and the union hall was as busy as a stock market trading floor. It was a scene of smoke-filled corridors, men shouting at each other, and musicians lining up at pay phones to locate accompanists. Some experienced job hunters stayed by the entrance door to get the jump on contractors as they entered. Subjective decisions, informal networks, and "good old boy" relationships were critical to scoring jobs on a regular basis. Oboist Sil D'Urbano described the qualification process for one gig: "I had an audition right at St. Botolph St. in the union building. He was an oboe player that did the audition. He took out a piece of music and I read it right off, you know, I had no trouble. He says, 'You pass. Go ahead.'"[18] Dave Fagin, who attended the scene with his father as a boy, says, "My dad was a local member since maybe 1923, '24. He played trumpet. And maybe I was four or five years old, he used to take me to the union on Mondays. It was a mad house, I mean, it was really a mad house," recalls the youth who would himself become a union member. "That's my memory. I like it, I enjoyed it. People running around—are you working this night, are you busy this night, is it OK?"[19]

Local 9 was the guardian of not only the occupational interests of musicians but also the cultural traditions of highbrow western music. It negotiated for musicians hired by the orchestras for the lucrative markets of theaters, concert halls, ballrooms, symphony orchestra, and the Boston Pops, among others. As such, the union musicians implicitly underwrote the biases of the canon of European traditions and Yankee standards. In May 1924, for example, after Boston University sponsored a symposium favorable to jazz, the *Globe* responded with condescending articles for months afterward. In August, the column "Music and Musicians" conducted a survey of critics of jazz like Frank Damrosch, director of the New York Institute of Musical Art: "Jazz is to real music what the caricature is to the portrait. Jazz may be clever, but its effects are made by exaggeration, distortions and vulgarisms."[20] Henry F. Gilbert, the folk music collector and composer of "The Dance in Place Congo," decried the "grotesque and burlesque effects on the saxophone, trombone, clarinet and other instruments."[21] Some traditionalists made exceptions for jazz appropriated by white bandleaders: George Ade, a writer on American culture, says, "Jazz can be a dreadful disturbance of the atmosphere when perpetrated by a cluster of small town blacksmiths and sheet metal workers, but it becomes inspiriting and almost uplifting under the magical treatment of Paul Whiteman. I suggest that every ragtime artist be compelled to take an examination and secure a license before he is permitted to fool with a saxophone."[22]

While the members of Local 9 conducted business in its neoclassical building, the Black musicians clustered in the tiny rooms above a South End sandwich shop. The Boston Colored Musicians Union, Local 535, evolved from the gathering of players at the record store of Harry Hicks in Frederick Douglass Square. Circa 1912, led by saxophonist Bill Smith (who would go on to become the union's first president), they began their organization to protect their interests by applying for a charter from the AFM. Drummer George Latimer, who joined the union at age sixteen, recalled the early days of the association activities in the record store: "I went in the union on Halloween eve 1917. I stayed active in the music until World War II. When I joined the union, Bill Smith was president and Harry Hicks was secretary-treasurer."[23] Latimer played with local bands led by Gene Goodrum, Harry Hicks, Charles "Skinny" Johnson, Bobby Sawyer, and Frankie Newton, among others. "The jobs then required that you read music and be able to accompany singers, especially for me as a piano player," Preston Sandiford described. "I had a very good band as far as reading music on sight.

We did general gig work. We played every club you can think of around here with the exception of the Ritz Roof." [24] The members included Howard Johnson, alto sax; Wendall Cully, trumpet; Buster Tolliver, tenor; Ray Cully or "Leggy" Taylor, drums; and a tuba player.

About 1927, the association moved from the Harmony music shop to the rooms above Charlie's Lunch, a dining room owned by Charlie Poulos on the ground floor in a small building at 429 Columbus Avenue. This space would remain the union hall for many years. The second-floor office was an extension of the gatherings that took place in the music shop and a harbor for musicians seeking information, and Charlie's Lunch became a hangout for jazz musicians.[25] Local 535 safeguarded its share of the music scene and agitated for a piece of the mainstream market. It handled the transfers of visiting musicians and enforced the rules of membership in the workplace. Dean Earl described one strong incentive for joining the union: "Prestige, you know; 'you got a card, man?' 'Yeh, I gotta card.' We also had to have a card to write music." He explained the sense of order that the union provided for "the musician and the person that hired you. I couldn't send somebody else in my place or anything like that." And he described how a union official would monitor clubs to enforce compliance. "Everybody said make sure the card was paid up, 'cause he'd get off the bandstand. He very seldom came in where I worked."[26]

Local 535 networked with the young players in the Frederick Douglass Square scene to help them improve skills and find gigs at college and society events. Mabel Robinson Simms decided to join in order to gain access to venues larger than salon parties. During the interwar years, she formed a trio for the house band at the Swanee Grill on Tremont Street. Simms, who would later become secretary of Local 535, appreciated the sense of camaraderie: "If I had not been in a union I don't think I would have been associated with as many musicians. So, I think it was an advantage." She found the union card provided leverage in the job market as well: "It did give me an advantage of earnin' a decent wage. And as the scale went up, my wages went up. That made a difference in my life."[27]

A small number of musicians and combos were regulars on the circuit of dance halls and ballrooms that hired Black orchestras. The names of some were found in the advertisements of the *Boston Guardian*: the Leroy Curtis Jazz Band (sometimes billed as the Leroy Curtis Orchestra), the Johnson-Jefferson Orchestra with Walter Johnson "the Jazz King" (the full name of the co-leader "Jefferson" could not be determined), Newton Ball's Orchestra, Henry Hicks Famous Jazz Band, and Bobby Sawyer and His Hotel Westminster Jazz Orchestra. Sawyer was a pianist and native of Frederick Douglass Square who held a prominent spot as the leader of the house band at the Westminster Hotel, located in Copley Square on the boundary of the Back Bay and South End. The hotel hosted a supper club with dancing and a society band. Sawyer hired talented young musicians from the neighborhood, like Johnny Hodges and Harry Carney, for an orchestra that performed between the 1910s and 1930s. He also worked as a booking agent yet does not appear to have left a discography legacy. He had a reputation for a flamboyant—perhaps even volatile—personality. He was reportedly associated with a street gang that was involved in an ugly incident at Mechanics Hall. The fracas occurred during a 1920s concert by Louis Armstrong, as described by pianist Hi Diggs: "A riot broke out because Bobby Sawyer was a leader of a gang, and that night he got part of his ear cut out."[28]

George Tynes was a popular trumpeter and bandleader known for ragtime swing and Chicago style jazz ensembles. He fronted orchestras in Boston from about 1925 to 1933 and took a combo to a New York recording studio—reportedly one of the first race record sessions by a Boston group. They went by the awkward name of the "Georgia Cotton Pickers" and included Tynes on trumpet; James Tolliver, piano; Bob Chestnut and Jay Smith, trumpet; John Cook, trombone; Wilbur Pinkey, clarinet and alto sax; Jackie Jackson, banjo; Albert Burse, tuba; and Eddie Deas, drums. In 1930, the

The Cotton Club was an afterhours speakeasy on Tremont Street run by the crime boss Charles "King" Solomon.

band recorded four sides for the Harmony label, founded as the discount label of Columbia records in 1925 (it is unclear if the label was related to the record store): "Snag It," "Twelfth Street Rag," "Cotton Pickers' Shuffle," and "Louisiana Bo Bo" by Ted Nixon, a raucous foxtrot. The Tynes band included additional members such as Don Pasquall, clarinet and alto sax; Ray Culley, trumpet; Jackie Jackson, banjo; and many others. The aspiring saxophonist Howard Johnson recalls the excitement of the band members, saying, "My main influence on alto saxophone was a fellow named Brownie, who used to play with George Tynes. Brownie was the hottest thing around, and we all used to marvel at his playing."[29] The George Tynes band performed at venues such as the Railway Club and the Copley Square Hotel.

The most prominent musician was pianist Walter Johnson, deemed the "Jazz King" of Boston and the eldest son of a South End musical family. His father played piccolo flute with the Colored Knights of Pythias band; younger brothers Bobby and George played guitar and banjo, and Howard played saxophone. All had professional experience either playing together or with popular orchestras. Walter contributed to the jazz scene as a pianist, composer, arranger, and bandleader. He reportedly studied at the Boston Conservatory and left the city to work as the house pianist at the Vendome Theatre in Chicago. When he returned to Boston, his bands went by the names "Walter Johnson's Orchestra" and "Walter Johnson's Celebrated Orchestra." It showcased neighborhood talents like Johnny Hodges in concerts at Ruggles Hall. Johnson, in addition to performance, was engaged in the commerce of jazz culture; he ran a booking agency with an office on Tremont Street, and in the midst of Prohibition, he opened a speakeasy under various names: "Walter Johnson's Social Club," "Phalanx Club," and "the Black and White Club." (The term "speakeasy" referred to the need to speak quietly about such places in public to avoid tipping off the police or informers.) It was an exclusive club for Black patrons that circulated its address on a "need-to-know" basis. The orchestra featured talents like saxophonists Johnny Hodges and Harry Carney, and may have been the setting where Duke Ellington first noticed them. While Johnson left a significant imprint on the jazz scene, he left no available recording legacy.[30]

Local 535 hosted rooms for business and for musician rehearsal space, recalled Simms. "I think there was about three rooms on the second floor. Upstairs was a filing room, books and what not. I think the piano was downstairs or upstairs on the second floor. They would rehearse there." And she describes the union hall environment as a predominately male setting: "I think I was one of the only women that attended the meetings that was there."[31] Here, older musicians like Benny Waters found time to mentor young aspirants like Harry Carney. Waters moved to the city around 1918 to be with one of his brothers and to take classes at either the Boston Conservatory or the New England Conservatory. He may even have been born in the city, but the record is confused—some sources claim Brighton, Massachusetts, and others Brighton, Maryland. What is clear is that he lived in the South End during his formative years as a musician.

Born about 1902, Waters played clarinet and saxophone and was a steady hand in the combos of Joe Oliver in Chicago and Charlie "Fess" Johnson in Harlem. Waters also played in the New York City swing bands of Fletcher Henderson and Jimmie Lunceford. During his years in Boston, he gave lessons to as many as seventy other youths in the South End and recruited Carney to accompany him at society parties. Among the musicians he performed with were Charles "Skinny" Johnson (pianist, bandleader, and booking agent); Bobby Johnson (banjoist and brother of Walter, George, and Howard Johnson); "Professor" Joe Steele (pianist); and Tom Whaley (pianist and bandleader). Waters teamed up with Johnny Hodges to play the Sunday afternoon tea room circuit. He gained the attention of radio listeners with a memorable solo performed with the John Bowles Orchestra. He left Boston in 1926 to pursue opportunities in Harlem.[32]

The influence of the musicians who migrated from New Orleans to Chicago and New York was felt in Boston as well, perhaps best represented in the mentoring relationship of the young saxophonist Johnny Hodges and the older master Sidney Bechet. Born in New Orleans, Bechet was an outstanding clarinetist, alto saxophonist, and composer soloist who migrated to Chicago and New York and played in Europe for many years. He was one of the most imposing figures in the art of improvisation and purity of tone, his significance to jazz development on par with contemporaries Joe Oliver, Louis Armstrong, Johnny Dodds, and others. Howard Johnson remembers the occasion when Bechet performed in Boston, saying, "Sidney Bechet came to Boston in a show. Now when a show comes to a small town, you know, *everybody* goes to see it, and when we were exposed to Bechet he became our idol."[33] Johnny Hodges became his protégé after watching him perform at a Scollay Square Theater in about 1924. He says, "I went to hear him at a theater in Boston. My sister knew him very well. Made myself known, had a little soprano under my arm. He asked me to play. I caught the show two, three times to catch as much as I could."[34] Bechet took Hodges under his wing and schooled him in the mastery of the reed instrument. Under such tutelage, Hodges brushed aside formal training in favor of head arrangements and on-the-job lessons from Bechet. "I had quite a few of his riffs," Hodges says. "Quite a few of his pets. My pets too."[35]

Boston jazz culture intersected with the manufacturing industry for audio consumer products. Through the production of records, the city had a small influence in the area of race record creation. Broome Special Records, started in 1919 by George Broome, a laborer who wanted to issue recordings of Black concert artists, is believed to be the first Black-owned record label in the country.[36] Broome distributed records by mail order from his home in Medford, Massachusetts. The discography for the 1919 "Broome Special" issue chronicles the high level of professionally trained musicians supporting the label. The session work during the fall of 1919 was an impressive outpouring of spirituals and art songs for the African American clientele: Harry Burleigh, a baritone concert singer and composer of spirituals as art songs, recorded "Go Down Moses." Edward Boatner, a bass-baritone concert singer and composer of art songs, did "Sometimes I Feel Like a Motherless Child" and "I Don't Feels Noways Tired." R. Nathaniel Dett, an Afro-Canadian pianist, choral director, and composer, recorded "Magnolia Suite-Mammy" and "In the Bottoms-Barcarolle." Florence Cole-Talbert, an opera soprano known as "The First Lady of Grand Opera," sang "Nobody Knows the Trouble I've Seen" and "Dell' Acqua: Vilanelle." Finally, Clarence Cameron White, a concert violinist and conductor, recorded his compositions on Black experience, "Lament" and "Cradle Song." Broome was one of the few opportunities for classically trained Black musicians to record, along with Harry Pace's Black Swan Records in Harlem. On that basis alone, the body of recordings merit study as part of the music recording history of Boston.[37]

There were a few independent studios making occasional records of jazz bands in the 1920s and 1930s, and more so in the 1940s and 1950s by supper clubs with touring swing and bebop artists like Storyville and the Hi-Hat. Overall, however, there is little evidence of an ongoing jazz recording legacy, although many musicians participated in out-of-town sessions for the race record and international labels. Preston Sandiford described the travails of one pioneer, Casper Gordon Studios, located downtown near Piano Row. "That was the first big New England recording studio right down the street here at 140 Boylston. They introduced me to another line: arranging for jingles," he said. "Our big hit was 'Time Out for Dawson's.'" He went on to describe the loss of royalties in the transaction. "The ad people threatened to take the account away from [Eddie] Casper, and he let them bully him into accepting a flat fee," Sandiford claimed. "So I had to watch fifteen to sixteen years of that jingle play and I only got a flat fee." Another studio was Ace Recording, which made inexpensive "instantaneous records" in a studio located on Warrenton Street near Stuart Street.[38]

While rarely profitable, records provided musicians with an opportunity to share their sound with a wider audience; market the band to the press, booking agents, and club owners; and hold a measure of prestige. For students of jazz, the records served as mediums of instruction and ways to discover new jazz licks. In the 1920s, Boston youths would have listened to cylinder and disc recordings of jazz combos from Chicago, society bands from New York, and Harlem solo pianists like James P. Johnson, Willie "The Lion" Smith, and Fats Waller. The records reinforced a learning process that relied on the "apprenticeship at the gramophone" as described by many jazz players and innovators.[39] The major race record labels—Black Swan, Paramount, OKeh, Brunswick, Gennett, Victor, Columbia, and others—captured the evolution of jazz music during the interwar years. Sales took off during World War

I from about $27 million in 1914 to $159 million in 1919, and they continued to grow as American consumers bought an estimated 100 million records in 1927.

Boston pianist and bandleader Preston Sandiford recalled an ill-fated recording opportunity with his society orchestras. He composed the song "Zulu Wail" that caught the attention of a record label on the West Coast: "They called up and wanted the band to go out there. They wanted us to record it, everything," he said. "But I was too chicken to go and wasn't sure that all the guys would go."[40] Years later, he recorded sides for the Canadian label, Cameo Records, including "Once in a While" and "Music Maestro Please." Sandiford recorded an album of piano ballads for the Solitaire label with "I'm Getting Sentimental Over You," "Manhattan Serenade," These Foolish Things," "Tea for Two," "Shine on Harvest Moon," "Music Maestro Please," "Once in a While," and "Where or When." Most of the labels were small independent operations and paid poorly; the lead musician could expect a flat fee of $30 to $75 for two sides of a 78 rpm record and no royalty payments. Some settled for no payment or in-kind compensation, like a bottle of whiskey. Fact is, the race record industry was unstable, and many labels ended up in bankruptcy.[41]

Boston jazz fans heard the faint broadcasts of orchestras on radio programs as early as 1921. The Hub had one of the few pioneer radio stations that offered scheduled programming, 1XE in Medford (renamed WGI the next year). By 1922, the station was joined by WNAC in the downtown Shepard's Department Store. At the time, people identified stations by either the name of the owner or location, such as "the Shepard Station." (It should be noted that the Westinghouse Electric and Manufacturing Company started WBZ in Springfield in 1921; however, few people in Boston were able to receive the signal. They had to open a second station in Boston a few years later.) Station 1XE was on the hilly campus of Tufts College in Medford; while located a few miles from the city, its hilltop antenna provided a strong signal that could be received as far as Chicago. Known as the "Medford Hillside Station," it was started during the war years by the American Radio and Research Corporation as a noncommercial experiment in "wireless telephone" technology.

The station programming featured live announcers, police reports, sports scores in Morse code, Tufts professors giving on-air lectures, and classical and jazz music on records bartered from a local store in exchange for the promotion. As a volunteer-run station, the station relied on music schools and conservatories for free talent—and a periodic source of jazz culture. They hosted live music performances ranging from amateur high school glee clubs to dance orchestras. They also recruited touring singers and actors from the vaudeville and dramatic stages of Boston. In 1922, for instance, the Black actor Charles Gilpin read from *The Emperor Jones* to promote a run of the play downtown. Clearly, the eclectic programming format of 1XE (WGI) created an opportunity for exposure to jazz culture and commerce in Boston.[42]

The audio consumer products bought by "radio bugs" included battery-powered crystal headsets, electric miniature radios, stylish Cathedral-shaped units, and elegant art deco consoles housed in mahogany cabinets. Purchases of radio equipment rose from $60 million in 1922 to $358 million in 1924—and soared to $430 million the next year. By 1929, the sale of radio equipment had reached nearly $850 million and was the main source of industry profit before advertising made station programming viable. It was common for local department stores to operate low-powered stations chiefly as a way to market radio sets. Popular models ran from $14 to $60, and Boston produced several portable models for enthusiasts. The Automatic Radio Manufacturing Corporation opened a factory at 122 Brookline Avenue near Fenway Park in 1920 where they made sleek vacuum tube models with names like Air Master, Autorola, Blue Bird, and Tom Thumb in wood, the opaque plastic Bakelite, and the colorful translucent plastic Catalin. They marketed the Tom Thumb radio, one of the smallest battery-operated radios, to the young generation. It featured an art deco design with cutout grill over the speaker and Catalin body in Azure Blue, Nile Green, Orchid, and other colors. Another portable model had a leather-bound cabinet with Catalin feet, oval dial with a cut-out grill, and carry handle. The level of Black employment at the factory is unknown, but perhaps some members of the community worked there. The Automatic Radio Manufacturing Corporation closed in 1957.[43]

The cultural and economic impact of Boston jazz radio is a subject that merits additional research. Certainly, the programs influenced the knowledge and preferences of audiences and the market for jobs in studios. Popular jazz acts would come to town and team with local musicians. The locals would get paid for concert work but not for any radio sessions. Dean Earl explained, "The main gripe is when they hire a name to play by himself that entails, a lot of times, broadcasting. A side man—[unclear]—you didn't get paid for broadcasting."[44] Musicians feared that radio would reduce audience interest in live performances and some thought it would diminish demand for orchestras in dance halls and nightclubs. The production of radio sets in the local factories no doubt impacted jobs and jazz culture; music stores and retailers probably thought it prudent to sell radio sets as a hedge. In all, the industry of jazz music gained traction in Boston with little financial benefit to the South End scene, but probably a lot of social and cultural value. People able to eke out a living as musicians held a status of favor in the community unlike that of porters, janitors, and laborers who may have earned more money.[45]

Frederick Douglass Square was a site of nightclub activity with suspected links to an organized crime syndicate. This is not a surprise during Prohibition, when from 1920 to 1933 the production, importation, transportation, and sale of alcoholic beverages was banned in the United States. Prohibition set off a lucrative illegal trade in the production, smuggling, and transportation (or bootlegging) of alcoholic beverages to circumvent the laws. It also created a demand for illicit establishments that sold alcoholic beverages, known as "speakeasies." Many of the criminal gangs were organized along ethnic lines that competed for territory.

The illicit alcohol racket supplied the speakeasies, brothels, supper clubs, dance halls, grocery stores, delicatessens, flower shops, and other legitimate establishments. In Boston, it funneled into the nightclubs and supper clubs in the Theater District and adjacent South End. Some musicians found working conditions in these establishments exploitative and even menacing. They played without contracts or with contracts forced upon them; some were subjected to intimidation, harassment, beatings, kidnappings, and threats against themselves and their associates.[46] One of the mob bosses was Charles "King" Solomon, leader of the Jewish syndicate that trafficked in alcohol, narcotics, and extortion of business owners. The gangsters also employed jazz musicians to perform in the venues, and Solomon had a reputation for being one of the more considerate employers among the racketeers—Sandiford revealed that at one time his band was "working then for Charlie Solomon, the gangster. He owned clubs, theaters, everything, and was a damned good guy to work for."[47]

Frederick Douglass Square hosted Boston's Cotton Club, a nightclub located at 892 Tremont Street and forever linked to the murder of the crime boss. Not much is known about the club itself—most stories about it focus on the singular event of Solomon's demise. He was gunned down in the men's room during a robbery in 1933. Apparently, the club had been started by the white impresario Tommy Maren to accommodate Black patrons in the city. It is reasonable to assume that the small club served as an outlet for illicit alcohol—and possibly narcotics—along with food and jazz from local musicians. In the 1930s, the club was housed in a drab two-story mixed-use brick building: a gospel hall was on the second floor and spaces may have been used for other services. On the ground floor was the corner grocer Sweet's Market, an unknown storefront named New Palace, and of course, the storefront of Boston's Cotton Club. The wooden door to the club was framed by brick walls and windows that reached floor to ceiling. Patrons would have looked out on a cobblestone Tremont Street lined with streetcar tracks, telephone poles, and parking spots. All in all, it appeared to be a modest establishment and contributor to the neighborhood jazz scene.[48]

Finally, booking agents were important actors in the commerce of Boston jazz. They supplied the orchestras and concerts for the summer dances in the string of waterfront ballrooms in New England. The booking and scheduling of bands was a lucrative branch of the live music business, and control of the booking service carried influence in the regional jazz culture as well. In cities impacted by the mass migration, according to Ted Vincent, independent Black booking agents emerged to represent the jazz music sprouting up in the various urban scenes. By 1920, a good number of Black talent agents were in a position to take advantage of the growing interest in jazz and blues music; they negotiated roles as suppliers of Black music as commodities for the mainstream markets.[49] In the South End, for instance, a promoter named Clement Thorn was known to manage dancers and musicians and stage "Battle of the Band" events that pitted one orchestra against another in downtown venues.

In New England, however, the most noted booking agency was run by brothers Charles and Simeon Shribman. Their company managed dance halls and theaters across the region and, in some cases, owned ballrooms and financed bands. The office was located on the tenth floor of the Little Building—today a part of Emerson College—at Boylston and Tremont streets in the Theater District. Two of their waterfront dance halls were Nutting-on-the-Charles in Newton and the Charleshurst in Salem Willows. In later years, they controlled the upscale Normandy Ballroom and the Roseland-State Ballroom in Boston. "He didn't own all the ballrooms in New England," recalls Duke Ellington, whose orchestra was scheduled by the agency. "But he had a very good association with the people who owned those he did not."[50]

The Shribman Company played a leading role in exposing audiences to jazz orchestras and filling a seasonal job market for local musicians. Preston Sandiford recalled, "They had 99 percent of the booking in this whole area of New England. What they used to do was bring in a name band from New York and would book them, maybe three dates. Sometimes between the dates, there were gaps and they would let my band in those gaps."[51] While a few South End bands and musicians were hired for intermission breaks, the white orchestras got the major engagements.

The Mal Hallett Orchestra was a popular Boston jazz band and a workhorse of the Shribman operation. Born 1896 in Roxbury, Malcolm Gray "Mal" Hallett trained as a classical musician on the violin and reed instruments at the Boston Conservatory. By 1922, he was known as a top bandleader and showman—a six-foot, five-inch mustached conductor who waved a baton to spur on talented soloists. His orchestra provided a stable stream of one-night acts for Boston revelers. While they never had a hit single, the group did record foxtrots and popular standards for major labels like Decca. Among the sides were "(Have You Forgotten) The You and Me That Used to Be," "Turn Off the Moon," "One in a Million," and "In the Chapel in the Moonlight."[52]

The Hallett Orchestra had an entertaining brand of performance that included bits of comedy. It was on full display in the 1930s Warner Brothers musical short *Mal Hallett School of Swing*. The scene was a classroom with Hallett posing as a music professor lecturing on the subject of "Swinglish." The band members were the students, sitting with instruments and following Hallett as he stood in front of a blackboard telling the history of swing. One by one, the students stand up to demonstrate jazz licks before the whole class breaks out in ensemble fury as Hallett bobs up and down and waves a baton like a crazed maestro. The short film was shown as a novelty reel between featured movies.[53]

Hallett employed musicians at the beginning of promising careers and the orchestra became a training ground for white musicians. Among the players who passed through the orchestra were Gene Krupa, Jack Teagarden, Henry "Boots" Mussulli, Jack Jenny, Lou McGarity, Brad Gowans, Buddy Wise, Mickey McMickle, and Nuncio "Toots" Mondello. As a small market band, however, Hallett was unable to hold on to musicians once they gained notice in the industry. The Hallett Orchestra was among the pioneer bands to inject swing into the respectable sweet jazz dance culture of Boston. They achieved a reputation as an orchestra that could stand its ground in "battles" against Duke Ellington, Paul Whiteman, Count Basie, and other top outfits. Ellington noted, "All these bands used to come up from New York, and Mal Hallett would blow them right out over the Charles River."[54]

The business of jazz in Boston generated employment and wealth in an overlapping fashion. Although Black musicians were at the vanguard of creating jazz culture, they enjoyed little of the wealth generated by an engine of entertainment commerce. As such, they were akin to sharecroppers in a lack of power to derive full benefits for their labor in the marketplace. David Suisman, in a study of the Harlem recording company Black Swan, examined the effects of race and industry practices on livelihoods and found that by 1919, composers and musicians had begun to speak out against such stolen wealth in a music industry valued at over $335 million. The commercial activity spanned the sale of musical instruments, sheet music, piano rolls, live performances, records, phonographs, and radio. Critics of the industry included James Reese Europe, William Christopher "W. C." Handy, and the founder of Black Swan, Harry Pace. Suisman concludes, "When music functions as a commodity, as it often does in American consumer culture, who makes it and on what terms are important questions of cultural and economic power."[55]

Boston Symphony Hall was a symbol of high-brow opposition to the spread of jazz music in the 1920s.

CHAPTER SIX

JAZZ TAKES THE BOSTON STAGE

Jazz infiltrated the culture of Boston through the theaters that hosted traveling shows and the highbrow advocates of the concert stage. Of particular importance were the musical comedies and dance revues of Harlem that infused acts with the sounds of ragtime, blues, and jazz standards—and sometimes hired musicians, dancers, and stagehands from the neighborhood scene. On occasion, Boston theaters were used to produce song and dance shows for the theaters of Broadway. By 1920, there was a cluster of about fifteen theaters in the city that staged performances with jazz-influenced acts of vaudeville, minstrelsy, talent shows, revues, and burlesque. Among the noteworthy houses were the Arlington Theater, the Tremont Theater, the Gaiety Theater, and Charles Waldron's Casino.

The Boston stages were part of the estimated 300 theaters that featured Black musical productions in the country, including about ninety-four controlled by Black owners and managers. While many shows were put on by local actors and musicians, at least 100 theaters hosted the productions of touring companies from New York City. The musical comedies of Harlem and Broadway were most in demand—and often were only modestly different from the earlier minstrel shows. Black musicals and revues were engines of show business activity sufficient to support a national circuit of theaters and talent. The 1910 US census provides a glimpse of the occupational benefit for some of the 5,600 Black musicians and 1,280 actors. By 1915, in fact, the former comedian Sherman H. Dudley was able to establish a booking agency for the Black theater circuit, the Theater Owners Booking Association, comprising about eighty venues and managing fifty production companies and 179 vaudeville acts.[1]

The music revues of Harlem played to audiences in Boston on the way to theaters on Broadway and other cities and in Europe. All the great Black productions of the jazz age came to Boston—and sometimes utilized local musicians and dancers. Among the noteworthy were *Shuffle Along*, *Running Wild*, *Chocolate Dandies*, *Blackbirds*, and *Hot Chocolates*. All featured songs with the latest jazz melodies and dance rhythms. The Arlington Theatre, located at 421 Tremont Street in the South End, carried live shows from 1921 until the end of the decade. The Arlington was located in the building of the former Castle Square Theatre, which hosted live shows and silent movies before it closed. The theater was noted for spacious foyers and an elegant auditorium. In April 1923, the Arlington Theater hosted the Broadway hit *Shuffle Along* for a two-week engagement. The *Guardian* announced the show as the "stupendous world's sensational record-breaking musical comedy." An advertisement published a full-page photograph of a chorus line and men in tuxedos and high hats. It promised blues singers, quartettes, comedians, girls, and jazz orchestras. "Never before in the history of the American stage has a musical production been such a success as Shuffle Along," the ad boasted. "It created more cheers, enthusiastic applause and uproarious laughter than had ever been heard on Broadway."[2]

The musical theater introduced Boston audiences to the talent of Nobel Sissle and Eubie Blake, among other Harlem acts. Sissle was a pianist, singer, and songwriter born in Indianapolis in 1889 who broke into show business when the manager of a hotel asked the young man to form a syncopated jazz band to tour in Europe. He went on to make recordings of ragtime and minstrel standards as early as 1917 and produced about 150 sides over twenty years. An example of his work for the minstrel stage is the 1920 side "Great Camp Meeting Day." In 1915, he teamed up with the pianist and composer Eubie Blake, whom he met at a Baltimore concert. Blake, born in 1883 in Baltimore, worked for the minstrel stage and had a desire to compose orchestral and show tunes that drew on the modern experience. He began to make recordings in 1917 with his group, the Eubie Blake Trio, for the Pathé label. Two that have survived are "Sarah from Sahara" and "The Jazz Dance." During the war years, he composed songs for the James Reese Europe Orchestra: "To Hell with Germany," "On Patrol in No Man's Land," and "No Man's Land Will Soon Be Ours." Blake and Sissle performed a minstrel act, the Dixie Duo, but declined to wear blackface makeup. In 1920, they teamed up with producers Aubrey Lyles and Flournoy Miller to develop musical comedies. One result was the aforementioned *Shuffle Along* in 1921.[3]

Blake composed more than 350 songs over his long career—perhaps none as popular as the 1920s golden age of jazz-inspired musical comedies like *Shuffle Along*. Among the favorites on stage and records were "I'm Just Wild About Harry," "Love Will Find a Way," and "Bandana Days." The show premiered at the 63rd Street Theatre in New York to grand reception, and the music appealed to fans as instrumental and lyrical products, incorporating a medley of minstrel acts, comedy skits, chorus line dancing, and catchy tunes. It featured the rarity of a love song by a Black couple, "Love Will Find a Way." It made stars of actors Adelaide Hall, Florence Mills, Paul Robeson, and Josephine Baker before branching out to audiences across the country.[4] In 1921, Blake recorded "Bandana Days" as a dance song by Eubie Blake and His Shuffle Along Orchestra. The Victor recording is an example of the "hot" syncopated music on the Harlem and Broadway stage. The opening melody resembles a march of a brass band then shifts to an uptempo one-step turkey trot, a popular dance of the 1920s; it includes a quotation from "Dixie" and a measure of the foxtrot, "I'm Just Wild About Harry." The session incorporated novelty sound effects like the clash of cymbals and the backbeat of handheld percussive "clackers."[5]

The Tremont Theatre, established in 1889, was a downtown playhouse at 179 Tremont Street that accommodated mainstream audiences. In 1915, it was the site of protests over the screening of D. W. Griffith's *Birth of a Nation*, a silent film that glorified the reactionary violence of the Ku Klux Klan during the Reconstruction. In the 1920s, the theater featured plays for mainstream audiences; among them was the popular production of George M. Cohan's *Little Nellie Kelly*. It debuted in the Tremont in 1922 before a year-long run on Broadway. In July 1924, the Tremont Theatre premiered a new Harlem revue by Sissle and Blake, *In Bamville*. It was an ambitious production with a cast of 125 actors, dancers, and musicians. The script was written by Sissle and Lew Payton and the music and songs by Sissle and Blake. The story revolved around a horse racetrack in a southern town named Bamville. The story was merely a framework for presenting comedy, songs, and occasional commentary poking fun at the minstrelsy tradition, though the play itself was a shadow of minstrelsy. After the Boston debut, Sissle and Blake took the show to Broadway under the new name *Chocolate Dandies*.[6]

The *Guardian* carried a full-page pictorial of "Sissle and Blake's newest musical comedy." The photo spread depicted Josephine Baker as the "eccentric dancer," Volada Snow as the "sensational dancer," Lottie Gee as the "prima donna," and Gee and Ivan Browning in spectacular regalia. Johnny Hudgins, Lew Payton, and the Four Harmony Kings were shown in a minstrel skit in blackface, white lips, and derby hats in comic poses. What made the production a vehicle for jazz music were the dance rhythms and intervals for improvisation in the solos and dances. A *Guardian* preview exclaimed, "The dancing now being shown far outdistances by its sheer originality and surpasses anything of a like nature seen there in years. The music of Eubie Blake is superior in quality, and tunefulness, from a strictly musical standpoint than the many so-called musical comedies of today."[7]

In addition to the playhouses, Boston featured two vaudeville theaters that hosted an estimated thirty-six Black or integrated variety shows during the 1920s. The Gaiety Theater and Charles Waldron's Casino were on Washington Street between the neighborhoods of Chinatown and Scollay Square—the Gaiety on Washington and Essex streets in Chinatown; the Casino on Hanover Street in the Square. The theaters featured many vaudeville-minstrel performances with the sounds of ragtime, blues, and jazz dance music. One annual spectacular was the *Big Black and White Show* with thirty-five Black actors and thirty-five white actors doing skits, comedy, novelty bits, songs, and chorus lines. It was common for a popular show to play at both houses on different dates. In the 1920s, the theaters were managed under the Columbia Entertainment Company of New York City. The theater chain was known as the "Eastern Wheel" of the burlesque circuit and catered to "clean" shows for working-class men. "Clean" was commonly understood as shows that allowed chorus girls to cover private parts and where dance routines stopped short of a full striptease. The theaters were considered proper venues to take the family and hosted two Broadway productions with the song and dance talent of Harlem: the music revue *Runnin' Wild*—and the musical comedy of the same name—were developed with acts from the revue.[8]

In April 1923, *Runnin' Wild*, the musical revue, was staged at Waldron's Casino as a top featured show. The revue of song and dance talent exposed audiences to the popular songs of composer "Cecil Mack." His real name was Richard McPherson, and he was born circa 1883 in Norfolk, Virginia. As a teenager, he planned to study medicine but instead followed his love of songwriting. Moving to Harlem, McPherson took the pseudonym of Cecil Mack when he was hired to compose for the minstrel team of Bert Williams and George Walker. Between 1901 and 1906, he wrote songs such as "Junie," "All in, Down and Out," "Good Morning, Carrie," and "He's a Cousin of Mine." Some of the odes were recorded by Williams and Walker for the Victor and Columbia labels. McPherson later founded the Gotham Music Publishing Company to protect copyrights and distribute the works. In either 1909 or 1911, he published "Too Much Mustard," a turkey trot hit record by the James Europe Society Band that also served as a transition song from ragtime to early jazz. His best-known song was "That's Why They Call Me (Shine)," written with Lew Brown. The dramatic ode for song and dance was recorded by the society band of Ford Dabney and covered by many musicians during the war years.[9]

By the 1920s, McPherson was one of the leading songwriters in the country and reportedly the first Black composer accepted into the American Society of Composers, Authors, and Publishers in 1925. The *Runnin' Wild* musical revue and later Broadway comedy laid the foundation for the second phase of his career: he teamed up with the South Carolina pianist James Price Johnson to create the music revue. The production that visited Boston showcased singer Daisy Martin debuting "Ginger Brown," "Old Fashioned Love," and "The Charleston" song. The *Boston Guardian* announcement raved that "the jazzy Colored revue will be presented by the most remarkable aggregation of Colored artists, experts in song, dance, jazz and harmony, ever assembled in one high class company." It highlighted that the show would showcase "the new dance craze, the Charleston, which promises to be the popular step this summer season."[10]

In November 1924, the Gaiety Theater featured the Broadway musical comedy *Runnin' Wild*. The *Globe* review made special note of actress Adelaide Hall by recalling her breakout performance in the musical comedy *Shuffle Along* two years earlier, noting, "The pretty little brown-skinned girl who created quite an impression in the 'Bandanna Days' number" and described that she was "possessed of a soprano voice of unusual mellow tone and quality."[11] Hall, born in New York City about 1901, came to the attention of Boston audiences at the beginning of her ascent to stardom. She was a prominent actress, singer, and dancer in vaudeville and musical theater. She had talent and the lighter complexion valued on the stage. She was the daughter of a white father and Black mother and went into show business after her father's early death. In the 1921 Broadway production of *Shuffle Along*, she was a dancer in the "Jazz Jasmines" chorus line and featured in a duet with Arthur Porter for the song "Bandana Days." She carried the song "Old Fashioned Love" in the 1923 revue of *Runnin' Wild*. She had a prominent career in musical theater and jazz recordings, like the 1927 "Creole Love Call" with the Duke Ellington Orchestra.

Outside of the vaudeville stage, jazz began to make itself felt in the concert halls of the city. Boston Symphony Hall was a grand theater that traditionalists held up as a citadel of highbrow culture. It represented the ascendance of Boston Brahmin families as leaders of American civilization and stood guard against the incursion of jazz influences in classical music. Opened with fanfare in 1900, Symphony Hall was the home of the Boston Symphony Orchestra and the Boston Pops, and a feat of architectural and engineering achievement. It was designed by the New York architects McKim, Mead, and White with acoustic engineering by Wallace Clement Sabine, assistant professor of physics at Harvard University. It was the first auditorium built on scientific acoustic principles: sloping walls to focus sound waves and shallow balconies to avoid sound traps, among other devices. The pretense of civilization was symbolized by the use of classical Greek statues to underscore the idea of "Boston, the Athens of America."[12]

By 1927, traditionalists around the world were in a state of alarm over the spread of jazz into classical realms. They demanded that the "jazz hounds keep their dirty paws off their betters" and spewed epithets that "jazz is dead from the neck up."[13] Critics were on high alert from the United States to Europe over the disgruntlement of the postwar "Lost Generation." Ernest Newman, a British music writer, declared in the *New York Times* that jazz composers had no right to "jazz" the classics, writing that "Strauss is Strauss and we are we."[14] In defeated Germany, however, young people gave way to the infectious dance songs. Eric Borchard, the leading jazz musician and promoter in Germany in the 1920s, noted that it was introduced in the country by Black soldiers during the war and reinforced by the circulation of records. "The Germans are wild about American jazz singing," he says. "So far they have heard it only on the phonograph. I am going to bring them the best quartet the United States can provide, as well as a brand new American band."[15] In April 1927, Borchard announced his trip from Bremen to New York to recruit Black musicians. A reporter noted that "The craze which suddenly developed in the country for phonograph records reproducing songs sung by negro quartets and other vocalists has inspired his trip."[16]

In June of 1927, the perception of jazz as an international contagion spurred a condemnation at the League of Nations. During a conference in Geneva, delegates traveled to Frankfort to attend a music exposition; some the delegates used the occasion to stand together in opposition to jazz. Among the critics were delegates from Austria, Poland, Italy, Switzerland, Czechoslovakia, Hungary, and Germany who expressed their objections to a reporter for the *New York Times.* For example, the German foreign minister Gustav Stresemann bemoaned, "I regret that negro rhythm has triumphed over harmony. We must protect our nerves from this drumfire and seek again that solemn hour of communion from which has come all the greatness ever created."[17]

In Boston, Alfred Casella, conductor of the Boston Pops, expressed similar concerns. He vowed to the *Boston Globe* that the orchestra would never perform a jazz program. He claimed that the music was offensive to concert audiences and that the "public is never wrong." He also admitted that "the orchestra lacks the necessary instruments and the special technique necessary to play jazz properly." Finally, he predicted a quick death for the jazz fad and its "early return to obscurity."[18] Meanwhile, highbrow cultural elites in the Black community spoke out against the menace of jazz as well. To understand their concerns, it is necessary to understand the politics of respectability in the Black community. Cultural leaders believed that tailoring behavior to mimic Yankee middle-class values was a way to defy stereotypes and better integrate into mainstream society. The politics was espoused by community leaders since the post-emancipation years and most prominently by Black New England writers like W. E. B. DuBois.

The old class of Boston Yankees exercised critical leverage through positions in teaching, journalism, politics, social clubs, the ministry, the professions, and by marrying among their own class. Of course, their middle-class status was more dependent on noneconomic factors than on personal wealth or family holdings. The factors included such elements as good reputation, sober behavior, reliable character, family standing, college education, and light skin tone. The politics of respectability was especially important to the efforts of women to debunk the stereotypes associated with the saloons and risqué floor shows of blues and jazz culture. Women's clubs in Boston, for example, tried to expose migrants and soldiers on leave to classical music and the concert hall. Many civic leaders worked hard to help migrants to assimilate as quickly as possible—although sometimes in ways that could be offensive to newcomers. In the desire to blend in, the critics could disregard the richness of Black music, and the strain to meet the standards of a different culture. Dean Earl, a member of Local 9, remembered the condescending attitudes of cultural elites, saying, "They always looked down on jazz musicians. I didn't like the way they said 'jazz.' 'Oh, you play *jazz*.' What do you mean? What the hell are you talkin' about?"[19]

With such fractures in public, Boston Symphony Hall became a front in the war between jazz and traditional culture. Gradually, the concert hall succumbed to the crusades of jazz promoters and occasional performances of blues and jazz orchestras. Among the pioneers at Symphony Hall were W. C. Handy, George Gershwin, and Paul Whiteman. The jazz music presented at Symphony Hall was a mere shadow of the real dance music, of course, but an introduction to the power of Black music. It began with the arrival of the blues orchestra of W. C. Handy. By 1920, the bandleader and composer was in the prime of his career, and his compositions and orchestra were in demand in major theaters. He spent the 1920s and 1930s promoting the blues to mainstream audiences and, in 1928, was the first conductor to present a program of blues at Carnegie Hall. The *Boston Guardian* proudly announced that in August of 1923, Symphony Hall would host a "night of syncopation" by the W. C. Handy Orchestra with Sara Martin, the "Queen of the Blues." The announcement promised that the Orchestra would perform "every recent hit of these two stars: everything from the soft, crooning lullaby, the darktown blues, the famous Handy march hits, foxtrots, one steps, on down to the ultimate in present-day 'blues' successes—both instrumental and vocal."[20] Concertgoers would have been treated to a live performance of "Aunt Haggar's Blues," a syncopated jazz tune that the Handy orchestra had recorded earlier that year for OKeh records. The session was a bluesy foxtrot with multiple lines of rhythm by trumpet, sax, tuba, clarinet, and xylophone, among others. The clarinet rises above the band with a blues melody. It is followed by a xylophone chorus and the background percussive sound of a rattle. [21]

The next year, Symphony Hall announced the hiring of a new Boston Symphony Orchestra conductor, Serge Koussevitsky. The Russian-born conductor would lead the BSO from 1924 to 1949 and whittle away the barriers imposed by the old Yankee elites. For one thing, he was more sympathetic to jazz for its "important contribution to modern musical literature. It has an epochal significance—it is not superficial, it is fundamental. Jazz comes from the soil, where all music has its beginning."[22] He commissioned jazz-inspired compositions from Ravel, Stravinsky, Aaron Copland, and others, even when such works sparked objections.

A *Globe* review of the 1928 Copland composition complains: "The last work of his heard here was a jazz concerto which roused much discussion [as to the] modernist style so obnoxious to musical conservatives."[23] Nonetheless, the shift in consideration made it easier for Symphony Hall to invite interpreters of orchestral jazz. In 1927, it presented a concert by George Gershwin, who performed a program of five works in an event deemed "something so unusual as to rouse comment, often hostile comment."[24] The challenge for Gershwin was to demonstrate how the dance music of African Americans was suitable material for the European orchestral framework. A *Globe* reviewer questioned whether the music could "stimulate the listener's imagination, touch his heart and satisfy his musical intelligence."[25] The writer concluded that Gershwin failed on all accounts! Of the five pieces presented, including "Rhapsody in Blue" and Concerto in F, the only composition this reviewer considered qualified to be on the concert stage was "The Man I Love," adding, "The song is a moving and beautiful expression of a simple human feeling, akin to that in Schubert's 'Gretchen am Spinnrade,' only less definitely tragic."[26]

Next, Symphony Hall presented a program of jazz selections by the Paul Whiteman Orchestra. Whiteman was a conflicted voice on the merits of jazz as a fine art and straddled the line on its value to American music versus its threat to Anglo-American culture. Whiteman's forte was the arrangement of melodic lines and syncopated rhythms for orchestration branded as "symphonic jazz." That was the jazz music he presented in Symphony Hall in December 1928. Serge Koussevitsky attempted to preempt doubters with a public endorsement of Whiteman—a risky move, given the hostility traditionalists felts toward Whiteman. To some critics, Whiteman's public assertion that jazz could help to revitalize American music made him akin to being a cultural traitor. He once argued, "Like the folk songs of another age, jazz reflects and satisfies the undeveloped aesthetic and emotional cravings of the great masses of people. Jazz is a spirit, not a manner."[27] He was an early supporter of George Gershwin's musical explorations, and commissioned "Rhapsody in Blue" for a 1924 New York concert. The Whiteman orchestra made the composition a standard over the years. In fact, he had performed the composition at Symphony Hall in 1925 for a social of the Bryn Mawr Club of Boston without criticism—but this concert was of a different scale.[28]

Despite the Koussevitsky endorsement, the Whiteman orchestra received a lukewarm reception at Symphony Hall. The program opened with a number that a critic thought aptly named: "Yes, Jazz is Savage." Whiteman included a performance of George Gershwin's Concerto in F—a composition that had failed to impress Boston audiences when Gershwin played it years earlier. A *Globe* reviewer sniffed that the Whiteman repertoire may be of "interest to those who believe there is a connection between jazz and the development of American music." The program was subjected to condescending remarks such as, "Much that Mr. Whiteman's orchestra played yesterday seemed nothing more than dance music of the type that is played in every cabaret in the country"; and was damned with faint praise as it regarded the presentation of the Gershwin concerto: "Its themes had individuality and pungency, were not mere deformations of popular sentimental tunes."[29]

While jazz themes were pressed by various orchestras, one singer did so in art songs for the concert stage. At Symphony Hall, a young Black man with a dream of becoming a concert singer brought the soulful melodies and stylish rhythms of the South End to Boston high society. That man was Roland Hayes, who would become the first Black tenor represented by the BSO. The child of former slaves, Hayes was born on a plantation in Curryville, Georgia, in 1887. He overcame obstacles social and personal to establish an international career as a concert singer. With a graceful voice and dramatic skills, he could move audiences to tears or laughter. His ear for song was developed by listening to the sounds of nature and the choirs in the church. He was drawn to the concert hall after listening to a recording of Enrico Caruso. Hayes developed his voice in choirs for the church, on street corners, and in railway stations. He teamed up with friends to form the "Silver Tone Quartet" to earn spare change. In 1911, he was a pageboy at John Hancock Life Insurance Company when he hired music teacher Arthur Hubbard for lessons—who tutored Hayes at his home to avoid inciting white students. Hayes pursued his passion despite the cautions from many that a career on the concert stage was unlikely. On two occasions, he self-funded recitals to burnish his credentials and public exposure. In 1916, he spent $200 to rent Jordan Hall for a program of European art songs. It was a waste of money as the performance failed to move even supportive guests.[30]

Yet, he rallied for another self-funded audition and spent the next year raising money by performing at schools and churches across the South. In 1917, he spent $400 to rent Symphony Hall for a program of art songs; he advertised the event in the newspaper, mailed out 3,000 invitations, and recruited friends at John Hancock to help promote it. As a result, he filled the 700-seat hall and gave a successful performance. The reception convinced Hayes that high-society audiences would support his career, saying, "I suppose I was unconsciously putting myself into competition with white singers, whose spotlight I wanted to share."[31] Following the concert, Hayes contacted record labels to gauge interest in a recording session. No major company expressed interest except Columbia, which offered to rent its local studio for a vanity recording. Taking up the offer, Hayes worked with George Broome of the Black-owned Broome Special Phonograph Records to cut sides. Broome was a laborer who started the company as a side business in 1919 to issue recordings of art songs by Harry T. Burleigh and Florence Cole-Talbert—Burleigh composed folk spirituals for the concert stage and Cole-Talbert was an African American opera soprano exalted as "The First Lady of Grand Opera." He oversaw recording sessions for Hayes under Columbia's vanity operation. Hayes sold his own recordings and used them to promote his career.[32]

The passion of Roland Hayes is best understood in the context of respectability politics and the role of Boston's Black upper class to model good taste and character in matters of culture and civics. His success was touted in the Black community and in the white press because he found a way to elegantly reconcile the Black folksongs that many people were ashamed of with the music of Yankee high-brow culture. In 1920, Hayes used his savings to move to London and take voice lessons and was swayed by conversations with Pan-African intellectuals over the intersections of colonial rule, race, and culture. This was a time of conferences of the Pan-African Congress held in London, Brussels, and Paris in the summer of 1921, as well as the debates among African students studying in London who formed the West African Students' Union (WASU) in 1925 under the leadership of Ladipo Solanke, a Nigerian student, and Herbert Bankole-Bright, an activist with the National Congress of British West Africa. WASU was the key political and cultural organization for West Africans in London and a gathering place for Pan-Africanists. In this cosmopolitan climate, Hayes revamped his program to include folk songs of the diaspora alongside European art songs. He came to view the spirituals as ancestral voices that "speak to me clearly, echoing the dim past—our ancient African ancestry and tribal memories."[33]

His new program featured songs that spanned the cultures of Europe and the African diasporic experience. It included European standards like "It Was a Lover and His Lass" from Shakespeare's *As You Like It*; "Where'er You Walk," an aria from George Frederic Handel's opera *Semele*; and "L'Absence" by Hector Berlioz; Afro-American folk standards like "Scandalize My Name," a traditional spiritual; "Weepin' Mary," by Harry T. Burleigh; "Mister Banjo" (also known as "Micheu Banjo"), a Louisiana Creole folk song; and the Afro-Brazilian chant to the war god "Xango" (Shango). The latter song begins with a low piano base riff like the beating of a ceremonial African drum. Hayes's rich tenor voice floats in over the rhythm with a chant to the ancient deity. The intervals between choruses added to the sense of mystical tensions—and Hayes ends with a yelp of ecstasy. Meanwhile, "Mister Banjo" is a playful folksong that one could imagine being sung in the barrelhouse saloons after a day of cutting sugar cane.[34]

In 1921, Hayes won over British audiences with his program that included authentic African songs. His concerts at Royal Chapel and Wigmore Hall led to an invitation to perform at Buckingham Palace for the royal court. From there, he successfully toured Vienna, Paris, Berlin, Rome, and Prague. He returned to Boston with an international reputation and gained the attention of BSO manager William Brennan—who a few years earlier had turned away the imitative program of Hayes. Now, in 1924, he offered to manage a national tour for the new program featuring authentic Black songs and booked 125 concerts, including Symphony Hall. One columnist told readers, "This writer has never heard another tenor with a voice as exquisitely beautiful and a musicianship as subtly perfect as that of Roland Hayes," adding that audiences should "not allow the fact that Mr. Hayes is a negro to affect in any way their judgment of his art. It is largely to his race that this country owes such native music as has been produced here."[35]

To fully appreciate the spread of jazz influence in Boston, one needs to look beyond the usual nightclubs and dance halls. The music was carried in the musical comedies and revues of vaudeville stage shows and in the classical programs and art songs of the concert hall. The musicians of the South End neighborhood jazz scene contributed to all these endeavors in various formats. As their voices reached into new corners of the city, they drew the attention—and ire—of white musicians curious about the emergence of these new sounds.

Art Deco radio and speaker decorated with the figurines of two dancers. The stylish radio set provided listeners with a variety of music and sound quality.

CHAPTER SEVEN

JAZZ ACROSS ETHNIC LINES

Jazz was an African American music that captured the imagination of young people across the lines of race and ethnicity; it did so during a time of anxiety over race and immigration, and a hardening of Jim Crow exclusionary practices in public accommodations, employment, housing, voting, policing, and music. Such was the case in Boston even though the Black community was a mere two percent of the population and relatively well integrated in poor white neighborhoods. During the interwar years, however, the racial groups separated into enclaves as native whites gained upward mobility; European immigrants claimed old housing in the West End, Roxbury, and Dorchester neighborhoods; and the Black sector forged a dominant presence in the South End and Lower Roxbury with the influx of migrants.

In theaters and auditoriums, concert dates could be scheduled by race, and rope lines were used to separate people at mixed events. For example, the popular annual vaudeville show known as the "Black and White Revue" featured thirty-five Black actors and thirty-five white actors, jazz battles of "sweet rhythm vs. Harlem swing," and other spectacles. It was hosted as a tent show and in venues like Charles Waldron's Casino in Scollay Square. The first show featured an all-white cast and the second show featured an all-Black cast. It is unclear how the theater managed to separate audiences for the two performances—quite likely people self-separated to watch the shows of preference in anticipation of being with audiences of the same kind.[1]

Along with theaters and auditoriums, the hotel ballrooms, supper clubs, and dance halls turned away Black patrons except on limited occasions. Such rules were enforced by doormen, bouncers, police, monitors, and by the indoctrination of the audience. Violations of the rules—such as crossing over the rope line—could result in disciplinary actions and even fights. The issue of gender was also a source of tension, and white women approaching Black men or vice versa could set off confrontations. Black women attending events could suffer the verbal abuse of police, monitors, and antagonists. Black combos hired for white dances were cautioned to avoid speaking with women and to avoid bringing girlfriends to the events. Black musicians could encounter threats, harassment, and attacks by customers and police alike. Some people took offense at the sight of well-dressed, confident jazzmen gaining prominence and felt the need to knock them down a notch. Interracial bands could incite the hostility of people in the audiences—and even white bands playing jazz could face harassment for promoting Black culture.[2]

One exception was the availability of "Black and Tan" cabarets or nightclubs in Black urban districts across the country. Such establishments provided jazz music and entertainment for Black and white patrons in New York, Chicago, Detroit, Pittsburgh and other places—in Boston a variation would have been Walter Johnson's Black and White Club. In Detroit, many of the cabarets were owned by Black businessmen to serve partiers after the closing hours of dance halls. They opened at 4 in the morning as a spot for musicians to hang out and "slumming" white audiences to have a good time. Many sites provided music, dancing, food, and whiskey disguised in coffee cups. Illicit activities like number running and prostitution were visible in some joints. Many clubs, like those in the Hill District of Pittsburgh, unintentionally contributed to the cause of civil rights by undermining racial barriers in the urban north.[3]

When it came to interracial orchestra work, most people accepted the practices of Jim Crow as a part of everyday life—but with occasional bruising experiences that cut deeply. In the case of orchestra leader Fletcher Henderson, for instance, the subjugation of his band to the whims of a white conductor in 1929 was scorned in the Black press. Henderson and his 12-member orchestra were contracted by a theater in Philadelphia to perform the music for the revue, Horseshoes. Upon arrival, Henderson was told to hire twenty additional musicians to enlarge the orchestra to thirty-two pieces. The new hires were all white and a white conductor was brought as well. Henderson gave way to the takeover even after the conductor fired six of his band members and refused to offer job security to the other six. For the Henderson band, the accommodation to an integrated orchestra was accepting the firing of half of the band and the reduction of Henderson's authority to pianist and arranger for the orchestra.[4]

There is the experience of pianist Teddy Wilson with the Benny Goodman Orchestra, the most prominent integrated jazz band in the interwar years. The Goodman dance combos with Wilson and Lionel Hampton on vibraphone thrilled audiences and served as a jazz counterpoint to the disciplined sections of the big band. When it came to touring, however, Wilson had to accept that "we all had to face the fact that in every category, and not only in entertainment, Negroes were not welcome in the majority of white hotels."[5] Wilson described the desire to avoid making a commotion for the band or promoters. He and Hampton got used to finding their own housing; he described how they would "get into our cars and drive straight away to the Negro ghetto in the town and find a Negro hotel, or some professional rooming house." And he explained how the practice of enforced separation was so engrained in society that it was accepted as a part of everyday life: "It was considered so normal in those days. People today should not forget that it had been like that since we were born."[6]

This being the case, white bands typically played for white audiences, and Black bands played for Black or mixed audiences in the establishments that served Black functions. White enthusiasts who wanted to hear the music of the Black South End had to venture out to after-hour joints. In these spaces, young people forged nodes of jazz appreciation and practice in their cliques, most especially in the working-class communities of Irish, Jewish, and Italian groups. Individuals within these circles became ambassadors to the South End scene. The Jewish trumpeter Max Kaminsky, for example, sought out the dives in the South End for camaraderie and validation. One noteworthy venue was the Railway Club located at 428 Massachusetts Avenue. It was a boarding house speakeasy that serviced visiting railroad porters, dining car waiters, musicians, and other Black travelers. It featured the George Tynes band and other local talent like Clement Jackson, a singer and violinist who later become president of union Local 535. Kaminsky remembered a friendly setting that made him feel welcomed. He was befriended by a fellow named Henry who played piano at the club and became an informal sponsor for Kaminsky and guide to the culture—a type of jazz apprenticeship that white enthusiasts have described repeatedly in memoirs.[7]

Max Kaminsky was among the generation of Jewish youths who took to jazz in the Boston neighborhoods. The son of Russian immigrants, he was born in Brockton in 1908. His family moved to Lower Roxbury when he was a boy and he early became aware of the music of the Black community. Among his earliest memories was the musicality of life on Williams Street in the "colored section" of the district: "On Sundays, my sister Rose would take me to the colored church to hear gospel singing, and I still remember the street cries of the Negro pushcart men on summer nights, as they hawked their wagonloads of watermelons or fresh-caught-crabs."[8]

His family also encouraged an appreciation for music, with one sister playing the piano and one brother the violin. One sister was married to a man who played trumpet in a symphony orchestra. This man, Henry Pollack, gave the eight-year-old Kaminsky his first cornet as a gift. Kaminsky writes, "The first time I blew it, I got that sound out of it. I'll never forget how nice it sounded to me." He later drew inspiration from playing race records as well. Another sister had a phonograph that came with complimentary race record songs by Bessie Smith, Maggie Jones, Ma Rainey, James P. Johnson, and Louis Armstrong. "They all sounded wonderful to me," Kaminsky recalled.[9]

Kaminsky became a "radio bug" at about eight years old when he learned that jazz could be heard on the crystal headset. He located the faint broadcast of Pittsburgh station KDKA and declared, "The first sound I heard when I turned it on was Ted Lewis's band playing 'Tiger Rag.' It was like finding diamonds, if you like diamonds."[10] During this time, South End youths began to use the new mediums of records and radio as tools of instruction. Harry Carney remembered that he and Johnny Hodges "used to get together and listen to records."[11] The boys spent many an afternoon gathering in close and listening to the records of bands from New Orleans, Chicago, and New York. Among the favorite recordings were those of Louis Armstrong, Sidney Bechet, the Clarence Williams Blues Five, the Fletcher Henderson band with Buster Bailey, and the Jean Goldkette band with Don Murray.[12]

The Kaminsky family was living in Dorchester when Max discovered Perley Breed's Shepard Colonial Orchestra, a local dance band that played in the tea room of Shepard's Department Store at Downtown Crossing, on radio station WNAC. The septet played a sweet style of Chicago jazz and included Warren Hookway on trumpet; Brad Gowans, clarinet; Frank Cornwell, violin and vocals; Newell Chase, piano; Junie Andersen, banjo and bass; George Dussault, drums; and Pearly Breed, clarinet and saxophone. The band recorded four sentimental sides for the Gennett label: in November 1924, "Tell Me, Dreamy Eyes" and "Where's My Sweetie Hiding?"; and in April 1925, "Honey, I'm in Love with You" and "Sweet Georgia Brown." The cover of "Sweet Georgia Brown" went unissued. The solo improvisations of Warren Hookway, in particular, won over Kaminsky. He wrote, "I thought this was the greatest band I'd ever heard, and up to then it was."[13]

In the early 1920s, Kaminsky formed the combo Six Novelty Syncopators. As he told the story, the boy band caught the attention of the manager of the Shawmut Theatre in Roxbury. Apparently, Harry Goldstein was the type of manager willing to engage in theatrical stunts to fill the house. He staged a Friday night "battle of the bands" competition that pitted his white band against an integrated band of professional musicians for a $50 prize. After a spirited contest, Goldstein declared the event a draw and announced a rematch for the next week—that contest ended in a draw as well! Several rematches followed with the same outcome until it dawned on Kaminsky that the whole thing was a gimmick to keep the audience coming. Kaminsky went to work as a fill-in accompanist with the house bands of dance halls and theater pits. He had little interest in high school courses except those related to music, and often missed classes due to fatigue from playing night gigs. One thing he did enjoy about school was meeting other students with an interest in music. He found a kindred spirit in Harry Carney from Frederick Douglass Square and recalls, "I was always so glad to see him and talk about music."[14]

Kaminsky told a story of encountering Louis Armstrong at the Railway Club one evening. He had met Armstrong in Harlem about a year earlier while exploring that jazz scene. He'd been down on his luck and short on cash and described the situation to Armstrong. Upon hearing the young trumpeter's story, Armstrong spotted him $10 to get back home. Seeing Armstrong in the Railway, Kaminsky approached him and offered to repay the money, but he declined to take it. Kaminsky insisted until Armstrong relented with the comment, "If you autograph it for me, daddy." To Kaminsky, the compliment was the ultimate validation of acceptance in the jazz fraternity.[15]

At the same time, many white musicians dismissed the idea that jazz originated in African American culture or that they were indebted to it. For some, their rejection of history was fueled in the interest of status preservation as white men fearful of being stigmatized in society. For them to acknowledge a hierarchy of racial culture was repugnant; it was better to deny, deflect, and substitute myths of white origination. On the other hand, there were white musicians who recognized the historical roots of jazz culture, like Kaminsky, Eddie Condon, Mezz Mezzrow, Artie Shaw, Hoagy Carmichael, Bud Freeman, and Jimmy McPartland. Some even respected the authority of Black practitioners and sought opportunities to collaborate with them. For this class of musicians, often coming from middle-class Jewish, Yankee, and German American families, the music was an act of rebellion. They turned to jazz in opposition to the expectations of middle-class society and the regimentation demanded by the experiences of the flu pandemic and World War I. Thus, the explorations of some musicians were equivalent to the motivations of "Lost Generation" novelists like Ernest Hemingway, John Dos Passos, and F. Scott Fitzgerald.[16]

A lot of Jewish youths used jazz culture as both a sword and shield for coping with a snobbish Yankee Protestant city. Some felt empathy with the music expression of another oppressed group whose position in American society bore resemblance to their historic experience in Europe. As such, jazz was used as a sword to penetrate the culture of a closed urban society. At the same time, it could be used as a shield to deflect the sense of estrangement in that society. Boston writers like Nat Hentoff noted the harsh experience of anti-Semitism, and young Jews grew up in fear of beatings from Irish Catholic gangs, public denunciations of their religion by the Catholic Church, and exclusions from elite Yankee institutions. Some turned to the jazz dens with a reverence for a music exotic, modern, and defiant. Moreover, they found ways to use the advantage of their white skin to leverage commercial opportunities denied to Black musicians, composers, producers, and other creative talents hindered by Jim Crow. Jewish talent was evident in all phases of the mainstream jazz industry of Boston by the 1930s.

In addition to an ethnic network, Kaminsky also stumbled upon a mentoring relationship with musicians in the touring orchestra of Jean Goldkette, the self-proclaimed "Paul Whiteman of Detroit." Goldkette was prominent in Detroit as a concert pianist, booker of jazz bands, and owner of the Graystone Ballroom. Born in France in 1899, he studied classical piano at the Moscow Music Conservatory before immigrating to the US in about 1910 or 1911. After a stint with Detroit society bands, he dedicated his work to the promotion of jazz. This included convincing investors to help buy the Graystone Ballroom, starting his own orchestra and managing others.[17] A 1924 reviewer for Detroit Saturday Night wrote, "He believes that it is the creeping infant that one day will develop into a true school of American music."[18]

In the mid-1920s, Goldkette hired some of the best white "hot soloists" for his orchestra. There were young men who had imbibed the riffs of pioneer Black musicians in the Chicago South Side and New York's Harlem. They incorporated the rhythms and melodies as their own voices. The fourteen-member Jean Goldkette Orchestra brought to the Graystone Ballroom an impressive line-up of jazzmen, including Bix Beiderbecke, Tommy and Jimmy Dorsey, Joe Venuti, Bill Rank, Don Murray, Steve Brown, Eddie Lang, Chauncey Morehouse, and Frankie Trumbauer, with saxophonist Trumbauer and cornetist Beiderbecke as featured soloists. The band was extensively recorded on the Victor label between 1924 and 1929, its new sound captured on standards like "In the Evening," "It's the Blues," "Where the Lazy Daisies Grow," "What's the Use of Dreaming," "Dinah," "Jigwalk," "She's Funny That Way," "Birmingham Bertha," and "Get Happy."[19]

The Goldkette orchestra played dance halls in cities and towns across the Midwest, Pennsylvania, New York, and New England, and proved itself formidable in battles against the leading bands of the age. By 1926, it earned a national reputation at the Roseland Ballroom in New York City during a memorable "Battle of Music" competition. The event pitted the orchestra of Fletcher Henderson against the Goldkette orchestra. The judges were musicians from over fifty big bands who deemed the Goldkette band the victory in the battle. Loren Schoenberg, artistic director of the National Jazz Museum in Harlem, says, "The event has gone down in jazz history as probably the first time a great white jazz band battled a great Black band." Rex Stewart, a trumpeter in Henderson's band—considered one of the best orchestras of the time—put it plainly: the Goldkette band was "the first original white swing band in jazz history."[20] During the concert (where Kaminsky was in attendance), the band played "Pretty Girl Stomp," "Ostrich Walk," "Tiger Rag," and "Clap Yo' Hands," among other hot numbers. Kaminsky mused, "Nobody had heard anything like this music before."[21]

Kaminsky made friends with the members of the band when he attended a concert at the rickety Nutting-on-the-Charles dance hall in about 1926. He found a mentor in Biederbecke, an older cornetist from the Midwest and protégé of the small combo jazz bands of Chicago. As Biederbecke told it, he first became aware of jazz music when hearing a New Orleans riverboat band playing on the Mississippi River steamboats in his hometown of Davenport, Iowa. He was subsequently inspired by the recordings of Nick LaRocca's Original Dixieland Jazz Band and King Oliver's Creole Jazz Band. Kaminsky was moved by the voicing of cornetist Biederbecke, writing, "I just sat there vibrating like a harp to the echoes of Bix's astoundingly beautiful tone. It sounded like a choirful of angels."[22] During intermission, Kaminsky welcomed Beiderbecke to the city and, knowing that he was a fan of baseball, offered to take him to a Boston Braves game. Biederbecke accepted the invitation and Kaminsky drove to pick him up, and they talked about music before heading out. Biederbecke took time to compose a thirty-two-bar chorus of the song "Blue Room" for Kaminsky to practice: "He explained about the use of passing tones to give color or tonal accent to a phrase, and he went on to discuss anticipation—playing notes of the melody a hair-breadth before the strict time," Kaminsky wrote, adding that the "use of anticipation, without rushing, which is all a part of making the music swing, was just getting to be understood then."[23]

Kaminsky recalled the thrill of being asked to sit in with the Goldkette orchestra during a performance at a dance hall in Salem circa 1926. Beiderbecke invited him to take his place, with Goldkette's approval. To dramatize the stunt, the stage lights were turned off as though there was a power outage. The orchestra continued to play in the dark as Kaminsky took Beiderbecke's seat. When the lights came on, the musicians feigned surprised at Kaminsky playing instead of Beiderbecke. Kaminsky blushed over the act: "I was so exhilarated by the musicians' kindness." One example of the small combo music of Kaminsky is the 1939 session of "Nobody's Sweetheart" with Eddie Condon's Chicagoans. The foxtrot dance featured Kaminsky on cornet; Condon, guitar; Pee Wee Russell, clarinet; Brad Gowans, valve trombone; Bud Freeman, tenor sax; Joe Sullivan, piano; Clyde Newcomb, bass; and Dave Tough, drums. It opens with a slick clarinet melody to introduce a foot-tapping interplay of instruments that breaks out into smart solo choruses. The saxophone chorus of Bud Freeman is especially well developed. [24]

The South End jazz scene caught the attention of a young man with roots in the immigrant Armenian community, pianist "Al Vega." Aram Vagramian was born in June 1921 in Worcester, Massachusetts, to parents of Armenian heritage, and entered the Boston scene during the interwar years. He came as a teenager to build a foundation for a long career as a player and bandleader in Boston jazz. Vega began his musical journey as a child with classical piano lessons; in high school, however, he discovered big band jazz through radio shows. He formed a group that covered the songs from the Kansas City scene of Count Basie. The sixteen-piece

Tabletop radio with a step pyramid design provided an elegant source of music and entertainment for South End listeners.

Basie Band, prolifically recorded by major labels like Columbia and Decca, gave rise to the hard-swinging ensemble style of territory bands and the shouting voice of Jimmy Rushing; Al Vega absorbed the records and arrangements.

As a result, his young band was hired to play Basie songs at college parties. He recalled those early years: "It was just a bunch of kids, you know, but we were playing Basie in those days."[25] Among the songs that Al Vega may have covered were "One O'Clock Jump," "Good Morning Blues," and "Topsy." The band was booked on the summer circuit of dance halls and ballrooms on the New England waterfront. "Every beach had a ballroom. Revere had a couple of Spanish gables. Wells Beach would have the Beach Casino, O'Logic Casino in Maine. Then the South Shore had its stuff," he described. His band even had an opportunity to fill in for the Count Basie Orchestra itself for one canceled date. Vega described being recruited for that gig by the booking agent, who said, "'Al, we need a band, Basie's bus broke down, he won't be able to get here for the gig tomorrow.' So I'd call up all the guys and we were all loyal to the band; even if we had a little joint job, we'd send subs in and play with the big band."[26]

The cross-over exchanges even had some reciprocal benefits for Black musicians of the South End. For example, the pianist Preston Sandiford recalled being hired for a recording session of Armenian songs at the downtown Casper Gordon Studios: "I did a lot of Armenian music with some brothers right over there by Chinatown. We did their recordings."[27]

Youthful jazz hounds in Boston's Italian American community embraced the musical expression of Black Americans, perhaps because the jazz age was a dismal time for Italian immigrants in the city due to a number of factors. Among these were the hysterical reactions to the trials of anarchists Sacco and Vanzetti, tabloid news reports on prohibition and mobsters, and the spread of pro-fascism clubs enamored with the 1922 rise of the charismatic Italian dictator Benito Mussolini. The trial of Sacco and Vanzetti probably had the most profound effect as a local event coming in the period of the "Red Scare"—the post–World War I years marked by fears of pro-union radicalism and anarchist bomb attacks against government officials.

The tribulations of Italian anarchists Nicola Sacco and Bartolomeo Vanzetti began in April 1920. As described by the state court system that tried and executed, the men were charged with committing robbery and murder at the Slater and Morrill shoe factory in South Braintree:

On the afternoon of April 15, 1920, payroll clerk Frederick Parmenter and security guard Alessandro Berardelli were shot to death and robbed of over $15,000 in cash. Eyewitnesses reported that two men committed the crimes and then escaped in a car containing two or three other men. Sacco and Vanzetti were arrested several weeks later on a trolley car. Both were armed, and Sacco possessed a flyer announcing that Vanzetti would speak at an upcoming anarchist rally. No other arrests were ever made; none of the stolen money was ever linked to them or recovered.[28]

Today the trial is viewed as a travesty of justice: "They were Italian immigrants and avowed anarchists. Their trials for armed robbery and murder occurred in this atmosphere of social tension and turmoil."[29]

In this climate, Boston's Italian American youths could identify with the music of a subjected group that also intersected with their own cultural history. The first commercial jazz recordings were made by New Orleans cornetist Nick LaRocca, an Italian American, and the Original Dixieland Jazz Band in 1917. In New Orleans, immigrant Italian entertainers blended the syncopated music of the opera with jazz rhythms on the vaudeville stages. In Italy during the war years, jazz culture was spread by association with soldiers, records, and radio and embraced as representative of youth and modernity. It won the admiration of Mussolini who proclaimed jazz as "the voice of Italian youth."[30] Italian American youths looked up to stalwart figures like Joseph Edward Filippelli of Brooklyn, New York. Taking the professional name of "Flip Phillips," he played clarinet and saxophone in the jazz orchestras of Frankie Newton, Benny Goodman, and Woody Herman, and performed for years in Jazz at the Philharmonic.

Boston's Italian neighborhoods nurtured an impressive array of jazz saxophonists. To name a few, there was Nuncio "Toots" Mondello, born in the city in 1911, who learned to play the alto and soprano saxophone with the mentoring of his father. He joined the union Local 9 at age fourteen and was a featured soloist in the Mal Hallett band and in Benny Goodman's radio band. He played a sweet style known as "the Boston sound"—a pure tone and slow tempo and well-rounded phrasing—a style that was advanced by alto and soprano saxophonist Charlie Mariano, born in Boston to Italian immigrant parents in 1923 to grow up in the Hyde Park neighborhood. He played in the jazz band of Stan Kenton, who himself was influenced by the recordings of Louis Armstrong and Earl Hines. Finally, the saxophonist "Boots" Mussulli—Enrico "Henry" William Mussulli—was born to immigrant parents in 1915. He started life in Milford, Massachusetts, but spent most of his long career in Boston. He was one of the top sax players in the city, featured in the bands of Mal Hallett and Stan Kenton.[31]

The Italian trumpeter Armando J. Correa contributed to the Boston scene on a number of levels. He emigrated from the Province of Catanzaro in the Calabria region in southwest Italy, which occupies the "toe" of the country's boot-shaped peninsula. Correa left this region of sun, mountains, villages, and coastline for the cold weather and cranky attitudes of Boston. He made a living playing with a Dixieland band for dances and clubs in the 1930s and 1940s. Beyond that contribution, he married Anna (Zaccone) Corea and fathered a musical son of the same name, Armando Corea Jr. Born in Chelsea, on June 12, 1941, the son would adapt the stage name of Chic Corea as a jazz keyboardist, composer, and bandleader.

The young Corea studied piano under the concert pianist Salvatore Sullo. He began to play publicly while in high school and formed a trio that covered the music of pianist Horace Silver, a Hartford jazzman with Cape Verdean roots. He also released a trio album, *Now He Sings, Now He Sobs*, with Roy Haynes and Miroslav Vitous. Corea was known for using a ring modulator to process the output of his electric piano. The technical savvy caught the attention of Miles Davis and they recorded together on the albums *Black Beauty: Live at the Fillmore West* and *Miles Davis at Fillmore:*

Live at the Fillmore East. Corea would go on to become a leading figure in the jazz fusion movement of the 1970s with the release of outstanding albums *Return to Forever* and *My Spanish Heart.*[32]

The Cape Verdean community of Afro-Portuguese heritage was known to make a valuable contribution to the jazz of the Hub and New England, not only through the bands and dances supported by its social organizations in the 1920s, but also by the several talented instrumentalists in the next generation. Hartford could boast of its hard-swinging pianist Horace Silver, for example; however, the South End could lay partial claim to the alto saxophonist Paul Gonsalves. He was born in Brockton in 1920 to Joao Jose Gonsalves and Maria Viera Fontes. Both of his parents emigrated from Djam d'Noli, Brava, Cabo Verde; Joao in 1905 and Maria in 1913. Gonsalves was the third of four children and the family moved to Pawtucket, Rhode Island, when he was about ten years old. His father encouraged the children to learn the guitar, which led Paul and his brothers to form a band that played traditional Cape Verdean music. However, Gonsalves fell in love with the alto saxophone after attending a concert by the Jimmy Lunceford Orchestra in Providence. He studied at the Boston Conservatory of Music and gigged with dance bands in Boston, including some dominated by Cape Verdean-American musicians. His work was cut short when drafted into the army during World War II. He returned to play in the Sabby Lewis Orchestra at the Savoy and drew the notice of a visiting Count Basie. He joined the swinging Basie Orchestra and then the bebop orchestra of Dizzy Gillespie. By the 1950s, he was hired by Duke Ellington and became a prominent solo voice in the orchestra.[33]

The restaurants of Chinatown probably were sites for the generation of jazz music and dance band activity—but the subject will require more research. In the 1920s, Chinese American cuisine became popular with non-Chinese patrons, and major cities experienced the fad known as the "chop suey craze." One result was an increase in the number of Chinese restaurant workers—ballooning from 11,500 to 45,600 nationally—as restaurants opened outside of the traditional Asian sectors at the same time as the overall population of Chinese workers declined due to the immigration bans. Much of the expansion was in the cities of the East Coast such as New York and Boston and the nearby municipalities in Long Island, New Jersey, and Connecticut. In New York, for example, Chinese restaurants opened in non-Chinese areas of Manhattan to satisfy the new curiosity over "chop suey." That city had fourteen "chop suey jazz places" between 42nd Street Times Square and 59th Street Columbus Circle, and some establishments featured jazz combos with Asian and Black musicians.[34]

There were relatively amicable relations between the Black and Chinese communities in New York dating back to the 1900s. Black diners showed their affinity by patronizing restaurants that opened in their historic Westside sectors in the Tenderloin District (34th Street), San Juan Hill (59th Street), and Harlem (125th Street and higher). One newspaper writer claimed that "Black Americans were among the earliest fans of eating Chinese."[35] While Afro-New Yorkers were reluctant to venture to Chinatown, they were regular customers of the restaurants in their neighborhoods. Among the reasons were their familiarity with ingredients like chopped chicken, barbecue pork, collard greens, and pig's feet, and the less overt racism against them than in white establishments. Meanwhile, the Chinese communities showed an affinity for jazz culture—pianist Dean Earl noticed the proliferation of bands in the chop suey houses, saying, "Man, almost every little Chinese joint had at least eight men. You could walk down the street and you pass bar rooms, the piano's going, they had drums, piano, and the bass."[36] In the 1920s, jazz musicians used the appeal of Chinese cuisine in the title of records like Louis Armstrong's 1926 "Cornet Chop Suey" and Sidney Bechet's 1925 "Who'll Chop Your Suey When I'm Gone?"[37]

The history of Boston's Chinatown restaurants is elementary, but evidence indicates a growing acceptance of the eateries by city authorities and an overlap with the nightclub and theater patrons in the bordering Theater District and South End. Why city authorities began to support the establishments is unclear after nearly fifty years of efforts to shut them down. During those years, Chinatown restaurants encountered objections from white labor unions and law enforcement, calling them "a serious menace to society." White workers viewed them as competitors with mainstream restaurants and exclusive employers of their own people. Unions supported boycotts and threats of violence against the restaurants in cities like Brockton. When boycotts failed, the objectors raised allegations of opium dens and prostitution rings and a threat to the morality of white women. The *Bridgeport Herald* wrote that "many a young girl received her first lesson in sin in Chinese restaurants."[38] In 1899, the Boston police commissioner ordered all Chinese restaurants closed by midnight; in 1910, the statehouse debated a "Yellow Peril Bill" that proposed banning women under twenty-one years of age from Chinese restaurants as either customers or employees and to require women patrons over twenty-one to have a male escort. The bill failed to advance after objections from the state attorney general and supreme judicial court. By 1920, Chinese restaurants in Boston faced little pressure from police and city authorities. Under Prohibition, organized crime gangs used restaurants to distribute booze under the protection of police. One might question whether this was the case in Chinatown as well.[39]

What is known is that the chop suey craze attracted celebrities of jazz like Bing Crosby. In Boston, one restaurant that merits research for the possible infusion of jazz culture was Ruby Foo's Den on Hudson Street. The eponymous Foo was a restaurateur whose association with celebrities in the theater business made her a topic in the newspaper gossip pages and her restaurant a bridge for curious Bostonians—the meals were designed for the palates of mainstream customers. In 1929, Ruby Foo and her brother George opened the one-room eatery at 6 Hudson Street for Chinese laundry workers seeking a "quick lunch" at small cost. It caught on with the cash-strapped actors and workers in the Theater District and nearby South End. The location was near the trolley and elevated train lines that increased the foot traffic of non-Asian patrons. One indicator that jazz dance music was incorporated in the operation was the regular mentioning of Ruby Foo's Den in the *Globe* column "Boston's Delightful Dining and Dancing Spots."[40]

Born Ruby Dare in San Francisco in 1908, Foo moved to Boston with her brother George sometime around 1923, where they discovered a small and ostracized community in comparison to the large San Francisco ghetto. Her migration is one example of how Boston's Chinatown was able to grow during the decades of harsh immigration laws. The Chinatowns across America had an imbalance of working-class males as a consequence of the laws that permitted a modest number of men and almost no women. In the 1900s, for example, Boston's Chinatown had an estimated population of about 1,000 residents—but only about fifteen or so were women![41] The community comprised older men working in the laundries and garment factories, overseen by families that owned grocery stores and restaurants along Harrison Avenue and Tyler, Beach, and Hudson streets. The public image was shaped by newspaper reports about opium, gambling dens, gang battles, speakeasy joints, and white prostitution.[42]

In the 1920s, the claustrophobic community began to unite behind the Goon, Moy, Yee, Lee, and Chin family associations. Neighborhood institutions stepped to the forefront, such as the Chinatown YMCA, the Chinese Consolidated Benevolent Association of New England, the Chinese Patriotic Women's Club, and the Nationalist Party office on Hudson Street. Mr. Yee Hay Wor was acknowledged as the "Mayor of Chinatown," and restaurants served an important function in the social fabric of the community. They were places of comfort and security where people could gather, entertain, and discuss important events in Chinese and accented English without shame. Among the popular spots were the Hon Hong Low and the Joy Hong Low restaurants, located at

25 and 8 Tyler Street, respectively. Ruby Foo broke the pattern with a restaurant that served mainstream patrons and created a brand name for similar restaurants in Providence; New York; Washington, DC; and Miami. It remains to be discovered whether jazz was used to attract patrons for dining and dancing. The question of dancing is especially intriguing because nowhere were the tensions of jazz and race more exacerbated than on the dance floor.[43]

The Copley Plaza Hotel featured jazz orchestras for the exclusive ballroom dances of the interwar years.

CHAPTER EIGHT

DANCING WITH ALL THEIR MIGHT

The Jazz Age was the age of dancing. In Boston, the sounds of small orchestras filled dance floors in the South End and in the hotel ballrooms, tea rooms, supper clubs, and dance halls of the city. Young people in Frederick Douglass Square mastered the latest dance movements in the course of everyday life, or as historian Jacqueline Malone explains: "Their academies are dance halls, house parties, social clubs, and the streets. In fact, formal dance studios are usually years behind the real source of America's major social dances: the black community." Neighborhood youths used dance as an instrument for collective "purification, affirmation, and celebration" in urban communities across the nation. As Ralph Ellison advised, "Keep to the rhythm and you won't get weary. Keep to the rhythm and you won't get lost."[1]

White youths looked to safe havens to learn the latest dance steps in Boston. For working-class couples, the arenas were often the speakeasy rooms in the downtown buildings and in neighborhoods that bordered the South End. Boston was home to an estimated 4,000 underground dance spaces that operated in tenement rooms, basements, garages, and out-of-the-way spaces in factories and commercial buildings for fear of attracting unwanted attention. Many existed on the fringes of the South End, Theater District, Chinatown, and Copley Square, where they offered a safe harbor to kids embracing gyrations reviled by traditionalists. Across the city, teenagers bounced on dance floors to a syncopated beat; they performed dances with the names of the bunny hug, toddle, black bottom, Texas Tommy, Lindy hop, and Charleston. Society band arrangements for dances like the foxtrot and turkey trot (holdovers from the prewar era) were adapted for new moves, and even ballroom standards like the waltz and the tango were modified.

Many of the new dances were influenced by African American styles from the rural juke joints of the south brought to the cities by migrants. A craze was underway among young people in New York City well before the war, as observed in a 1913 issue of Variety: "Since the turkey trot craze the colored musicians in New York have been kept busy dispensing syncopated music."[2] The foxtrot of dancers Vernon and Irene Castle became a popular symbol of the relaxed social standards of the modern era. Their dances were considered dazzling for the time to the music of James Reese Europe's society orchestra. By 1914, they were part of the emerging society jazz scene of New York, opened a dancing school, and staged a thirty-five-city dance tour with the Europe orchestra. As such, they served as ambassadors of jazz dance to many people and especially to respectable white America.[3]

The dance that most resonated with young people was the Charleston, which captured their imagination in the neighborhoods of the South End, all around Boston, and across the country. The dance was rooted in the old ring shout culture of the "Gullah" people of coastal Carolina and Georgia. Composer Will Marion Cook described the evolution of the dance in a December 1926 letter to the *New York Times*. His intent was to correct the false impression in a review that gave credit to a white theater producer. In it, he explains that the Charleston was "African in inspiration" and practiced "in the South, especially in the little islands off

Charleston, SC, for more than forty years to my knowledge. The dance reached New York five years ago. In Harlem any evening a group of Negro children could be seen 'Doin' the Charleston' and collecting pennies."[4] As for its adaptation for the theater, he writes: "This dance was first staged in a real production by Frank Montgomery in *How Come*. Leonard Harper, a colored man, used a few steps of the dance. The first music with this fascinating rhythm was the 'Charleston Strut,' written by Tommy Morris and published by Jack Mills, Inc., about four years ago (1922). Jimmy Johnson, a Negro songwriter, first conceived the idea of a Charleston song, and in his score of *Runnin' Wild*, for Miller and Lyles, wrote the famous 'Charleston,' which was staged by Elida Webb, and the craze was on."[5]

The children dancing on Harlem streets were likely recent migrants from the seacoast islands. The Gullah people lived in relative isolation on the far spread islands of a region with a history of independent Black settlements created by runaway slaves. The Gullah people spoke in a dialect of African and English languages, much like Black people in the West Indies. The culture, as it related to music and dance, was reflected in the performances of regional bands like the Jenkins Orphanage Boys, which arranged the coastal dances to entertain audiences in the urban North. In Harlem, band members were known to perform the "strange little dance" as people shouted out, "Hey Charleston, do your Geechie dance." As Cook noted, the street dances caught the attention of Harlem stride pianist James P. Johnson, himself a migrant of Charleston, who composed eight tunes based on the Gullah dances for Broadway shows. One number, "The Charleston," was a collaboration for the Broadway theater between composers Johnson, Cecil Mack, and Maceo Pinkard, and dancers Maude Russell and Rufus Greenlee.

The evolution of the popular dance started when Pinkard composed the "Charleston Dance" for Russell and Greenlee to perform in the Broadway revue *Liza*; it had a successful run on

Broadway in 1922 and 1923, even though the dance number was a small part. It was then adapted for the musical comedy *Runnin' Wild* by writer-producers Flournoy Miller and Aubrey Lyles, where it involved singer Elisabeth Welch and a chorus line, and sparked a national craze among people unaware of its origin in spiritual rituals. At the same time, it drew the ire of traditionalists in Boston who were alarmed at the sight of youths performing wild dance steps and body movements.[6] Nonetheless, youths embraced jazz dances as a rite of passage and rebellion against the conservative culture of Boston.

Boston religious and civic authorities engaged in campaigns to extinguish the fire: opponents spoke out against the threat of jazz contaminating the morality of young people. In Saugus, for example, town leaders banned swing dancing at the high school junior prom. Students were warned to "watch their step" on the floor, and chaperones were assigned to monitor for violators. Of particular concern was the influence of jazz style on society women. Influenced by figures like the Boston aviator Amelia Earhart, middle-class white women were emboldened with a new sense of confidence and liberation. It was increasingly acceptable to challenge norms in ways small and large, such as going out on dates rather than waiting for men to call on them at home. The new attitudes toward dance and dating, fashions of bobbed hairstyles, rakish hats, short skirts, and other accoutrements culminated in the "flapper girl" style, and moved traditionalists to declare a state of emergency.[7]

Across the nation, traditionalist forces mobilized in a crusade to denounce jazz as a corruption to the American soul. By the mid-1920s, cities passed laws requiring club owners to obtain a dance license or face closure. The most alarming fear was of white girls dancing with Black boys in free spirit. In Pittsburgh, city leaders banned jazz dancing in public parks, dance instructors refused to teach the "vulgar steps," and Black ministers blamed jazz for declining church attendance. One educator bemoaned of the youth, "we dance to it, we sing to jazz, we eat to jazz and worst of all, our morals, our religion and our thoughts are turned to jazz."[8]

In 1922, as jazz dance enthralled youths across New England, traditionalists gathered at Tremont Temple Baptist Church at 88 Tremont Street to declare jazz a threat to the social order. In May, opponents sponsored a conference on "The Young People and the Church." One prominent speaker was the Reverend Ralph A. Sherwood of First Baptist Church in Salem, who denounced jazz culture from the pulpit: "I am against jazz; first, because I don't believe there is any music in it; and second, because it is a device of the devil, and undermines all that is sacred, pure, and good," he proclaimed, adding, "Is it any wonder that the dancing masters have come forward and announced that it must go, and that our leading periodicals have said so too." He closed the sermon with an admonishment of the debate teams at Holyoke High School and Salem High School who had, after a competition, held an inter-school jazz dance. Sherwood bellowed, "By what right and propriety should you end such an affair by a dance?"[9]

The outrage expressed by the Rev. Sherwood was applauded by the audience of clergymen. They meant for the conference to be a warning light for the culture of Boston. They urged parents to be better role models and called on the young to respect the authority of parents, teachers, and the church. What concerned them most was the rapid spread of jazz dancing as white teenagers copied their impressions of Black dance. The sentiments of the clergymen were carried forward in society groups across the metropolitan area. In Cambridge, for instance, a group that went by the name "Ye Old Tyme Club" attempted to revive old-fashioned contra dances, square dances, and quadrilles along with the Virginia reel, the polka, and the waltz. The club boasted 175 followers and met on Thursday nights under the direction of the widow Mrs. Josephine Farrell. "We don't think much of the jazz stuff. It usually doesn't appeal to the middle-aged and older people. The young folks, of course, don't have any use for the old, graceful dances," she said, adding in lament that even her son preferred jazz dances: "It's because he doesn't know the old ones."[10]

Boston newspapers carried nostalgic articles about "the good old days" like "When Grandma Danced," a 1925 polemic by a Portland, Maine, scribe with the pen name "The Stroller." It looked back to the era of square dances enjoyed by "those with an all-white thatch or grey around the temples." The essay waxed nostalgic for the old line and circle dances of social etiquette adapted from European dance socials. Common were the waltz, polka, schottische, quadrille, lancers, and contra dances performed at assemblies, balls, and social affairs, the writer notes: "When grandma danced the minuet, long ago, next mother danced the quadrille and now daughter dances the Charleston, etc. There were not bobbed hair flappers and no patent leather haired lads in their teens and in the adult class or dancing at the balls."[11]

Car maker Henry Ford acted to promote a revival of traditional (read: Anglo-American) dance by hiring Boston-area dance instructor "Professor Lovett" to lead the crusade. Benjamin Lovett, born in Swanzey, New Hampshire, in 1876, was raised in Hudson, Massachusetts, where he started a folk-dance academy with his wife, Charlotte Cooke, after he met Ford at the historic Wayside Inn of Sudbury. A 1925 news article observed of Ford, "The industrialist is striving to reawaken an interest in the various old-fashioned, open dances. He frankly rejects the modern modes as immoral." The traditionalist offensive did create renewed interest in folk dancing among the older set; in Boston, enthusiasts practiced English country dance in particular: "Whole neighborhoods in Greater Boston have gone rural, and it is an unusual school or community center that doesn't have its classes in country dancing."[12]

Tragedy struck at a white dance party as if in retribution for engaging in sinful practices. The incident occurred in an after-hours speakeasy called the Pickwick Club on the border of Chinatown and the South End. The incident happened on the morning of July 4, 1925. The club was located in the Dreyfus Hotel on

Beach and Washington streets and was open to "members only"—meaning white patrons—on the third floor of the five-story hotel. It was an easy walk from the raucous shows of the Gaiety Theater and probably catered to theater-goers leaving the burlesque shows. Billy Glennon played that night, known for his hot jazz music. At about three in the morning, some 200 young people crammed into the club for a "night before the Fourth celebration." The crowd danced the Charleston with people joining hands, kicking up their legs, and jumping about to the music. Frank Decker, a band member from Melrose, recalled: "The dancers, hilarious and gay, were leaping about vigorously. The orchestra speeded up the rhythm and the dancers moved faster and faster. They jumped higher and higher, until, almost simultaneously with the last notes of the musical instruments, the lights went out. Imagine the force of fifty couples leaping up and down in unison. The heavy tramping set the floor swaying, then it cracked."[13]

A moment later, the floor fell through and the walls collapsed as the building crumpled around them. Forty-four people died in the wreckage and scores were injured in the worst building collapse in Boston history. In a logbook entry, the Boston Fire Department noted the following: "The so-called 'Pickwick Club Disaster' occurred during the early morning of July 4, 1925, when the building housing a dine and dance establishment, known as the Pickwick Club and located at 12 Beach Street, collapsed, resulting in the death of forty-four persons. No fire resulted, but apparatus was called to aid in removing the debris and locating the injured and dead. Box 1471, Washington Street, opposite Boylston Street, was transmitted at 3:00 a.m., with all-out at 9:00 a.m." A Suffolk County grand jury investigation led to the indictment of twelve authorities believed responsible, with charges ranging from negligence to manslaughter. The accused included two city inspectors as well as a contractor, foreman, and others involved in the excavation work for a garage project next to the hotel. Investigators noted the rotting pilings and concrete of the building and claimed that the pounding of the excavation work created undue instability. While the structural causes were open to debate, the cultural implications were clear to observers like Boston columnist "Uncle Dudley": "The flooding expression of the people in these steps cannot be dammed. They are venting emotions produced by the disturbing civilization in which they live. They are responding to the fundamental rhythm of life."[14]

The tragedy did little to stem the popularity of jazz dance. It had become an unstoppable force and spread to enthusiasts in the middle class and high society, albeit with a more formal presentation. Into this milieu entered dance instructors ready to open studios to groom the middle-class youths in the physical accompaniments to jazz music. One was Mildred Davenport, known as an "Evangelist of the Dance," who founded dance studios in the Black community during the interwar years. Born 1900 in the South End, she attended dance recitals with her mother, Mamie Dandridge, a private maid and secretary to various actresses. She remembers, "We'd sit way up in the top of the opera house and I'd take notes on what they were doing."[15] Davenport graduated from Boston Girl's High School in 1918; she later developed an interest in physical education when studying at Sargent College at Boston University. In 1920, she opened the Davenport School of Dance at 522 Columbus Avenue in the South End; in the 1930s, she opened the Silver Box Studio. While teaching jazz dance, Davenport organized community programs that showcased the girls in her studio. She collaborated with the Women's Service Club at 464 Massachusetts Avenue in the South End to produce its annual "464 Workshop Follies," a musical revue fundraiser for community needs. This evolved into the "Bronze Rhapsody" series of annual performances that she directed and staged at theaters like Jordan Hall. One former student recalled, "Everyone who thought they were anybody, and who could afford it, went to Mrs. Davenport's."[16]

Davenport was hired as a fill-in dancer by the musical revues of Broadway that toured in Boston. During the interwar years, she worked for musical comedies and revues in Boston and New York like *Hot Chocolates*, *Fast and Furious*, *Flying Colors*, and *Blackbirds*. She performed an interpretive dance to the spirituals under Arthur Fiedler and the Boston Pops, and made history as the first Black woman dancer to do a solo performance in Symphony Hall. In 1932, she reopened the dance studio as the Silver Box Studio on Columbus Avenue. A few years later, she stopped touring to settle into work in the neighborhood and became a respected civic leader.[17]

Meanwhile, Stanley Brown was a jazz "hoofer" who opened a studio in the South End in 1929. Born in 1902 on Andros Island in the Bahamas, he immigrated to Harlem to establish a career as a professional dancer of tap and soft shoe. By the 1920s, he had become a master of tap rhythms and style, and brought his unique talent to a cranky Boston. The city in those years, he recalled, kept Black dance at arm's length: "Jazz dancing was a mongrel. There were no names for the steps; jazz dancing wasn't accepted downtown, it was more for theaters in Harlem."[18] He started in the circuit of Harlem rent parties and advanced to the Apollo Theater and the Hoofers Club. "All the acts came to the Hoofers," he remembered. "Everybody had almost the same routines, and you learned from them." He worked as a single act and on vaudeville chorus lines. He danced at the Cotton Club, Harlem Opera House, and Palladium, among other forums in the US, Canada, and Europe. He trained with Josephine Baker, Honi Coles, Bill "Bojangles" Robinson, John "Bubbles" Sublett, and other tap pioneers. He developed a style of flash dance that combined tap with acrobatics. "The Negro did not invent tap dancing," he said, explaining that the Dutch clog dancing and Irish jigs were sources of origin. However, the Black dancers expanded on the range of body movement for interpretative expression: "Negroes didn't have the patience with the slow tempo—we would call it 'un-soul' today. Negroes started hoofing and the buck and wing. The audience went wild. There was speed and daring to it."[19]

The Stanley Brown Studio was in the Gainsborough Building on Huntington Avenue and Gainsborough Street, on the edge of the South End and Back Bay. Brown became a father figure to young dancers and musicians in the city. For example, he tutored Preston Sandiford on how to arrange music for dance routines. Sandiford recalled, "He really gave me a good start on how to write for dance routines properly. He had definite ideas, and they were all good about what kind of a background I would put on for these people."[20] The studio also hired orchestras to play for recitals, including racially mixed band members. Dean Earl recalled playing in one with Preston Sandiford and local white musicians: "I worked with Stanley Brown's dance studios during the season, that's like September to June. We had Jimmy Moses Band for Stanley's recitals and they were mixed. Sandy played piano. The musicians themselves didn't pay it any mind."[21] The Stanley Brown Studio was a touchstone for pioneers of jazz dance, such as Bill "Bojangles" Robinson and Cab Calloway, who stopped by to rehearse and scout talent in the neighborhood. His studio trained the next generation of dancers, among them Jimmy Slyde Godbolt, the dancer who created a daring slide step routine. Brown promoted tap dancing as a part of jazz culture and "one of the few truly American dances."[22]

For affluent families of Beacon Hill, the Back Bay, and the metropolitan area, the place to go to learn jazz steps was the Arthur Murray Dance Studio in the posh Statler Hotel in Park Square. Murray began teaching the art of ballroom dancing in about 1912 through mail-order lessons, and his name brand was well regarded by the jazz age. He was able to open studios in many cities and trained instructors in his methods. In Boston, the studio gained prestige from its location in the Statler and taught the popular dances of high society like the Foxtrot, Quick Step, and the Boston Waltz for couples to use at tea rooms, supper clubs, and ballroom affairs. As members of Boston society, they wanted to dabble with more daring steps with a proper air of decorum in light of the city's history of suspicion toward social dancing. The most well-known

Louis Armstrong stayed in Frederick Douglass Square when visiting the city.

controversy involved the waltz: around 1834, it was introduced to Boston society by Lorenzo Papanti, an Italian dance instructor who opened a studio in then-fashionable Scollay Square, where he designed a simplified version of the Vienna waltz for youths of well-to-do families. However, critics decried the waltz as a scandalous form of Italian dancing that compromised the morality of single women. The dance was modified with a dip-step to accent separation and renamed "the Boston Waltz" or simply "the Boston." It caught on with Harvard students and, in the 1920s, was modified further with a ragtime cross-step. This made the Boston feel new and stylish—but once again drew the ire of traditionalists.

Popular sites for jazz dancing were the tea rooms, supper clubs, dance halls, and ballrooms of hotels and resorts in Boston and coastal New England. Like other such spaces around the country, they operated under the practices of Jim Crow and prohibited Black patrons or restricted their access to certain days and hours, with exceptions for the bands and others. Most galling among the exclusive jazz clubs that used the Black community as a type of theme park for white patrons. Clubs like the Savoy in Harlem and the Hi-Hat in the South End were examples of upscale entertainment located in the heart of Black communities, with Black orchestras and floor shows, that excluded Black patrons except on occasions.

The Shepard Colonial Tea Room combined the music of society bands with a fashionable setting for light meals. Located at 30 Winter Street in Downtown Crossing, it became known as a place to meet Harvard men and women of the suffrage age and as a generator of jazz culture in the city. The room was opened as part of the retail business of the Shepard's Department Store, which had deep roots in Boston commercial history. It began as Shepard-Norwell & Co. in 1865 when retailer Jon Shepard opened a dry goods store with Henry Norwell on Hanover Street in the City Hall Plaza area. In later years, he expanded the inventory to meet the demands of a growing urban consumer market. By the early twentieth century, the Shepard Store was one of the city's more popular shopping destinations in the region. He raised his son, John Jr., in Boston and brought him into the family business to oversee a second Shepard's Store opened in Providence, Rhode Island. The son experimented with a new shopping concept where customers could find "under the one roof practically all the necessaries of life, as well as the luxuries."[23] Shepard's Department Store hosted an information bureau, post office station, and nursery with trained nurses so mothers could shop at ease. By 1911, Shepard Jr. was in charge of the stores in Shepard's Boston and Shepard's Providence and later turned over management to his own sons, John III and Robert.[24]

They opened the tea rooms to take advantage of the new buying power of middle-class women. The 400-seat Colonial Tea Room in Boston became a haven for Yankee society with a house band that played the "sweet" jazz of romantic ballads and easy dance songs. The Boston Tea Room sponsored the Shepard Colonial Orchestras—the most popular being the Perley Breed Colonial Tea Room Orchestra. The Shepard Tea Rooms disseminated jazz culture through the hosting of music, dancing, records, and radio broadcasts. By 1922, the Boston store founded radio station WNAC to build its brand under "The Shepard Stores Broadcast" with all-day programming of music, talk, news, and weather. The *Boston Globe* column "Radio Broadcasts" provides a guide for the WNAC schedule on October 19, 1927: programs ran for 30 minutes from 10:30 a.m. to midnight and began with a women's talk show, news and weather, church service, and a luncheon concert with the Shepard Colonial Orchestra. In the afternoon, it had a similar mix with the Shepard Colonial tea dance; then WNAC provided an evening of music with Murray Hockburg's Orchestra, "Dok" Eisenbourg's Sinfonians, and a piano recital. At night, it presented jazz with the Hotel Brunswick Orchestra and with Jimmie Gallagher's Orchestra. In 1929, the Boston and Providence stores combined to create the Yankee Radio Network with programming in music, news, and sports. The network included affiliated stations in New Bedford, Worcester, Hartford, Bridgeport, Manchester, Bangor, and Portland.[25]

Meanwhile, Boston saw a proliferation of nightclubs and supper clubs that conspired to operate under the radar of Prohibition. The establishments used meals and jazz culture to attract middle-class patrons with alcoholic beverages disguised in teapots. The Cocoanut Grove joined the supper club circuit in October 1927, located at 17 Piedmont Street near Charles and Stuart streets in the old Park Square district. It was managed by the orchestra leader Jacob Stavinski (also known as Jacques Renard) and was apparently controlled by the mob boss Charles "King" Solomon. Renard also recorded with his fifteen-piece orchestra for the Victor label. The club offered dining, dance, and entertainment acts in a setting designed to represent a tropical landscape: "The sides of the room are terraced, with a Spanish tile covering, and the ceiling is worked out to represent a star-strewn sky."[26] The 500-seat club was open from 5:30 p.m. to 2 a.m. all week and was one of the most popular clubs in the city. It has been memorialized for a horrendous fire that left 492 people dead in November 1942. A tribute plaque is placed at the site of the old club in the Bay Village neighborhood near the South End.[27]

The Seaglades opened in September 1931—as the Depression deepened—in the Hotel Westminster at St. James and Clarendon streets in Copley Square, where it boasted a nautical concept in design and costume. The design concept was conceived by owner Emile Coulon Jr., who came up with the idea after viewing marine life through a glass-bottom boat during a visit to Catalina Island. He commissioned architect Harold Kellogg to bring the scheme to life as a supper club. Kellogg described his design as a mission to "reflect in the room by marine life and scenery the present age of rhythm and jazz."[28] Patrons entering the room felt like they were stepping aboard such a glass-bottom boat, with the peal of an ocean liner bell announcing their entry. They passed panels of glass fish tanks with live fish, marine vegetation, and fragments of old ships. Lights beamed from the acoustic shell of the bandstand onto dancers on the floor and created the illusion of an aurora borealis. "I want to show music in the walls, music in the lights, rhythm in the ceiling," Kellogg wrote. "The primary idea of Seaglades is to show a room in constant motion."[29]

The two clubs, however, drew fire from traditionalist opponents as purveyors of sin, among them the colorful evangelist Sister Aimee Semple McPherson, who founded the Foursquare Church in Los Angeles where she held revivals in tents and on radio and newsreels; the sister soon became a cult figure. Born in Ontario, Canada, in 1890, she began preaching as a teenager and made it a lifelong career. She barnstormed small towns and cities and drew audiences large enough to fill stadiums. Yet she herself was known for controversy: in 1926, for instance, she was kidnapped and held for ransom in a shack in Mexico. Critics suspected the crime was a publicity stunt to raise money. She inspired the character "Sister Sharon Falconer" in Sinclair Lewis's 1927 novel *Elmer Gantry*, in which the characters of Falconer and Gantry team up to bamboozle the simple folk. In 1931, Sister Aimee visited Boston to lead a revival of 10,800 followers at the Boston Garden, accompanied by her third husband—the first died, the second deserted—together, they toured supper clubs to shame patrons. She was allowed to speak at the Cocoanut Grove and the Seaglades and used the occasion to condemn jazz culture. At the Seaglades, she delivered a message of rebuke to the polite applause of inebriated patrons. She poked fun at the club's nautical decor and teased a waiter dressed in a sailor's uniform: "What ship are you from?" At the Cocoanut Grove, she said, "I have come here to get the missing." She denounced jazz as "music with the lure of liquid velvet" and jazz dancing as a "waste of time."[30]

Still, Boston supper clubs drew tourists from across New England who flocked to the Hub in search of jazz dances to celebrate the holidays. Many scheduled annual visits for the big college football games and converged at hotel supper clubs near the South End train stations. Hoteliers competed to attract party groups for New Year's, Halloween, and Thanksgiving. The year 1927 was a stand-out for the hospitality industry as hotels drew in an estimated $300,000 spent on food, entertainment, and dancing by 40,000 revelers. The cash flowed beyond the hotels and clubs to the tip-dependent workers like waiters, cigarette girls, hat checks, elevator operators, and taxicab drivers. The top hotel dining rooms could accommodate about 7,500 visitors with cover charges from $5 to $10 per person. On New Year's Eve, 1928, for example, the hotel clubs, dining rooms, and ballrooms were packed with celebrants; among the downtown hotels, the Statler on Arlington Street hosted 1,000 celebrants, the Elks on Tremont provided for 1,000 guests, and the Parker House on Tremont had 400. In Copley Square, near the Back Bay and Trinity Railroad stations, the Hotel

Westminster had 800 revelers, the Hotel Brunswick had 700, and the Copley Plaza Hotel hosted 1,500 diners and dancers between the State Ballroom, Swiss dining room, and banquet hall.[31]

It was customary for the hotel ballrooms to lower the lights for the final countdown to the New Year. At midnight, the lights would return as the orchestras played "Auld Lang Syne." Throughout the night, the bands would keep the party going; in 1929 at the Copley Plaza Hotel, New Year's Eve merrymakers were hosted in three large ballrooms. As the New Year started, two jazz combos led revelers in a snake dance parade out of the ballrooms, through the lobby, and onto the streets, where people rallied in Peacock Alley with musicians and dancers whirling and twirling. One reporter observed, "The swarms of beautiful jeweled women and their escorts created the most colorful, gayest procession imaginable."[32] Meanwhile, the Elks Hotel, located at 275 Tremont Street on the border of the Theater District and South End, was known for holding rooftop dance parties. It was owned by the Benevolent and Protective Order of Elks, a fraternal order founded by white male entertainers for the minstrel stage. The hotel served as the headquarters of its Boston Lodge 10 and featured the Cascade Roof, a fifteenth-floor rooftop dining room that seated 400 guests with dancing to the music of the Elks Dance Band. Like most hotels, the Elks hired white bands and excluded Black patrons and orchestras. There were also supper clubs and ballrooms in the Touraine Hotel at Boylston and Tremont, and the Ritz-Carlton on Newbury and Arlington streets—which rarely featured jazz entertainment because the managers believed it beneath the dignity of their guests.

The Egyptian Room was a prominent Art Deco supper club in the Brunswick Hotel in Copley Square, one of the first big clubs to open during World War I, with 1,300 seats. The Brunswick Hotel was a six-story building of ornate brick with corner turrets located at Boylston and Clarendon streets, at the current site of the John Hancock skyscraper. The Egyptian Room was located on the ground floor of the hotel and featured themed decor based on the ancient kingdom during a time of public fascination with King Tut and archeological digs in the Nile Valley. Among the depictions were the costumes, cosmetics, jewelry, architecture, farms, temples, and pyramids of the ancient African civilization. Newspaper ads featured illustrations of dynastic icons such as the Great Pyramid of Giza, the Sphinx of King Khafre, and obelisks, scarabs, and pharaohs altered to look like a Boston Yankee.[33]

The Egyptian Room hosted parties for society groups, Ivy League football fans, and celebrants of major holidays. Like other clubs during Prohibition, the room could run afoul of the authorities. In 1920, for instance, federal police swept the room after the Harvard–Princeton game, confiscated three quarts of liquor from customers, and arrested the manager on charges of aiding and abetting violation of the Volstead Act. Featured amid this chaos was the Leo Reisman Orchestra, a society jazz band that made the room a "living legend of the glory of the twenties." Reisman was born in Boston in 1897, studied violin, and worked for the Baltimore Symphony Orchestra before abandoning the concert hall for jazz. After Baltimore, Reisman returned to Boston to lead a society orchestra considered by many to be the most popular in the city. He also served as the music instructor for a 1924 symposium on jazz at Boston University.[34] Reisman was known for his eccentric antics in imitation of classical conductors. Max Kaminsky, who played cornet in the band, recalled how Reisman created a public persona with "long bushy hair which was always falling over his eyes, and his beat-up, crushed hats. Those were the days of full-dress suits and satin evening gowns." He entertained the audience with antics such as "lying down on the bandstand and swinging up his legs and hollering "Yeah!" This was the closest we ever came to swinging in society bands."[35] The band played moderate-paced standards of violin-heavy waltzes, foxtrots, and popular songs such as "Bright Eyes," "Bye Bye, Blackbird," "Indian Love Call," "Here in My Arms," and "Ain't Misbehaving."

Reisman was a promoter of jazz and an admirer of the Duke Ellington Orchestra. He covered one of Ellington's standards, "The Mooche," in an eight-minute film titled *Rhythms*. The short reel was produced by Warner Bros. in 1929 and featured Leo Reisman and the Hotel Brunswick Orchestra in the Egyptian Room. To achieve the sultry Ellington sound, Reisman hired the trumpeter James "Bubber" Miley who played for Ellington in 1924. He was known for playing bluesy tones and using a plunger mute to make a "wa-wa" sound. The film copied the "scrim" method of silhouette projection that Ellington used in live performances in New York's Cotton Club. Miley's "shadowgraph" imaging projected his figure as a dark shadow against a white screen, obscuring the faces of the orchestra members and avoiding any controversy over the promotion of a racially mixed band. After the song, the film cut to the scene of a waterfall as the band played the "Waters of Perkiomen." When the camera returned to the orchestra, it showed the faces of players but without Miley. Instead, the spotlight was on the white singer Smith Ballew, dressed in tuxedo and performing "If I Had You." The ensemble went on to do a medley of "Hyo-Mio," "Milenberg Joys," "Lonely," and "Some of These Days." At the end, it reverted to the scrim effect for a jazz sequence with a woman dancer.[36]

Reisman led other bands in the city and recorded for the Victor, Columbia, Vocalion, Decca, and Brunswick labels. He also wrote a column for *Melody Magazine* where he defended the merits of jazz against traditionalist critics like Henry Ford. In one entry, he debunked a popular argument that jazz was an immoral influence on the young generation, arguing that jazz was no more a cause of risky teenage behavior than the Ford cars they used to make out in. By 1924, his society band had reached audiences around the city with radio broadcasts from the Egyptian Room on station WBZ located in the hotel, further incorporating the Egyptian Room as an important element in the jazz culture of Boston. "It wasn't the idea of its elegance so much as that it was a place where the new music was being played," Kaminsky noted. "It was all so exciting, this beginning of the feeling of a little jazz seeping into the white man's orchestra."[37]

DUKE ELLINGTON AT HIS PIANO

Duke Ellington sits at the grand piano with hand held high for dramatic effect before striking a perfect note.

CHAPTER NINE

THE TRIUMPH OF THE SOUTH END SHOUT

In the 1930s, Black swing bands gained a degree of recognition by mainstream audiences and venues in Boston. During the earlier decade, the gatekeepers of the industry largely neglected the talents of these orchestras in favor of heralding the slow, melodic white "sweet jazz" bands; increasingly, however, audiences exposed to the night spots, records, and radio broadcasts of hot jazz grew bored with the formulaic approach of the style and demanded that theaters and dance halls feature authentic performers. Such demands played into the politics of jazz and race as musicians in the South End scene found the chance to present their music in Boston's culture.

In the 1930s, orchestras shifted from the varied rhythmic accents of small combinations and society bands to big bands of 12 or more pieces under the direction of savvy conductors. These ensembles featured slick rhythm sections and frontline wind and brass sections and relied less on the interweaving rhythmic lines, short solos, and head arrangements of early jazz. The new musical style was known as "swing." According to historian Sam Charters, "For most of the musicians the essence of the new style was the rhythm, a driving, unaccented 4/4 that maintained its steady pulse against varied melodic accents. It was the swinging rhythm that gave the style its name."[1] The rise of swing bands was associated with a consolidation in the jazz entertainment business due to the financial constraints of the Great Depression. While much of the innovation of swing took place in the Black territory bands of the Midwest, the industry looked to a small number of orchestras capable of appealing to national audiences on tours, records, radio, and movies. Among the popular national bands were the Benny Goodman Orchestra and the Duke Ellington Orchestra. Such bandleaders developed "books" of arranged compositions for the coordination of instrumental sections; in particular, the reed section grew in importance as a primary voice of the orchestra, with strong interplay with the brass section. In the rhythm section, the guitar displaced the banjo and the double bass replaced the tuba; moreover, bass players innovated a "walking bass line" that gave the music a feeling of forward propulsion.[2]

Harlem bandleader Edward Kennedy "Duke" Ellington was in the process of revamping his orchestra for an original sound. He found the right combination for the reed section in clarinetists and saxophonists Harry Carney and Johnny Hodges. Teddy Wilson described the rigor of the big band format: "To get that effect you'd have to rehearse and rehearse and rehearse. Only then would you get seventeen or eighteen men playing like one man. When the reed section played, everybody would breathe and phrase in exactly the same way as the lead alto. The same applied to the brass."[3] Boston critics would come to esteem the talented musicians in the Ellington band even as they continued to hold up the fading symbols of jazz excellence.

They continued to tout the Paul Whiteman Orchestra as the defining standard of jazz, placing him on a pedestal. Whiteman himself was a conflicted advocate who spent many years trying to ignore or diminish the Black origins of his music. His mission was to see the genre accepted by elite society in a hybrid format, crafting African American folk tunes with Anglo-American orchestral sophistication. In 1924, he performed a program of modern American music at Aeolian Hall in New York City and proposed that jazz "sprang into existence about ten years ago from nowhere in particular."[4] His 1926 history book *Jazz* ignored the Black roots and surmised that it arose from syncopated classical music. He was featured in the 1929 fictional film *The King of Jazz*, in a story that largely dismissed the African American contributions—and suggested that their music required the intelligent refinements of classical conductors. Whiteman deemed jazz "the folk music of the machine age" and attempted to mold it to classical forms that he branded "symphonic jazz."[5] His orchestra was in demand for society balls, theaters, and concert halls in the United States and Europe, as well as on records and movie reels; among his popular recordings were "Wang, Wang Blues," "Mississippi Mud," "Grand Canyon Suite," "Hot Lips," and "Wonderful One." A 1928 Victor recording of "Mississippi Mud" (featuring Paul Whitemen's "Rhythm Boys" with Bing Crosby, vocals; Bix Beiderbecke, cornet; and Frank Trambauer, saxophone) opens with Beiderbecke's rich cornet voice introducing the melody with the scat singing of Austin "Skin" Young. Some versions altered the 1927 minstrel lyrics of Harry Barris from "when the darkies beat their feet on the Mississippi Mud" to "when the people beat their feet."[6]

Whiteman was aware of Duke Ellington's musical innovations and would surveil his band in the New York clubs. The two bandleaders even developed a collegial association when Ellington discovered that Whiteman was a frequent visitor to his performances at the Kentucky Club on 49th Street and Broadway: "It was the afterhours hangout for all the musicians who played in the plushier Broadway places. Paul Whiteman came often as a genuine enthusiast, listened respectfully, said his words of encouragement, very discreetly slipped the piano player a fifty-dollar bill, and very loudly proclaimed our musical merit."[7] To his credit, Whiteman hired Black musicians even over the objections of unions and studios, and devised ways to use their talents that minimized offending white sensibilities. For example, he hired saxophonist and composer Jimmy Mundy and bandleader Fletcher Henderson to write arrangements; mostly, however, he relied on a talent pool of white soloists trained in the styles of the Black combos. In 1927, he raided the cash-strapped Jean Goldkette Orchestra to lure away players steeped in the Chicago and Detroit jazz scenes like Bix Beiderbecke; in 1929, he featured singer Mildred Bailey, who had studied the recordings of Bessie Smith and Ethel Waters.[8]

In 1927, Paul Whiteman defended jazz against traditionalist critics and became a lightning rod in the politics of race and culture in America. To traditionalists, the obese, thrice-married bandleader was a cultural traitor; to jazz purists, he was a charlatan who co-opted their desires to rebel against conventions. Nonetheless, Whiteman ended up in the position of validating jazz as an original American art and an expression of the national character. Jazz, he wrote, "is an American flavor, an American spirit. It is the only art Europe has ever accepted from America." And in a rebuttal to critics, he taunted, "Jazz scorers have gotten more things out of wind and brass than are dreamed of in symphonic scores. Many of these discoveries are musically valuable." Finally, Whiteman conceded: "I certainly believe it to be a genuine musical force, a trend, an influence: perhaps a form that is bound ultimately to affect, in one respect or another, the music of the future."[9]

The Metropolitan Theater—now the Wang Theater—was a symbol of popular culture achievement in the city. Located on Tremont and Stuart streets and bordering the Theater District and the South End, the Metropolitan was the largest theater in the city. With 4,400 seats, it was a house that only the most magnetic acts could dare to fill—and the Whiteman orchestra barnstormed the theater to great acclaim in 1927. Trumpeter Max Kaminsky attended the packed concert and described it from the perspective of an authentic jazz musician: "Whiteman tried to make jazz acceptable and respectable by attempting to raise it to a symphonic level, and though this wasn't the real thing, Whiteman was a tremendous factor in bringing it to public attention."[10] To a *Globe* attendee, the concert represented the ultimate in jazz entertainment: "The audience is fond of Whiteman, and at every performance the corpulent yet graceful orchestra leader has come in for much personal approbation. Whiteman is a great figure in national jazz circles, and he is an undoubted box-office success."[11]

That year, as the Whiteman orchestra reigned supreme, the rumble of a jazz earthquake could be felt in the coming of the Duke Ellington band. With the addition of horn men from the South End, his orchestra was on the verge of shaking up the status quo—and planting the flag of the neighborhood scene—by showcasing ensemble jazz capable of crossing over to the mainstream. He owed a debt of gratitude to the young men of Frederick Douglass Square and their saxophone brilliance that laid the foundation for the distinctive Ellington orchestral sound. The ascendance of the Ellington band was the culmination of years of building a presence in New England that began around 1924 when he relocated from New York City for a six-week engagement at the Charleshurst dance hall in Salem. At the time, the Kentucky Club—Ellington's home base in New York—was shut down due to fire damage, and the Charles Shribman agency recruited the band to play in Salem. Ellington found the Charleshurst space too small for the regular ten-piece orchestra and formed a six-piece combo with trumpeter Bubber Miley, trombonist Joe Nanton, guitarist Freddy Guy, bassist Wellman Braud, and drummer Sonny Greer. The group was booked for the ballrooms and dance halls in the Shribman circuit of summer concerts; however, the band was still missing a few key ingredients in the formulation of a dramatic horn section.

Recordings of the Ellington orchestra produced between 1924 and 1927 lack the command of later years, which evolved with revamped reed and brass sections capable of powerful dynamics, swinging solos, and lovely melodies. After 1927, the voices of saxophonists Harry Carney and Johnny Hodges were key to the Ellington orchestra brand and marked the beginning of a wave of about

160 recorded sides between 1928 and 1931. The contribution of the Boston musicians to the orchestra sound is distinguished in trademark songs like "Solitude" with Carney's soulful baritone cry, and "Sophisticated Lady" where he employs the use of "circular breathing" to create an uninterrupted tone. Hodges became renowned for the pure beauty of his tone and mastery of ballads and blues.[12] As lead alto, Hodges guided the reed section with imaginative solos backed by the big sound of Carney.

Harry Carney was a seventeen-year-old journeyman working gigs in places like the Bamboo Inn, an afterhours chop suey joint in Harlem, before he teamed up with the Duke. His talent was noted by Ellington, who frequented the restaurant and approached him for a discussion: "One day I bumped into Duke on the street. He inquired as to what I was doing," Carney explains. "That's when he made me the offer to join him. He was taking a band up to New England, which was my old stomping ground. I'd been away from home long enough to be homesick." In 1927, Ellington led a six-piece combo with Bubber Miley, Joe Nanton, Freddy Guy, Wellman Braud, and Sonny Greer, which he decided to expand to an eight-piece band by adding Rudy Jackson and Carney. Returning to Boston, Carney introduced Ellington to his mother, saying, "Duke, always a fluent talker, out-talked my mother and got permission for me to stay with the band."[13]

At the time, Carney played alto and clarinet but decided to switch to baritone to better complement the Ellington band. He explained, "Rudy was playing clarinet and tenor so both of us were playing clarinet all night long, which was pretty much the same sort of thing. I got the idea of trying a baritone to get a different color and sound, so I took it on the job and it went down so well with the guys and the people I've been stuck with it ever since!"[14] To many jazzmen, the baritone sax was considered a ponderous and muddy-sounding instrument. Carney recalled, "At the time the baritone was not very popular. Most baritone players doubled—it was usually alto and baritone. The instrument was only used to play parts in an arrangement. In fact I was trying to make the baritone sound like a bass. I used to try to make it sound like a tenor as well!"[15] He worked hard to make a smooth transition until it paid off: "My mother came down to see us one night and she thought I'd blow my brains out because I was such a skinny kid and the instrument was bigger than me. She said I should quit!" Instead, Carney turned the instrument into a voice of the balladeer with techniques like circular breathing. His big sound became a defining mark of the horn section: "I was only seventeen. I thought it had such a big sound and this made me feel like a mature man. I felt grown-up because of the attention it commanded."[16]

In 1927, the twelve-piece Ellington orchestra was booked for nine engagements on the circuit of Charles Shribman ballrooms. He selected nearby Salem as the "home base for lengthy periods as we worked around the New England territory."[17] Meanwhile, the easygoing Carney became a trusted confidant of Ellington as he used his Chrysler to taxi the Duke from city to city and give him time to unwind. Carney stayed with Ellington for forty-seven years; his big melodic lines and clean phrasing defined ballads like "Sophisticated Lady." "I think with me making records with the instrument it might have been an incentive for some guys," he said, hinting at an influence on white contemporaries like Pepper Adams, Gerry Mulligan, and Serge Charloff. "We made so many records and I usually had a solo on them."[18]

Carney encouraged Ellington to bring his boyhood friend Johnny Hodges into the orchestra. The soprano and alto saxophonist had left Boston in 1924 to play with an old mentor, Sidney Bechet, when he opened Club Bechet in New York. Hodges used the exposure to develop a reputation for original ideas, beautiful tones, and soulful blues. He played with various bands, including the Chick Webb Orchestra, before joining Ellington. He became a valued soloist and leading voice in the reed section. His ability to shape mood and tell story is evident on songs such as "Jeep's Blues" (Jeep was a nickname from the band), "Confab with Rab" ("Rab" was short for Rabbit, a boyhood nickname), and "Prelude to a Kiss." Ellington recalled Hodges as "a player of "pure artistry [. . .] a beautiful giant in his own identity."[19] By 1928, the young men from Frederick Douglass Square had infused the sounds of the Boston jazz scene in the Ellington orchestra, and the band went from playing the summer circuit ballrooms to theaters with huge followings.

By 1931, the elegant orchestra of Duke Ellington was ready to wrest away the crown of the "jazz king" from the Paul Whiteman orchestra. Scheduled to play in the same Metropolitan Theater that Whiteman once bestrode, the Ellington band arrived to make a declaration of the South End shout. In February, Duke Ellington and his Cotton Club Orchestra—proclaimed by his press agent as "the hottest band on earth"—was booked for a weeklong engagement on a bill that included the movie *Once a Sinner*. A *Globe* review noted the orchestra of "twelve excellent and versatile musicians gives a fine demonstration of pep and ability. Many in the audience actually got to their feet during the applause for this long-awaited appearance, and regretfully watched the curtain fold for the final number."[20] During the tour, Ellington stayed true to his fan base in the Black community and scheduled a concert for a mixed crowd at the Ambassador Palace, located at Berkeley Street and Warren Avenue.

This unique event brought together two of Harlem's top bands in pitting the Ellington orchestra against Charlie Johnson and his Victory Recording Orchestra from Small's Paradise. It was a homecoming for musicians of the South End as well. Johnson led one of the most popular bands of Harlem and his personnel included another product of Frederick Douglass Square, the banjoist Bobby Johnson (unrelated to Charlie Johnson) of the prominent musical family. The *Chicago Defender* covered the battle of the bands, reporting that it "drew the largest throng of both races ever gathered in this city when they played at the Ambassador palace."[21]

The Metropolitan Theater booked Ellington for a two-week return engagement in November 1931. He had succeeded in claiming the crown, and the Boston press had to acknowledge the knockout. A *Globe* review stated that Ellington's "popularity has increased since he last come to Boston, it would seem from the repeated applause that the famous Cotton Club leader and his men received yesterday." It continued, "No other orchestra can quite parallel it" and predicted that the "colored orchestra" would transform modern music.[22] During the visit, the orchestra was booked for a gig at the Harvard–Dartmouth Intercollegiate Ball in the Copley Plaza Hotel ballroom. Back then, Harvard football games were among the most prestigious events in the city, and home games loomed large on the calendar of banquet activities. One of the biggest annual festivities was the Harvard–Yale game, followed by the Harvard–Dartmouth game. Parties went on for days and drew tens of thousands of people to the hotels. In 1925, for instance, the Harvard–Yale game attracted 40,000 people to downtown with motorcades and street celebrations. Crowds of rowdy fans swarmed the nightclubs and ballrooms with impunity, as chronicled by a 1926 headline: "Flask-Toting Football Rooters Denounced at Dartmouth Dinner." The *Globe* article reported on an event for 600 Dartmouth alumni at the Copley Plaza Hotel where speakers condemned the widespread drinking at football games.[23] Second to the Ivy League competitions were the Catholic college football games, when hotels and restaurants filled with crowds during the battle between Boston College and Holy Cross.

The Copley Plaza Hotel straddled the South End with proximity to the major railroad stations at Back Bay. The hotel rented private dance space to colleges and conventions that hired Black jazz orchestras. Events were easily accessible to out-of-town travelers with the New York, New Haven, and Hartford train line as well as to locals on the Huntington Avenue trolley line. In 1931, for example, the Harvard–Yale Intercollegiate Ball featured a dance with the orchestra McKinney's Cotton Pickers for an estimated 1,200 students and alumni. McKinney's Cotton Pickers was the most influential jazz orchestra in the Midwest territories in the 1920s. It was founded by drummer William McKinney in Springfield, Ohio, in the early 1920s and became a hot dance band in the late decade under the arrangements of Don Redman. The band blended the hot syncopated rhythm and solo freedom of a jazz combo with the formality of the society orchestra. In 1925, the Detroit booker-bandleader Jean Goldkette hired the band to play in the ballrooms of the city and around the country.[24]

The night Ellington was to perform at the hotel, rumors surfaced of a plot to ruin the concert and embarrass the band at its moment of victory. The incident involved two dances sponsored by Dartmouth College students and alumni, with the largest one held at the Copley Plaza Hotel. This was a traditional affair to bring together Dartmouth and Harvard football fans after the big game. However, a competing group plotted to undercut the Copley affair by organizing a dance with two bands at the Hotel Statler.[25] Allegedly, the sponsors of the rival dance planned to torpedo the Ellington orchestra by various schemes. One scheme relied on inciting racial anxieties in the music industry; according to the *Globe* report, the group tried to "prevent Ellington from appearing by appeals to the [white] musicians' union and theatre management."[26] The plot led Irving Mills, Ellington's manager, to publicly express concerns that timid sponsors would cave in to the demand. There were even fears that taxi drivers would be bribed to kidnap the band and drop them off in the hostile ethnic enclave of South Boston, an Irish working-class neighborhood with a reputation for racial hooligans. The *Globe* noted that "As a precaution against their being 'led astray into South Boston or somewhere,' the Ellington band was given a police escort from the Metropolitan Theatre to the hotel."[27] After the theater concert, the band was "whisked in a fleet of six taxicabs to the hotel" where they were celebrated by an estimated 1,500 revelers in the hotel ballroom.[28] As a result, the shout of the South End jazz scene ruled the night.

By the 1930s, musicians of the South End were venturing to New York City to seek better opportunities, developing a migration of

The Duke Ellington Orchestra wind and brass sections played like one man.

talent known as the "Boston–New York Pipeline." One advantage of the Harlem scene was the nondiscrimination policy of the New York chapter of the American Federation of Musicians. Unlike the Boston union, New York had accepted Black players as early as 1886 with the registration of violinist Walter Craig. Although the union cherry-picked Black musicians for theater and orchestra work, the city offered a larger market in the size of the Black community specifically and in the scope of work opportunities generally. Boston's Black community of 20,500—about two percent of the population—was outmatched by New York's Black population of 328,000 (about six percent).[29] Moreover, the New York scene was a wide-open jazz outlet compared to Boston under Prohibition. By comparison, the New York clubs served alcohol from 8 a.m. to 4 a.m. daily except Sunday, when service began at noon. In contrast, Boston prohibited the sale of liquor after 11 p.m., and none at all in the dance halls. Such constraints led the *Boston Herald* jazz columnist George Frazier to write, "Boston may be great, but New York—New York is the varsity."[30]

Bobby Sawyer, the pianist and bandleader, was one of the early participants in the pipeline and recruited his friends Harry Carney and Johnny Hodges to join him. They, in turn, shared the information with friends such as Charlie Holmes, Howard Johnson, and Preston Sandiford. The seventeen-year-old Hodges began visiting New York around 1924: "I used to come from Boston just for pleasure and stay a week. New York was a real terrific town then, really a nightlife town. All night long you'd go from one place to another. Nothing was expensive," he recalls, noting "a club on every corner in those days. There were five clubs on 134th Street. I'd come back, probably three or four weeks later, join another band, get some new ideas, go back to Boston."[31] He was followed by jazz scene peers like drummer Eddie Deas, pianist Joe Steele, and saxophonist Buster Tolliver, among others. Benny Waters left around 1925 at the invitation of friend Bobby Johnson, who was the music director of the Charlie Johnson Band (no relation) at Small's Paradise. Carney described that "Hodges was in New York before I came there. He was instrumental in getting me my first job in New York. That was in 1927."[32] The gig was an intermission band at the Savoy Ballroom in Harlem. By 1928, Max Kaminsky had joined the exodus to New York City, saying, "Here I was, nineteen years old, and though I had always had my own little way of playing, I still felt I couldn't play the way I wanted. There was only one thing I was sure of—that it was hopeless for jazz in Boston."[33]

To a lesser degree, the pipeline enriched the Boston jazz culture as players returned and as New York musicians played for the boutique market of Boston. Thus, the pipeline had a hand in fortifying the local jazz scene as well. Pianist Preston Sandiford, for example, went to New York with Eddie Deas to work at the Lafayette Theater. Deas, known as "Thunder Mouse" in reference to his small stature and loud drumming, led the ten-piece Boston Brownies between the 1920s and 1930s after playing in the bands of George

Tynes and other musicians.[34] Among the sidemen were Sandiford; Jabbo Jenkins and Chet Burroughs, trombone; George Matthews, Wilbur Pinkney, and Walter Sisco, reeds: Dave Chestnut, drums; George Jones, bass; Buster Daniels and Kenneth Roane, trumpets; Buster Tolliver, saxophone; and Victor Hadley, banjo and guitar. The orchestra recorded four sides on the Victor label in 1931: "Jes Shufflin," "Little Mary Brown," "All I Care About is You," and "Signs of the Highway." In the session for "Jes Shufflin" the band resembles the sound of a Midwest territory band with hot trumpet introduction by Chester Burrell, balanced interplay between the reed and brass sections, steady piano rhythms of Sandiford, and drums and vocalizing by Deas.[35]

The barriers of race in jazz began to decline in the Boston market in the 1930s as white musicians and venues recognized the accomplishments of musicians from the South End and Lower Roxbury. Pianist and bandleader Preston Sandiford, when living in Harlem, advanced his mastery of the keyboards from associating with pianist Art Tatum. When he opted to return to Boston, he brought new insights gleaned from the experience and a new sense of obligation to the local scene: "I stayed in New York for two years, but didn't like it. In fact, I hated New York, still do."[36] As newspaper writers published positive reviews, new opportunities arose for jazz musicians in the city. George Latimer, for example, performed on a regular basis with pianist Hi Diggs and his brother, violinist George Diggs, for a radio program on station WEEI.[37]

As Boston prepared for the Second World War, the cluster of venues with dance orchestras expanded to the downtown: the Karnak Club, Cocoanut Grove, the Latin Quarter, Casa Mañana, Lido Venice, Club Touraine in the Hotel Touraine, and the Terrace Room in the Hotel Statler. In Copley Square, there was the Music Box in the Copley Plaza Hotel and the Egyptian Room in the Hotel Brunswick. Clubs for jazz combos opened along the Massachusetts Avenue stem in the South End. Between Huntington Avenue and Tremont Street arose a new jazz scene derived from the social environment of fraternal halls, street concerts, speakeasy joints, music stores, the Pioneer Club, the Cotton Club, and the Railway Club. The new establishments included names like the Royal Palms, Savoy, Hi-Hat, Big M, and Little Harlem, among others. Clearly, the South End scene had laid a foundation for the culture of jazz in the culture of Boston.[38]

The Hi Hat Club was renowned for barbeque dinners and bebop music in the post-war South End.

CODA

SKETCHES OF POSTWAR TRENDS IN THE JAZZ SCENE

After the Second World War, the Frederick Douglass Square jazz scene included live houses with big band swing, "Dixieland" jazz, small combo bebop, piano bars with women balladeers, and rhythm and blues acts. After the victory celebrations, however, there was a growing economic anxiety as the Charlestown navy yard and defense factories cut back and the wartime military demobilized. The Black middle class in the South End discovered better housing and commercial opportunities in Dudley Square, Roxbury. During the wartime wave of migration, Boston's Black population more than doubled from 23,700 in 1940 to 51,500 in 1950. (During this time, the white population continued to grow and to relocate to suburbs that excluded Black middle-class buyers.) As Black commerce shifted to Roxbury, the properties in the South End and Lower Roxbury fell into disrepair; however, its music scene continued to appeal to a white clientele seeking an authentic jazz scene. What follows are a few stories of the notable musicians and clubs that anchored the postwar era.

Big band swing continued to have a popular following in postwar Boston. The acknowledged leader of swing was pianist and bandleader William Sebastian "Sabby" Lewis. The Lewis band was one of the rare Black orchestras with a steady following in the mainstream clubs and theaters as well as on records and radio. His 1975 album *Boston Bounce* captured the style of the orchestra and the bluesy influence of territory bands like the Count Basie Orchestra. Lewis was born in Middleburg, North Carolina, in about 1914 and raised in Philadelphia before migrating to Boston around 1932. He had been an accomplished pianist since boyhood and began playing professionally with the Tasker Crosson band The Ten Statesmen. From the 1920s to 1940s, Crosson fronted this ragtime combo on banjo, guitar, and bass, and recruited neighborhood musicians Harry Carney, Johnny Hodges, Joe Booker, Eugene "Sugar" Caines, and of course, Sabby Lewis, who stayed with the band for two years before organizing his own combo.[1]

In 1936, Lewis formed an eight-piece dance combo that was popular across the region and a training ground for South End and Roxbury musicians. It had a regular booking in the string of "Mass Ave clubs" like the Roseland-State Ballroom, the Savoy, and Egleston Square Gardens. Lewis promoted the band as the "Fitch Bandwagon Orchestra" after winning a national radio contest sponsored by the hair product company F. W. Fitch. The contest was held at the Hotel Statler in 1942 with the prize of being promoted on the Fitch network of 120 radio stations. With Lewis on piano, the band included Al Morgan, double bass and vocals; Joe Booker, drums; Eugene Caines, trumpet; Maceo Bryant, trumpet and trombone; and Jerry Heffron, Elliott "Ricky" Pratt, and Jackie Fields, tenor and baritone saxophones. Sabby Lewis conducted the regular band at the Savoy, located at 410 Mass Avenue, and was booked for concerts across New England and New York. The story goes that Count Basie went to see the band perform at the Famous Door in New York City. The next day, Lewis received a telegram of admiration from Basie in his usual economic style: "Rock' em, Pops."[2] An example of the Sabby Lewis output was the 1947 recording of "Bottoms Up" by Illinois Jacquet that incorporated elements of the uptempo "jump blues" and extended solo choruses of bebop. The session featured the thumbing rhythmic lines of bassist Al Morgan, ensemble voicing by trumpeters "Gene" Caines and Maceo Bryant, tenor saxophonists Dan Turner, Jimmy Tyler, and Bill Dorsey on baritone sax. It captured a powerful solo performance by Tyler with honking exclamations.[3]

The Sabby Lewis Orchestra was prominent in the effort to integrate the upscale nightclubs in the South End. Lewis broke the decade-long color bar at the Hi-Hat supper club, which opened in 1937 as a place to dine on barbeque chicken and dance to the music of a society jazz band. It was located at the corner of Columbus and Massachusetts Avenue in a node of emerging postwar clubs, including the Savoy and Wally's Paradise, and admired in the 1950s for being "the Jazz Corner of Boston." The Hi-Hat was owned by "Julie Rhodes"—whose real name was Julian Rosenberg but may have been changed to avoid the stigma of the notorious Cold War spy Julius Rosenberg—who desired to run a high-end jazz dance spot. Rhodes was reluctant to book African American or integrated orchestras for fear of attracting their fans—or "go colored" as the term was known—and scare away the lucrative white business. The Hi-Hat featured a restaurant on the ground floor and nightclub on the second floor. The street entrance was characterized by a scarlet awning, red carpet, and doorman dressed in top hat, cloak, and cane to welcome white customers—and turn away others. The club hired white society orchestras for a "dine and dance" experience well into the postwar years. [4]

By 1948, Rhodes witnessed other integrated clubs operate with success on the Mass Avenue strip and decided to end the Jim Crow policy. And he did not look far to hire a band that could appeal to the new generation of mixed audiences. He hired the Sabby Lewis Orchestra, the house band at the nearby Savoy, where it thrilled audiences with the incorporation of modern bebop in the swing band format. The incorporation ranged from performing compositions by Illinois Jacquet to hiring soloists like Sonny Stitt. From then on, the Hi-Hat became a premiere spot for small combo bebop and nationally renowned musicians.

The jazz of the postwar era introduced "Bebop" and a new style of solo artistry. Bebop emerged from the innovations of musicians in the territory swing bands and their estrangements from the limitations of swing. The best-known laboratories for bebop experimentation were the famed cozy nightclubs of Harlem, Minton's Playhouse and Clark Monroe's Town House. There, musicians like Thelonious Monk, Charlie Parker, Dizzy Gillespie, Charlie Christian, Bud Powell and others constituted a pantheon of jazz heroes. However, the creative solo style was honed by musicians in other cities as well. The Boston South End has standing to claim partial rights to saxophonist Edward "Sonny" Stitt, one of the leading bebop innovators, with over 100 albums to his credit including vintage South End recordings. He was born on February 2, 1924, to Edward Boatner, a classical composer, and Claudine Wickes, a piano teacher. His father migrated to Boston from the Midwest to study classical music during the great migration and in 1919 helped to produce recordings of sacred songs for Broome Specialty Phonograph Records. Edward Boatner arranged recording sessions for Burleigh's rendition of "Sometimes I Feel" and other compositions of folk spirituals as art songs. The Boatner marriage dissolved in later years, but the family remained in the city.[5]

Claudine Boatner moved to Saginaw, Michigan, with Edward Jr. and married Robert Stitt, a tavern owner, in the mid-1930s. Edward took his stepfather's surname and later the professional name "Sonny." He learned to played piano, clarinet, and saxophone at Central Junior High and Saginaw High School, where he was in the school bands. After graduating in 1942, he played in the Saginaw nightclubs and in the nearby factory cities of Flint and Pontiac. He toured with the Bama State Collegians orchestra before heading to Detroit to join the Tiny Bradshaw band. Stitt returned to Boston to work for the Sabby Lewis Orchestra when it commanded the Savoy Café as the house band in the mid-1940s.

Among the featured instrumentalists were Frankie Newton, Paul Gonsalves, Jimmy Tyler, Bill Dorsey, and Big Nick Nicholas. Stitt went on to establish his style with the Billy Eckstine Band and the Dizzy Gillespie Orchestra and in Detroit contests like the "Special Bebop Session" at the Mirror Ballroom. In 1947, he won the Esquire Award for "New Star" on the alto saxophone.[6]

By 1949, Stitt had mastered the tenor and baritone saxophones and became the most proficient bebop musician on all three instruments. In 1953, he returned to Boston for a tour de force engagement, and his 1954 recorded concerts at the Hi-Hat were bebop history for the city. The sessions were broadcast by remote radio to audiences across the region on a regularly scheduled program; they were overseen by emcee Symphony Sid Torin from 10 p.m. to midnight on WCOP and were also recorded as live albums. Among the musicians who were recorded this way are Dizzy Gillespie, Charlie Parker, Erroll Garner, Thelonius Monk, Oscar Peterson, Miles Davis, Ruth Brown, Carmen McRae, and Sarah Vaughn. Sonny Stitt was booked for extended engagements in 1953 and 1954. The February 1953 concert was a two-week booking that took place during his twenty-ninth birthday, which he celebrated with a quartet that included pianist Horace Silver and debuted the song "Massachusetts Ave Swing" (later renamed "Symphony Hall Swing"). In February 1954, he returned and teamed up with local talents Dean Earl, piano; Bernie Griggs, bass; and Marquis Foster, drums. They produced a compilation of fifteen sides that captured the power of Stitt in his prime: *Sonny Stitt Quartet—In Boston '54 Live at the Hi-Hat.*

Stitt delivered on alto, tenor, and baritone sax during the live recording session. One reviewer concluded, "It was one of the few occasions when he had all three of his instruments on stage with him and it seems to be the last time he recorded on the baritone saxophone." The session includes Stitt's compositions "Baritone Blues" and "Wigwam"; two compositions by Count Basie: "Every Tub" and "Blue and Sentimental"; and three by composers James

Trumpeter Frankie Newton led the Savoy Café orchestra and was a mentor to young jazz fans in post-war Boston.

"Jimmy" McHugh and Dorothy Fields: "How High the Moon," "I'm in the Mood for Love," and "Tri-Horn Blooz." (Both Fields and the Boston native McHugh were white writers who composed for the Black bands of Harlem between 1920 and 1940.[7]) The 1954 release of Jazz at the Hi-Hat with Sonny Stitt, volume 1, recorded February 11, 1954, features twelve sides, including "Tri-Horn Blues," "Indiana," and "Wigwam." He demonstrates his mastery of alto sax bebop on the composition of "Wigwam." He performs an extended solo flight of pure notes coming at rapid intervals and phrasing with mathematic precision. The solo is backed by the pulsing rhythms of a walking bass line and accented drumbeat. Stitt's vocal runs ascend and descend until coming to a landing with a honk! Boston audiences could have easily mistaken the session for one of the famed jam sessions at Minton's.[8]

The postwar "jump blues" musician Paul "Fat Man" Robinson was a leader of that genre of jazz in the city. The saxophonist and singer led a quintet that performed uptempo rhythms in the style of Louis Jordan, Amos Milburn, and Eddie "Clean Head" Vinson. Little is known about the early life of the gregarious bandleader; it appears that he migrated to Boston from Cleveland and began to perform after the war. Robinson played alto and sang and clowned with the audience between his novelty songs backed by an infectious bassline and soaring alto sax. He was described as "an obese, marvelous Black R&B alto player/singer, who would chant periodically between tunes, 'I'm as cool as a fool in a motor pool.'"[9] His quintet (and sometimes septet) included Oscar Dunham, trumpet; Sam Rivers and Andy McGhee, tenor saxophone; Bill Tanner, bass; Charlie Cox, piano; and for a while in 1952, J. C. Higginbotham on trombone.

Fat Man Robinson played in the honky-tonk joints downtown for the boisterous soldiers and sailors on leave and in the jazz clubs in the South End. He was a regular act at the Knickerbocker Café, 117 Stuart Street; the Silhouette Room, 243 Tremont; Petty Lounge, 233 Tremont; 4-11 Lounge, 411 Columbus Avenue; and at the Hi-Hat and Wally's Paradise. According to sideman Andy McGhee, they worked an "eight-day" week that included seven nights and a Sunday matinee: "Fat Man worked all the time. I was with him for four or five years with no time off at all."[10] The combo recorded for the Decca and Regent labels as well as the independent Motif label in Cambridge. Among the novelty jump blues songs recorded were "Lavender Coffin," the humorous lament of a hard-luck gambler that was a hit on the rhythm and blues charts in 1949, "Sophronia Jones," "Fill That Gap in Your Mouth with Teeth 'Cause Daddy Tired of Kissing Gum," and "My Bucket's Got a Hole in It." The latter recording opens with a foot-tapping double bass rhythm and ensemble riffs of saxophone and trumpet. Robinson croons nonsense lyrics to responsorial piano chords. The band fell out of favor when interest in small combo R&B declined after the 1950s. He reportedly left Boston to return to Cleveland and passed away in the early 1960s.[11]

In the late 1940s, the South End supported a few Black-owned music rooms with a compelling enough mystique to draw the curious away from mainstream audiences. The Pioneer Club was one such key location of the jazz scene in the 1920s that was still active under the ownership of the brothers Shag and Bal Taylor, located in a red brick three-story building on the former Westfield Street in Frederick Douglass Square. No longer a center of jazz culture for the Black community, by the 1940s it had transitioned to serve as an after-hours spot for mixed audiences and featured the pianist Mabel Robinson Simms. She led the house band in the 1950s and was popular with audiences in the metropolitan area while also serving as secretary of Local 535, the Black musicians union. She recalled, "I first started workin' the Pioneer Club, I think it was 1951—this is before the Pioneer Club became popular as an after-hours club. Well, I stayed there quite a few years. In fact, I opened it. Then gradually it became very popular."[12] The club was frequented by white fans including university students; one recalled, "If you were a regular, you rang the bell and waited for the doorman to move back a sliding wooden cover to the glass peephole. It was as dark as a pocket in the doorway, but in most cases you were recognized. On those occasions when the doorman could not recognize you, he opened the door, but kept the burglar chain fastened."[13]

The Professional and Business Men's Club, located at 543 Massachusetts Avenue, was founded by a group of civic leaders in

1946 and became known for its support of community programs, for hosting small combo jazz bands, and for its lively after-hours scene in the 1950s. The regular attraction was singer Mae Arnette, a migrant from Harlem who was billed as "Boston's First Lady of Song." Arnette was raised in a show business family; her parents taught her to tap dance and sing as a child. She won the Harlem Amateur Hour at the Apollo Theatre and was singing at a Harlem nightclub in 1952 when she was invited to a gig in Boston by her uncle, who managed the Celebrity Club with the Sabby Lewis Orchestra and recruited her to fill in. She decided to stay in town, and when that uncle became manager of the Professional and Business Men's Club, he hired her as the house singer. She captivated audiences with renditions of jazz standards like "Bye, Bye, Blackbird," "The Masquerade is Over," "Don't Get Around Much Anymore," and "Wee Small Hours of the Morning." She performed the tempo-changing song for the Aurora label with Jack Raymond's Balalajka Trio and a backup group identified as "The Academics."[14]

She recalled the period of audience transition during the late 1950s by saying, "I was there doing the regular hours. 'Cause a lot of the students would come down and try to get in, you know the college crowd. They'd come afterwards, but a lot of musicians came through there." She worked six days a week, from 7 p.m. to midnight, until the end of the decade, noting, "I stopped for about ten years to raise my kid you know." She concludes, "I didn't know that I was gonna be spending the rest of my life in this town. But having done so it's been, I must say, it's been an education and it's been a love in a way."[15]

Wally's Paradise emerged as the most renowned Black-owned jazz spot in the postwar South End. It lacked the resources and networks of the prestigious white clubs but harbored an advantage in the vision of founder Joseph L. Walcott. Born in the British colony of Barbados, Walcott immigrated to Boston in about 1908 during the early phase of West Indian immigration. His first business was as a driver and manager of a South End taxi service. After World

War II, he saw opportunity in the expansion of jazz clubs along Massachusetts and Columbus avenues. In 1946, he bought the liquor license from Little Dixie's nightclub at 428 Massachusetts Avenue, and Wally's Paradise was founded in January 1947. The club was more than a music room able to compete with better resourced white clubs—it was a symbol of Black self-determination.

The West Indian community was an important source of intellectual and cultural support for the Pan-African development ideas of Booker T. Washington, W. E. B. DuBois, and Marcus Garvey. In Walcott's time, the community was active in the local chapters of the National Negro Business League, NAACP, and Universal Negro Improvement Association. The Jamaican Marcus Garvey's Universal Negro Improvement Association (UNIA) was especially embraced for its appeal to self-reliance, economic nationalism, and African decolonization. His stirrings of Black pride ignited a movement among the common folk in the US, the West Indies, and Africa, as recalled by resident Ken Guscott, whose parents emigrated from Jamaica: "Garvey was our leader. He said, 'Stand up Black Man!' He was the leader and he, you know, he bought a ship and started a ship line. The ship line failed but started us to think about doing it yourself."[16] The headquarters of the Boston chapter was Butler's Hall near Northeastern University—which was renamed by followers of Garvey as "Liberty Hall" in allegiance with the UNIA headquarters in Harlem. The building hosted dances, a grocery store, and community activities. "I was probably two or three years old," Guscott recollects. "I remember that on Saturday they would march around with the robes. They had white robes that they used and then they had a headscarf and those were the Black nurses of Garvey. They would march around up Hammond Street and around Madison Park."[17] Guscott would go on to become one of Boston's most prominent Black developers. In 1972, he, along with brothers Cecil and George, founded Long Bay Management, a business encompassing property management, development, and construction. By 2000, the firm would own or manage 3,000 units and play a leading role in the revitalization of the greater Roxbury area.

Walcott, in founding the jazz club, became a stand up "race man" who did not waste time complaining about exclusions when he could be creating alternatives to the white establishments that shunned his people. Wally's Paradise became a cultural beacon for the Black community across the street from the white clubs that denied them—and it did the job for decades, so well that it eventually attracted the money of white patrons seeking an authentic jazz scene. Wally's gave a platform to the bands of Sabby Lewis, J. C. Higginbotham, Jimmy Tyler, Fat Man Robinson, Jaki Bayard, and many more neighborhood musicians. It sponsored remote radio broadcasts on WVOM and WBDA, and in later years, attracted the aspiring musicians at Berklee College. As the South End declined as a scene in the Black community, Wally's became a touchstone for young white jazz hounds like Nat Pierce, Charlie Mariano, Teddi King, and Herb Pomeroy, who developed reputations in Boston's jazz community in the 1960s. "What kept the club in business all those years?" ponders his daughter, Elynor Walcott. "My father's tenacity. This club was his life, and he worked hard to keep it going."[18]

In the postwar era, South End jazz increasingly catered to young white audiences from the colleges and other neighborhoods. This was the time when white writers assumed the role of interpreters for a cultural history outside of their own. Many, like the white jazz musicians of old, shared a sense of alienation from their own ethnic cultures and sought an escape in the jazz environment. They discovered in the Black dives a novel scene that satisfied their notions of rebellion and belonging. Take the case of George Frazier, born in Boston in 1911 and reviewer for "Sweet and Lowdown," a pioneer jazz column in the *Boston Herald*. He assumed the persona of a Yankee Brahmin when in fact he grew up in a middle-class Irish Catholic household in South Boston. However, he absorbed the characteristics of the elites while studying at Harvard. His jazz reviews had an impact on a generation of young jazz hounds like Nat Hentoff. "In Boston there was a writer in jazz named George Frazier," he wrote, noting, "What compelled me to read Frazier wherever he appeared was his daring." Among those dares was a willingness to challenge critics on questions like whether Benny Goodman was a better clarinetist than Charles Ellsworth "Pee Wee" Russell.[19]

Hentoff was born in Boston in 1925 and grew up with a sense of estrangement from his own community in Roxbury. He was part of a working-class Jewish immigrant enclave in a city with anti-Semitic tensions, and he was at odds with the old-world culture of his Russian parents. He discovered in jazz an American artform that spoke to the experience of exclusion. He studied the records and looked to Black jazzmen as interpreters. In the late 1940s, he found solace in the bohemian crowd at the Savoy Café, a jazz club started by impresario Steve Connolly in 1942. Hentoff wrotes, "Except for cops, the whites who crossed over the line and into the Savoy were the jazz-crazed, of almost all ages, from Boston and its environs."[20] Hentoff commended the Savoy for giving him an education in life as valuable as his courses at Northeastern University: "Behind the closed doors of the Savoy, I felt more at home than anywhere else I had ever been, including home. I could not get enough of the music, the deep warmth and the surprise of it. And I could not get enough of the musicians."[21]

Hentoff was befriended by Frankie Newton, whom he described as a "tall trumpet player, much admired for his concise lyricism."[22] In fact, Newton was an underrated trumpeter, singer, songwriter, and bandleader of the interwar years. Born in Virginia about 1911, Newton migrated to Harlem about 1929 and began to play in the swing bands of leading musicians including Charlie Johnson, Andy Kirk, and Chick Webb; over more than a decade, he recorded with Cecil Scott, Willie "The Lion" Smith, Bessie Smith, Billie Holiday, Art Tatum, Maxine Sullivan, Mary Lou Williams, James P. Johnson, Sidney Bechet, Buster Bailey, and Teddy Wilson. He also recorded with the interracial studio band of Mezz Mezzrow and His Swing Gang as well as with his own Frankie Newton and His Uptown Serenaders. He led the Café Society Orchestra in Greenwich Village and recorded with Billie Holiday on the John Hammond sessions of 1939 that included the famed elegy of "Strange Fruit." The Café Society attracted the leading cultural and political figures of New York City New Dealers. The club was noted for appearances by actors like Judy Holiday and Paul Robeson, comedian Zero Mostel, singers Lena Horne, Peggy Lee, and Bing Crosby, writer John Steinbeck, and conductor Arturo Toscanini. Newton was believed to be a member of the Communist Party and was a known advocate for cooperative bands. He was acquainted with the leftist British historian Eric Hobsbawn, who took the liberty of writing a jazz column for the *New Statesman* under the pen name "Francis Newton"—supposedly in honor of the trumpeter.[23]

By the 1940s, Newton was part of the flow of jazz talent in the New York–Boston Pipeline and led a quintet at the Hotel Pilgrim in Plymouth in 1942. Newton played at the Savoy in the Sabby Lewis Orchestra and his own band during the late 1940s and 1950s, when he impressed upon numerous white youths the hard path of Black jazz musicians. He was generous about emotional travails and shared some of the mean experiences he had encountered in the industry and society. By then, Newton appeared to embrace the politics of Pan-Africanism that was in circulation during the 1950s period of anti-colonialism; he espoused a view of jazz as a cultural platform capable of appealing to audiences of the diaspora and African continent while building bridges of mutuality with other racial groups. Such outlooks were reflected in the debates of the community of Black thinkers over the merits of Pan-Africanism versus socialism and communism. Hentoff, for instance, recalled: "He thought Black—in terms of history, politics, culture. And language."[24]

George Wein also suffered from the melancholy of alienation and turned to jazz for solace. He was born in Boston in 1925, the son of a respected doctor, and faced the prospect of a contented but numbing life of upper-middle-class Jewish expectations. His family discouraged the interest in jazz, which in their minds was associated with tales of alcohol, drugs, prostitution, gangsters, and burlesque women. Wein made a pilgrimage to the South End scene during the late 1940s, with stops including the Savoy, Pioneer Club, Slade's, Estelle's, and occasional rent parties under the tutelage of friendly musicians. Wein also benefitted from the friendship of Frankie Newton and described his physical deterioration from the jazz life: "Once a proud, distinguished-looking man, he was now a confirmed alcoholic, and his posture and countenance were wracked with a feeling of futility. His playing bore similar signs of decay."[25] In 1950, Wein opened Storyville in the Copley Square Hotel on Huntington Avenue and Exeter Street. With 200 seats to fill, the club had a rocky trial period and closed within months; he opened a second Storyville in the Hotel Buckminster in Kenmore Square that was successful.

Wein came to understand the racial lens used by audiences in gauging jazz authenticity. He noted, for example, that the British pianist George Shearing—a blind musician with the gift of an exquisite sound—drew larger audiences than foundational icons like Billie Holiday! She performed at Storyville when it was located in the Hotel Buckminster in Kenmore Square for a one-week engagement in October 1951. The program was split with saxophonist Stan Getz playing an early set; however, he sometimes waited around and sat in on a few songs with Holiday. During the concert, Holiday did extra sets for radio broadcast on station WMEX as well.[26] Wein would later innovate the packaging of multiple acts in the economical format of annual festivals and started the jazz festival in Newport, Rhode Island.

After World War I, the spirit of jazz drumming in the South End was enriched by the presence of musician and army veteran Herbert Wright, the infamous killer of conductor James Reese Europe. The drummer served his time and became a Boston resident and mentor to young drummers in the neighborhood like Roy Haynes. The legacy established a tradition of drumming excellence that continued in the postwar era with the presence of George "Alan" Dawson.

Born in 1929 in Marietta, Pennsylvania, Dawson was raised in Roxbury as the fourth child of James W. and Eva Dawson. They encouraged his study of the multi-piece drum set under Charles Alden, a respected white drummer in New England. Dawson was one of his students in the early 1940s. (In 1953, Alden formed the Charles Alden Music Company in Westwood, Massachusetts, the exclusive distributor of the Sonor drums and accessories for the eastern seaboard.) Dawson began to play professionally as a fourteen-year-old freelancer in the South End. He gained the attention of Sabby Lewis who hired him to fill in for gigs at the Hi-Hat and other clubs. In a short time, Dawson gained a reputation for a melodic approach to drumming and an advanced level of hand and foot coordination. His fledgling Boston career was interrupted by military service during the Korean War. He played in the army dance band at Fort Dix, New Jersey, from 1951 to 1952, then joined the Lionel Hampton Orchestra for a three-month tour of Europe. He returned to Boston and rejoined the Sabby Lewis Orchestra before branching out to play with local musicians such as trumpeter Frankie Newton, baritone saxophonist Serge Chaloff, and pianist Jaki Byard, among others. In 1957, Dawson was the house drummer at Wally's Paradise, then worked the Stables club with trumpeter Herb Pomeroy from 1959 to 1960, and from 1963 to 1970 was part of the house band with pianist Ray Santisi and bassist John Neves at the famed Lennie's On The Turnpike in Peabody. Dawson backed a pantheon of jazz heroes in the mid-twentieth century including Oscar Peterson, Charles Mingus, Dexter Gordon, Dave Brubeck, Frank Morgan, Hank Jones, Teddy Wilson, and Sonny Stitt. His 1972 album with Stitt, "Tune Up!," is considered one of the best recording sessions for both musicians.[27]

In 1957, Dawson joined the faculty of Berklee College of Music in the South End. The school established a formal education system for jazz musicians that replaced the old system of individual mentorship to a large degree. Dawson emphasized students' learning music as a whole and simply the drumming parts. In this regard, his students played over jazz standards while singing the melody to avoid letting technique override expression. He also encouraged students to use brushes to reduce stick rebound. He published his method for learning the drum set in a 1960s textbook, "The Drummer's Complete Vocabulary." Dawson, as a musician and teacher dedicated to Boston, offered up precious knowledge and experiences to many students; most notable, the aspiring drummer Tony Williams:

> "I met Mr. Dawson when I was nine years old. He went out of his way to encourage me, help me and to see that I had opportunities to develop my meager skills. For example, on Saturday night he would drive one hundred miles out of his way to pick me up in Roxbury, drive to Cambridge to let me perform with his trio and gain valuable experience, and then return me safely home before returning himself to Lexington. I was twelve years old."[28]

Born in 1945 in Chicago, Anthony Williams moved to Roxbury with his family as a toddler. His father, Tillmon Williams, was a jazz saxophonist who played in the South End clubs on weekends and introduced the young "Tony" to the scene. "I would sit in the audience when I was a kid and just watch the drummer," he recalls.[29] He studied drummers on records and expanded his knowledge of what the instrument could do, he said, adding, "When I was a kid, I would buy every record I could find with Max Roach on it and then I would play exactly what he played on the record—solos and everything."[30] At nine years old, Williams accompanied his father to a club and was invited to sit in with the band. His education was furthered by the mentoring of Alan Dawson, associating with touring drummers like Max Roach and Art Blakey, and gigging with saxophonists Sam Rivers and Jackie McLean. His novel style of playing was described as "freeing up of the hi-hat from its traditional role of maintaining beats two and four and a more pulse-oriented approach to the ride cymbal."[31] Others noted his "volcanic style of drumming" and awareness of the whole band.

At age seventeen, Williams was hired by trumpeter Miles Davis to form one of the influential combos of the 1960s with Wayne Shorter, saxophone, Herbie Hancock, piano, and Ron Carter, bass. Over a six-year period, the quintet produced outstanding classic albums as *Four & More*, *Nefertiti*, *Sorcerer*, and *In a Silent Way*, with memorable sessions like "E.S.P.," "Miles Smiles," and "Live at the Plugged Nickel." The body of work produced is considered among the most important in that era of jazz. Williams then branched out as a leader of a fusion movement with the avant-garde band, Lifetime, with guitarist John McLaughlin and organist Larry Young. The band integrated elements of jazz, funk, and rock into an original mix. He recalled, "On those first records with Lifetime, I was just trying to do something that no one else had done."[32] In this way, Tony Williams rose from the jazz clubs of the South End and Roxbury to become one of the most important jazz drummers of his generation.

In closing, the cultural politics of the South End shout was anticipated by the observant Malcolm Little. The man who would become Malcolm X studied how the enjoyment of the music was also an indication of the power of the music. Malcolm X long searched for a platform that would allow Black people to speak to broad publics from a position of authority. While he ultimately embraced a world religion, he nonetheless perceived the spiritual value of jazz music. He had migrated to Boston from Lansing, Michigan, in 1939 and lived intermittently in the metropolitan area until 1952. In the early 1940s, he resided at 72 Dale Street in Roxbury, the new Black residential neighborhood as people moved out of Frederick Douglass Square or arrived from other places. The center of the new Black commercial district was Dudley Square (known today as Nubian Square). Frederick Douglass Square remained a vital scene for live jazz but increasingly the neighborhood was disinvested and left in a state of disrepair.

As a teenager, Malcolm was employed as a bathroom attendant in the Roseland State Ballroom on Massachusetts Avenue and Burbank Street. The dance hall was managed by the Charles and Simeon Shribman brothers and straddled the borderline of the South End and Back Bay. He shined shoes and established a side hustle of distributing hand towels, condoms, liquor, and arranging for white patrons to solicit prostitutes. In the confines of the men's room, he made the acquaintance of Duke Ellington, Count Basie, Lionel Hampton, Cootie Williams, Jimmie Lunceford, Jimmie Rushing, Lester Young, Harry Edison, and Johnny Hodges—who apparently stiffed him over a fifteen-cent shoeshine.[33]

Malcolm recalled the transformational rituals that occurred on the dance floor, writing, "Most of Roseland's dances were for whites only, and they had white bands only. The fact is that very few white bands could have satisfied the Negro dancers." He noted the collective release of emotions that reached a level of a spiritual rapture: "Some couples were so abandoned—flinging high and wide, improvising steps and movements—that you couldn't believe it. I could feel the beat in my bones," he continued. "Then a couple of dozen really wild couples would stay on the floor, the girls changing to low white sneakers. The band now would really be blasting, and all the other dancers would form a clapping, shouting circle to watch that wild competition as it began."[34]

In 1945, Malcolm moved to Cambridge and fell in trouble with the law—arrested on felony charges. In February 1946, at age 21, he was convicted of robbery and sentenced to serve eight to ten years in the Charlestown State Prison. During incarceration, he worked to improve his education and was transferred to the Norfolk Prison Colony that offered inmate education programs sponsored by local colleges. He studied world cultures and religions and strengthened his vocabulary. With new understanding, he joined the debating club and mastered the skills of oral communication like a musician on a drum set. During this period of intellectual growth, he became a Muslim and joined the Nation of Islam; upon his release in 1952, he was appointed a national minister. Years later, he looked back on the experience in the Boston jazz scene with a new perspective. What stood out was the cathartic ritual of dance and movement to the music of the Black dance orchestras; it led him to make this observation on the power of the South End shout: "I see the time when the Black culture will be the dominant culture."[35]

Notes

INTRODUCTION

1. Lars Bjorn with Jim Gallert, *Before Motown: A History of Jazz in Detroit*, XIII.
2. Travis A. Jackson, *Blowin' the Blues Away: Performance and Meaning on the New York Jazz Scene*, 57.
3. Michael C. Heller, *Loft Jazz: Improvising New York in the 1970s*, 30.
4. Burton W. Peretti, *The Creation of Jazz: Music, Race, and Culture in Urban America*, 54.
5. Court Carney, *How Early Jazz Got America's Ear*, 135.
6. Boston Landmarks Commission, *Connolly's Bar* (report, 1997), 10.
7. Ro Jackson, *Blowin' the Blues Away*, 29, 38.
8. Jialu Chen, "Back Where He Started," *Boston.com*, July 26, 2011; Cintia Lopez, "Berklee Announces End of Beantown Jazz Festival," *WBUR*, April 2, 2019.
9. "I'm Shouting Again—Count Basie," uploaded to YouTube by Johnnystaccata, May 28, 2018, accessed 21 June 2021, https://youtu.be/8LQe5JG7omk/.
10. Teddy Wilson, "Teddy Wilson Talks Jazz," 33.
11. William Grimes, "Eric J. Hobsbawn" [obituary], *New York Times*, October 9, 2012.

CHAPTER 1

1. M. E. Lasseter, *Jonkonnu, Jankunu, Junkanoo, John Canoe: Reorienting North Carolina's Practice in the American Mediterranean* (University of North Carolina, 2014), https://docsouth.unc.edu/; Robert Farris Thompson, *Flash of the Spirit*, 18–33; Maultsby, Portia K. "Africanisms in African American Music," 326–49; Samuel Floyd, Power of Black Music, 38.

2. "Free African American Population in the U.S.: 1790–1860," University of Virginia Library, http://fisher.lib.virginia.edu/collections/stats/histcensus/; James Oliver Horton and Lois Horton, *In Hope of Liberty*, 31.
3. Horton and Horton, *Liberty*, 32.
4. James Horton, *Black Bostonians*, 30.
5. Horton, *Black Bostonians*, 30.
6. Horton, *Black Bostonians*, 33.
7. Robert Woods, *Americans in Process*, 247; Kerri Greenidge, *Boston's Abolitionists*, viii.
8. Horton, *Black Bostonians*, 37; Robert Woods, ed., *Americans in Process*, 218.
9. Con Chapman, *Johnny Hodges*, 7.
10. Court Carney, *Cutting Up*, 12.
11. Maud Cuney Hare, *Negro Musicians*, 162; Tim Brooks, *Lost Sounds*, 30–33.
12. "Attractions at the Theatres," *Boston Daily Globe*, September 13, 1908 (via ProQuest archive).
13. Jeffrey Perry, *Hubert Harrison*, 251–54.
14. Bert Williams, "Nobody," recorded May 22, 1905, uploaded to YouTube by "Remember Our Music," May 23, 2017, accessed 11 June 2022, https://www.youtube.com/watch?v=LGnlmWTNBbk/.
15. Clarence Cameron White, "Chant," *The Bandanna Sketches*, recorded 1921. Performed by The Paragon Ragtime Orchestra, Rick Benjamin, director, *Black Manhattan* vol. 3 (2019), accessed June 11, 2022, https://www.youtube.com/watch?v=u8H1A7wkDkI/.
16. Reid Badger, *Ragtime*, 26.
17. Sam Charters, *Jazz: A History of the New York Scene*, 14–17; Jacob Goldberg, "Black and White United," np.
18. Maud Cuney Hare, *Negro Musicians*, 139–40.
19. Badger, *Ragtime*, 260, 268, 289.
20. Stephen Robinson, "Basketball in 1920s Harlem," Digital Harlem Blog, June 3, 2011, accessed June 12, 2022. https://drstephenrobertson.com/digitalharlemblog/maps/basketball-in-1920s-harlem/.
21. Badger, *Ragtime*, 73–77.
22. Badger, *Ragtime*, 73–77; Hare, *Negro Musicians*, 138–39.
23. Hare, *Negro Musicians*, 138.
24. Badger, *Ragtime*, 235–36.
25. David Kyvig, *Daily Life*, 201–03.
26. Tim Brooks, *Lost Recordings* [liner notes], 51; Badger, *Ragtime*, 236.
27. Badger, *Ragtime*, 136, 289; "Jim Europe Wears Jazz Garb," *The New York Sun*, May 14, 1919.

CHAPTER 2

1. Maud Cuney Hare, *Negro Musicians*, 137; Court Carney, *Cuttin' Up*, 82.
2. "Jazz Band Created Big Stir in France," *Philadelphia Evening Public Ledger*, March 21, 1919, 15.
3. "Jazz Band Created Big Stir in France"
4. "Jazz Band Created Big Stir in France"; Eileen Southern, *Music of Black Americans*, 289.
5. James Reese Europe's 369th U.S. Infantry "Hell Fighters" Band, "The Darktown Strutters' Ball," The Orchard Enterprises (January 2015), accessed June 11, 2022, https://www.youtube.com/watch?v=HwkisCEOndo/.
6. Preston Sandiford, "Through the Years with Preston Sandiford," interview by Dan Kochakian, *Whiskey, Women and . . .* (December 1985).
7. Reid Badger, *Ragtime*, 237–39.
8. Court Carney, *Cuttin' Up*, 130.
9. Jeremy Eichler, "The Rise and Fall," *Boston Globe*, Nov 8, 2009 (via Boston.com archive).
10. Badger, *Ragtime*, 237.
11. "Concerts by the Famous 369th U.S. Infantry Band," *Boston Daily Globe*, March 23, 1919 (via ProQuest archive).
12. "Boston Opera House," *Boston Daily Globe*, March 27, 1919 (via ProQuest archive).
13. "J.R. Europe, Band Leader, Murdered," *Boston Daily Globe*, May 10, 1919 (via ProQuest archive).
14. Thomas O'Connor, *The Hub*, 193–94; "All Set for the Great Parade," April 25, 1919 (via ProQuest archive); Kerri Greenidge, *Black Radical*, 234–35.
15. "All Set for the Great Parade," *Boston Daily Globe*, April 25, 1919 (via ProQuest archive).
16. "How Yankee 26th Fought Its Way to Fame," *Boston Daily Globe*, April 25, 1919 (via ProQuest archive).
17. O'Connor, *The Hub*, 193–94.
18. O'Connor, *The Hub*, 193–94; "Colored American Made Lasting Record," *Boston Guardian*, May 16, 1919.
19. "J.R. Europe, Band Leader, Murdered." *Boston Daily Globe*, May 10, 1919, 1 (via ProQuest archive).
20. "J.R. Europe, Band Leader, Murdered"; Frederick Spencer Jr., *Jazz and Death* (University of Mississippi, 2002), 63–70.
21. "J.R. Europe, Band Leader, Murdered"; Spencer, *Jazz and Death*, 63–70.
22. Spencer, *Jazz and Death*, 63–70.

23. "J.R. Europe, Band Leader, Murdered."
24. Spencer, *Jazz and Death*, 63–70.
25. Caroline Alexander, "The Shock of War," *Smithsonian Magazine* (September 2010).
26. "Drummer Who Killed Europe," *Baltimore Afro-American*, April 9, 1927.
27. David Kyvig, *Daily Life*, 71–75; Burton Peretti, *Creation of Jazz*, 154; "Lois Deppe: First African American Swing Band in Pittsburgh," accessed May 2021, http://pittsburghmusichistory.com/.
28. "Drummer Who Killed Europe"; Kyvig, *Daily Life*, 71–75.
29. "Roy Haynes," Interviewed for Berklee Oral History Project, April 2009; Ron Herd, producer, "Jazz Great Roy Haynes," *W.E. A.L.L. B.E. News*, March 20, 2016.

CHAPTER 3

1. *Boston Daily Globe*, "Would Name Square After Douglass," January 30, 1917; Burton Peretti, *Creation of Jazz*, 43–45.
2. "From the Great Migration to Boston's Charlestown Navy Yard," Boston National Park Service, accessed June 6, 2022, https://www.nps.gov/articles/great-migration-to-charlestown-navy-yard.htm.
3. John Daniels, *In Freedom's Birthplace*, 364.
4. Daniels, *Freedom's Birthplace*, 365–67; Kerri Greenidge, *Black Radical*, IX–X.
5. *Boston Guardian*, ad for Hotel Melbourne, January 24, 1920; Robert Hayden, *African Americans*, 80; Daniels, *Freedom's Birthplace*, 365.
6. *Boston Guardian*, ad for Mary E. Moore Co, January 10, 1920; *Boston Guardian*, ad for Bay State Pharmacy, March 31, 1923.
7. *Boston Guardian*, ad for Star Lunch, January 10, 1920; Hayden, *African Americans*, 80–81.
8. *Boston Guardian*, ads for David Crawford and John O'Brien, January 24, 1920; *Boston Guardian*, ad for Gamer's Music, April 7, 1923.
9. Ron Bailey, *Lower Roxbury*, 63.
10. Kenneth Guscott, Lower Roxbury Black History Project, May 14, 2008, Northeastern University.
11. *Boston Guardian*, ad for Douglass Square barber, January 10, 1920; *Boston Guardian*, ad for Modern Hair, January 24, 1920.
12. Charles Thomas, Lower Roxbury Black History Project, January 23, 2008, Northeastern University.
13. *Boston Guardian*, ad for Farm Outlet, January 10, 1920, and editorial, July 28, 1923.

14. Kevin McNatt and Andrew Todesco, "Boston Tigers, New England's top African-American baseball team, met Mansfield team on diamond in 1927," Wickedlocal.com, February 22, 2022, accessed June 3, 2022; Bijan C. Bayne, "Black baseball in Boston: recovering a lost legacy," Bay State Banner, April 27, 2006, accessed June 3, 2022, baystate-banner.com.
15. James Oliver Horton and Lois E. Horton, *Black Bostonians*, 66–67.
16. *Boston Daily Globe*, "Would Name Square After Douglass," January 30, 1917; City Documents, Volume 3, Issues 33–49, 211 (May 2021).
17. *Boston Daily Globe*, "Boston Honors Douglass Today," February 14, 1917.
18. Darlene Clark Hine, *African American Odyssey*, 86.
19. Horton and Horton, *Black Bostonians*, 61, 130.
20. William Cole, "Introductory," in *The City Wilderness*, ed. Robert Wood, 3; Albert Benedict Wolfe, *Lodging House*, 104.
21. Wolfe, *Lodging House*, 10.
22. Wolfe, *Lodging House*, 82.
23. Wolfe, *Lodging House*, 27; Wood, *City Wilderness*, 82–89.
24. Wolfe, *Lodging House*, 6–7, 99–100, 167–68; Wood, *City Wilderness*, 86–89.
25. Wolfe, *Lodging House*, 102.
26. Wolfe, *Lodging House*, 91.
27. Wolfe, *Lodging House*, 91.
28. Wolfe, *Lodging House*, 91.
29. Con Chapman, *Rabbit's Blues*, 10.
30. James R. Green and Hugh Carter Donahue, *Boston's Workers*, 68–69.
31. Green and Donahue, *Boston's Workers*, 69.
32. Frederick Bushee, "Population," in *City Wilderness*, 45; Daniels, *Freedom's Birthplace*, 384; Chapman, *Rabbit's Blue*, 9.
33. "Frederick Douglass Square Historic District," Boston Landmarks Commission report, August 27, 1996; Bailey, *Lower Roxbury*, 1–6.
34. Bailey, *Lower Roxbury*, 59, 62.
35. Bailey, *Lower Roxbury*, 60, 63.
36. Bailey, *Lower Roxbury*, 57–58, 63.
37. Charles Thomas, Black History Project, January 23, 2008.
38. Bailey, *Lower Roxbury*, 7, 26.
39. Green and Donahue, *Boston's Workers*, 69–70.
40. Daniels, *Freedom's Birthplace*, 320–21; Frederick Bushee, "Population" in "City Wilderness," 45.
41. Daniels, *Freedom's Birthplace*, 321.
42. Daniels, *Freedom's Birthplace*, 320.

43. Daniels, *Freedom's Birthplace*, 333; Albert Benedict Wolfe, "Lodging House," 94.
44. Daniels, *Freedom's Birthplace*, 343.
45. Guscott, Black History Project; Chip Deffaa, *Voices of the Jazz Age*, 30–31.
46. Wolfe, *Lodging House*, 87; Bailey, *Lower Roxbury*, 59; Daniels, *Freedom's Birthplace*, 337.
47. Horton and Horton, *Black Bostonians*, 82.
48. Bailey, *Lower Roxbury*, 63; Pauline Thomas, Lower Roxbury Black History Project, January 23, 2008, Northeastern University.
49. Bailey, *Lower Roxbury*, 58–62.
50. Daniels, *Freedom's Birthplace*, 346.
51. Daniels, *Freedom's Birthplace*, 352–54.
52. Daniels, *Freedom's Birthplace*, 363.
53. Daniels, *Freedom's Birthplace*, 128–29.
54. Patricia Hoskins Morton, "National Negro Business League," *Encyclopedia of Alabama*, May 6, 2009, accessed May 29, 2021, http://encyclopediaofalabama.org/.
55. Daniels, *Freedom's Birthplace*, 392–93.
56. Daniels, *Freedom's Birthplace*, 244–48.
57. Daniels, *Freedom's Birthplace*, 244–48; Church of God and Saints of Christ, "Leaders," accessed May 29, 2021, https://www.cogasoc.org/.

CHAPTER 4

1. Travis Jackson, *Blowin' the Blues Away*, 70; Ron Bailey, *Lower Roxbury*, 15.
2. Roy Haynes, "Jazz Great Roy Haynes," *W.E. A.L.L. B.E. News* (podcast), March 20, 2016, https://www.blogtalkradio.com/weallbe; Roy Haynes, interview for Berklee College oral history, April 2009.
3. Roy Haynes, interview for Berklee College oral history, April 2009.
4. Haynes, Berklee College interview.
5. Haynes, Berklee College interview.
6. Haynes, Berklee College interview.
7. Preston Sandiford, "Through the Years with Preston Sandiford," interview by Dan Kochakian, *Whiskey, Women and . . .* (December 1985).
8. Stanley Dance, "Charlie Holmes," in *The World of Swing: An Oral History of Big Band Jazz*, 248–49; Con Chapman, *Rabbit's Blues*, 13.
9. Dance, *World of Swing*, 241–48.
10. Dance, "Howard Johnson," in *World of Swing* 241–42.

11. Dance, "Charlie Holmes," in *World of Swing*, 248–49;
12. Dance, "Charlie Holmes," in *World of Swing*, 248–49;
13. Chapman, *Rabbit's Blues*, 12—4.
14. Chapman, *Rabbit's Blues*, 12—4.
15. Jackson, *Blowin' the Blues Away*, 78;
16. Jackson, *Blowin' the Blues Away*, 78; Loraine Elena Roses, *Black Bostonians*, 51–54.
17. "Announcements," *Boston Guardian*, May 16, 1919; June 14, 1919.
18. "Announcements," *Boston Guardian*, March 31, 1923.
19. "Announcements," *Boston Guardian*, January 10, 1920; April 7, 1923.
20. James Horton, *Black Bostonians*, 32; John Thompson, "Fraternal Orders," Oklahoma Historical Society, https://www.okhistory.org (accessed May 30, 2021).
21. John Daniels, *In Freedom's Birthplace*, 207–09.
22. Bailey, *Lower Roxbury*, 15; Preston Sandiford, "Through the Years with Preston Sandiford," interview by Dan Kochakian, *Whiskey, Women and*... (December 1985).
23. Eric Jackson, "Riff Tide," *Boston Magazine*, May 15, 2006.
24. "Announcements," *Boston Guardian*, May 16, 1919; April 12, 1919.
25. "Announcements," *Boston Guardian*, March 31, 1923.
26. "Welcome I.B.P.O.E in Faneuil Hall," *Boston Daily Globe*, August 23, 1921.
27. "Welcome I.B.P.O.E in Faneuil Hall."
28. "Welcome I.B.P.O.E in Faneuil Hall."
29. "Welcome I.B.P.O.E in Faneuil Hall."
30. "Colored Knights of Pythias Parade," *Boston Daily Globe*, May 21, 1923.
31. Jackson, *Blowin' the Blues Away*, 84; "Announcements," *Boston Guardian*, May 16, 1919.
32. "Announcements," *Boston Guardian*, April 12, 1919; May 16, 1919.
33. "Harry Hicks" under "History—Major Contributors" of *Boston Jazz Scene*, last updated February 26, 2014, https://bostonjazzscene.blogspot.com (accessed June 24, 2021).
34. Bailey, *Lower Roxbury*, 15; Chapman, *Rabbit's Blues*, 11.
35. Dance, "Howard Johnson" in *World of Swing*, 241—2; "Harry Hicks," *Boston Jazz Scene*; Chip Deffaa, *Voices of the Jazz Age*, 31–32.
36. Charles Thomas, interview for Lower Roxbury Oral History Project, Northeastern University library.
37. Thomas, Lower Roxbury Oral History Project.
38. Kenneth Guscott, interviewed for Lower Roxbury Oral History Project, Northeastern University library.

39. "Jenkins Orphanage Band," Jenkinsinstitute.org, accessed June 8, 2022, https://jenkinsinstitute.org/index.php/the-music.
40. James Hutchisson, "The Cradle of Jazz," *Charleston Magazine*, April 2005.
41. Haynes, Berklee College oral history; see also the Haynes interview in "Jazz Great Roy Haynes," *W.E. A.L.L. B.E. News* (podcast).
42. Robert Hayden, *African-Americans in Boston: More than 350 Years* (Boston Public Library: 1991), 20.
43. Bailey, *Lower Roxbury*, 62.
44. Guscott, Lower Roxbury Oral History Project; Chapman, *Rabbit's Blues*, 17.

CHAPTER 5

1. Burton Peretti, *Creation of Jazz*, 185.
2. Preston Sandiford, "Through the Years with Preston Sandiford," interview by Dan Kochakian, *Whiskey, Women and . . .* (December 1985).
3. Con Chapman, *Rabbit's Blues*, 14–15;
4. Mabel Robinson Simms, interviewed March 30, 1999, Boston Musicians Association oral history transcript.
5. Simms, Boston Musicians Association oral history transcript.
6. Sandiford, "Preston Sandiford."
7. Chapman, *Rabbit's Blues*, 15–16;
8. Simms, Boston Musicians Association oral history.
9. Dean Earl, interviewed February 12, 1999, Boston Musicians Association oral history transcript.
10. Simms, Boston Musicians Association oral history.
11. Dean Earl, interviewed February 12, 1999, Boston Musicians Association oral history transcript.
12. Sandiford, "Preston Sandiford."
13. David Hajdu, "Who's Got the Blues?," *Mother Jones*, September/October 2003, 77–105.
14. Sandiford, "Preston Sandiford."
15. Teddy Wilson, *Teddy Wilson Talks Jazz*, 37.
16. Peretti, *Creation of Jazz*, 157–58; Earl, Boston Musicians Association oral history transcript.
17. Chapman, *Rabbit's Blues*, 19.
18. "Sil D'Urbano," Boston Musicians Association oral history webpage, bostonmusicians.org.
19. "Dave Fagin," Boston Musicians Association oral history webpage, bostonmusicians.org.

20. "Music and Musicians: Musicians' Views on Jazz," *Boston Globe*, August 24, 1924 (via ProQuest archive).
21. "Music and Musicians," *Boston Globe*.
22. "Music and Musicians," *Boston Globe*.
23. George Aaron Cuddy, interview with George Latimer in *Where Hash Rules: The Story of Charlie's Sandwich Shoppe in Boston* (2015)
24. Cuddy, *Where Hash Rules*; Sandiford, "Preston Sandiford."
25. Cuddy, *Where Hash Rules*.
26. Earl, Boston Musicians Association oral history transcript.
27. Simms, Boston Musicians Association oral history transcript; "Pianist/Vocalist Mabel Robinson Simms," *Troy Street Observer*, Troystreet.com.
28. Chapman, *Rabbit's Blues*, 18; Event announcements, *Boston Guardian*, June 14, 1919, January 10, 1920, and March 31, 1923; "Bobby Sawyer" under Stu Vandermark, "History—Major Contributors" of *Boston Jazz Scene*, accessed June 24, 2021, https://bostonjazzscene.blogspot.com.
29. "George Tynes," under Stu Vandermark, "History—Major Contributors" of *Boston Jazz Scene*, accessed June 24, 2021, https://bostonjazzscene.blogspot.com.
30. "Walter Johnson" under Stu Vandermark, "History—Major Contributors" of *Boston Jazz Scene*, accessed June 24, 2021, https://bostonjazzscene.blogspot.com; Stanley Dance, "Howard Johnson," in *World of Swing*, 241–48; Chapman, *Rabbit's Blues*, 18.
31. Simms, Boston Musicians Association oral history transcript.
32. "Benjamin 'Benny' Waters" under Stu Vandermark, "History—Major Contributors" of *Boston Jazz Scene*, accessed June 24, 2021, https://bostonjazzscene.blogspot.com.
33. Dance, "Howard Johnson," *World of Swing*, 241–48
34. Don DeMichael, "Double Play: Carney to Hodges to Ellington," *Downbeat* (June 1962), reproduced at confabwithrab.blogspot.com (accessed June 29, 2021).
35. DeMichael, "Double Play."
36. "Broome Specialty Phonograph Records," *78RPM Club*, accessed June 29, 2021, https://78rpm.club/record-labels/broome-special-phonograph-records/.
37. "Worth Reading and Hearing: "The Blue Sky Boys" and "Black Swans,"" Mainspring Press, December 11, 2019, accessed June 12, 2022, https://78records.wordpress.com/tag/broome-special-phonograph-records/.
38. "Broome Specialty Phonograph Records," *78RPM Club*; Sandiford, "Preston Sandiford."
39. Travis Jackson, *Blowin' the Blues Away*, 97; Sven Bjerstedt, "Stealing Knowl-

edge in a Landscape of Learning: Conceptualizations of Jazz Education," *British Journal of Music Education* 33, no. 3 (November 2016), accessed June 12, 2022, https://www.cambridge.org/core/journals/british-journal-of-music-education/article/stealing-knowledge-in-a-landscape-of-learning-conceptualizations-of-jazz-education/.

40. Sandiford, "Preston Sandiford."
41. Peretti, *Creation of Jazz*, 152–53; "Preston Sandiford," discogs.com.
42. Donna Halper, "Boston Radio in the Early 1920s," https://www.oocities.org (https://www.oocities.org/uridfm/r/earlybostonradio.htm).
43. Carole Scott, "The History of the Radio Industry in the United States to 1940," https://eh.net/encyclopedia.org; "Automatic Radio Mfg. Co.," https://www.radiomuseum.org. (https://www.radiomuseum.org/dsp_hersteller_detail.cfm?company_id=1932)
44. Earl, Boston Musicians Association oral history transcript.
45. Peretti, *Creation of Jazz*, 154–55.
46. Peretti, *Creation of Jazz*, 146–47.
47. Sandiford, "Preston Sandiford."
48. Stephanie Schorow, *Drinking Boston*, 102–03.
49. Ted Vincent, "The Window of Opportunity," *The Black Scholar* 22, no. 4, Black Culture 1992 (Fall 1992): 6–16.
50. Sandiford, "Preston Sandiford"; Duke Ellington, *Music Is My Mistress*, 98—9.
51. Sandiford, "Preston Sandiford."
52. "Malcolm Gray 'Mal' Hallett" under Stu Vandermark, "History—Major Contributors" of *Boston Jazz Scene*, accessed June 24, 2021, https://bostonjazzscene.blogspot.com; Richard Vacca, *Boston Jazz Chronicles*, 47–48; "1936 Mal Hallett: In The Chapel In The Moonlight (Jerry Perkins & chorus, vocal)," uploaded by the78profto YouTube, May 3, 2019, accessed June 11, 2022. https://www.youtube.com/watch?v=qdy3WUDdo4E/.
53. "Teddy Grace w/ Mal Hallett & His Orchestra," uploaded by derekbjenkins to YouTube, Oct 3, 2007, accessed June 11, 2022, https://www.youtube.com/watch?v=ehqGJ3l3ra4/.
54. "Malcolm Gray 'Mal' Hallett," *Boston Jazz Scene*.
55. David Suisman, "Co-Workers in the Kingdom of Culture," *Journal of American Music* (March 2004): 1296.

CHAPTER 6

1. Jacqui Malone, *Steppin' on the Blues*, 79, 83; Gregory Lamb, "Drama Unfolds," *Christian Science Monitor* (March 7, 2003).

2. "Castle Square Theater" entry in Cinema Treasures, accessed May 30, 2021, http://cinematreasures.org/theaters/15773; "Shuffle Along," advertisement in the *Boston Guardian*, March 31, 1923.
3. Tim Brooks, *Lost Sounds*, 36.
4. Henry Louis Gates Jr. and Evelyn Brooks Higginbotham, eds., "Blake, Eubie" in *Harlem Renaissance Lives* (NY: Oxford University Press, 2009), 55–57; Brooks, *Lost Sounds*, 52–53.
5. "Eubie Blake and his 'Shuffle Along' Orchestra—Bandana Days (1921)," uploaded to YouTube by ASACurator, January 2021, accessed June 11, 2022, https://www.youtube.com/watch?v=SmsTrhxQTGI/.
6. "Tremont Theater," African American Trail Project, Tufts University, accessed July 2, 2021, https://africanamericantrailproject.tufts.edu/.
7. "In Bamville," advertisement in the *Boston Guardian*, July 13, 1924.
8. "Gaiety Theater Study," Boston Landmarks Commission, 2003.
9. Gates and Higginbotham, "Mack, Cecil" in *Harlem Renaissance Lives*, 334–35.
10. "Runnin' Wild," advertisement in the *Boston Guardian*, April 28, 1923.
11. Gates and Higginbotham, "Hall, Adelaide," in *Harlem Renaissance Lives*, 233; "Notes About the Players," *Boston Globe*, September 2, 1923 (via ProQuest archive).
12. "History of Symphony Hall" entry in "History/Archives," accessed May 30, 2021, https://www.bso.org/.
13. Paul Whiteman, "In Defense of Jazz," *New York Times*, March 13, 1927 (via ProQuest archive).
14. Whiteman, "In Defense of Jazz."
15. "German Coming to Seek," *New York Times*, April 8, 1927 (via ProQuest archive).
16. Whiteman, "In Defense of Jazz"; "German Coming to Seek," *New York Times*.
17. "Jazz is Not Music," *New York Times*, June 12, 1927 (via ProQuest archive).
18. Stephen Somervell, "Public Never Wrong," *Boston Globe*, May 5, 1927 (via ProQuest archive).
19. Dean Earl interview with Boston Musicians Union, February 1999.
20. "The King of Jazz is Coming," *Boston Guardian*, July 28, 1923; Victor Okocha, "W. C. Handy (1873–1958)," *Blackpast*, March 19, 2007, accessed July 2, 2021, https://www.blackpast.org/african-american-history/handy-w-c-1873-1958/.
21. "Jan. 5, 1923 recording 'Aunt Hagar's Blues' W C Handy's Orchestra," uploaded to YouTube by Remember Our Music, January 5, 2017, accessed June 11, 2022, https://www.youtube.com/watch?v=AiAV70gRujw/.
22. "Music Notes and Comment," *Boston Globe*, December 9, 1928 (via ProQuest archive).

23. "Music Notes and Comment," *Boston Globe*.
24. "George Gershwin at Symphony Hall," *Boston Globe*, January 17, 1927 (via ProQuest archive).
25. "George Gershwin at Symphony Hall," *Boston Globe*.
26. "George Gershwin at Symphony Hall," *Boston Globe*.
27. Whiteman, "In Defense of Jazz."
28. Whiteman, "In Defense of Jazz."
29. "Whiteman's Band at Symphony Hall," *Boston Globe*, December 10, 1928 (via ProQuest archive).
30. Robert Hayden, "Not to Be Forgotten," liner notes to *The Art of Roland Hayes* (Smithsonian Collection, 1990).
31. Hayden, "Not to Be Forgotten."
32. Hayden, "Not to Be Forgotten"; "Broome Specialty Phonograph Records," *78RPM Club*, accessed July 2, 2021, https://78rpm.club/record-labels/broome-special-phonograph-records/.
33. Hayden, "Not to Be Forgotten."
34. "The Art of Roland Hayes," with Reginald Boardman (piano), Smithsonian Collection of Recordings B000017SF, 2007, compact disc; "American Tenor Roland Hayes: Two Songs (1942)," uploaded to YouTube by CurzonRoad, July 30, 2013, accessed July 2, 2021, https://www.youtube.com/watch?v=qWqkb4alznl/.
35. "Music Notes and Comment," *Boston Globe*.

CHAPTER 7

1. Con Chapman, *Rabbit's Blues*, 13; "Black and White Revue," public domain posters available at https://picryl.com/.
2. Burton Peretti, *Creation of Jazz*, 178–83.
3. Lars Bjorn, *Before Motown*, 39–44; Richard Gazarik and Karen Anthony Cole, *A History of Pittsburgh Jazz*, 75.
4. Sam Charters, *Jazz: A History of the New York Scene*, 182.
5. Teddy Wilson, *Teddy Wilson Talks Jazz*, 44.
6. Wilson, *Teddy Wilson Talks Jazz*, 45.
7. Max Kaminsky, *Jazz Band* (Da Capo Press, 1963), 49; Dean Earl, interviewed February 12, 1999, Boston Musicians Association oral history transcript; Eric Jackson, "Riff Tide," *Boston Magazine*, May 15, 2006, https://www.bostonmagazine.com/2006/05/15/riff-tide/.
8. Kaminsky, *Jazz Band*, 2–3.

9. Kaminsky, *Jazz Band*, 2, 10.
10. Kaminsky, *Jazz Band*, 2.
11. Don DeMichael, "Interview with Johnny Hodges and Harry Carney," *Downbeat* (June 1962).
12. DeMichael, "Interview with Johnny Hodges and Harry Carney."
13. Kaminsky, *Jazz Band*, 10–12; Brian Rust, *The American Dance Band Discography, 1917–1942* (New York: Arlington House Publishers), 192.
14. Kaminsky, *Jazz Band*, 7–9, 14.
15. Kaminsky, *Jazz Band*, 49; Dean Earl interview; Eric Jackson, "Riff Tide."
16. Peretti, *Creation of Jazz*, 85–90.
17. Lars Bjorn, *Before Motown*, 28; Sam Charters, *Jazz: A History of the New York Scene*, 153.
18. Lars Bjorn, *Before Motown*, 28.
19. Sam Charters, *Jazz*, 146; "Jean Goldkette Orchestra," *Discography of American Historical Recordings*, UC Santa Barbara library, accessed July 3, 2021, https://adp.library.ucsb.edu/index.php/mastertalent/detail/323277/Jean_Goldkette_Orchestra/.
20. Scott Yanow, "Jean Goldkette—Artist Biography," *Allmusic.com*, accessed July 3, 2021, https://www.allmusic.com/artist/jean-goldkette-mn0000224739/biography/.
21. Kaminsky, *Jazz Band*, 13–15.
22. Kaminsky, *Jazz Band*, 13–15.
23. Kaminsky, *Jazz Band*, 13–15; David Hudson, Marvin Bergman, and Loren Horten, eds., s.v. "Beiderbecke, Leon Bismarck 'Bix,'" *Biographical Dictionary of Iowa* (University of Iowa Press Digital Editions), accessed 3 July 2021, http://uipress.lib.uiowa.edu/bdi/DetailsPage.aspx?id=22/.
24. Kaminsky, *Jazz Band*, 18; "Nobody's Sweetheart—Eddie Condon's Chicagoans," uploaded to YouTube by Godfrey Daniels, April 26, 2014, accessed June 11, 2022, https://www.youtube.com/watch?v=DALWy2H5VTg.
25. Al Vega, interview for Berklee Oral History Project, May 19, 2005; Jeff Tamarkin, "Boston Pianist Al Vega," *Jazztimes*, April 25, 2019.
26. Al Vega interview, Berklee Oral History Project.
27. Preston Sandiford, "Through the Years with Preston Sandiford," interview by Dan Kochakian, *Whiskey, Women and . . .* (December 1985).
28. "Sacco and Vanzetti: Justice on Trial." Commonwealth of Massachusetts website, accessed June 6, 2022, https://www.mass.gov/info-details/sacco-vanzetti-justice-on-trial.
29. "Sacco and Vanzetti: Justice on Trial."
30. Anna Celenza, "Our jazz is culturally black, but its global dissemination owes

a lot to Italians," *The Lens*, May 17, 2017, accessed June 6, 2022, https://thelensnola.org/2017/05/01/our-jazz-is-culturally-black-but-its-global-dissemination-owes-a-lot-to-italians/.

31. NECA 18.20, "Nuncio 'Toots' Mondello Papers," New England Conservatory Archives, accessed July 3, 2021, https://necmusic.edu/archives/nuncio-toots-mondello/.
32. "Chick Corea, Jazz Keyboardist born," accessed June 12, 2022, https://aaregistry.org/story/chick-corea-jazz-keybordist-born/.
33. "CV Black History Makers – Paul Gonsalves (1920–1974)," The Creola Genealogist, March 4, 2018, accessed June 13, 2022, https://thecreolagenealogist.com/2018/03/04/cv-black-history-makers-paul-gonsalves-1920-1974/.
34. Haiming Liu, "Chop Suey as Imagined Authentic Chinese Food," *Journal of TransAtlantic American Studies* (February 2009); Gabriel Chin and John Ormonde, "The 'War' Against Chinese Restaurants," *Regulation* (Summer 2017), 32–38.
35. Liu, "Chop Suey."
36. Dean Earl interview.
37. Liu, "Chop Suey."
38. Chin and Ormonde, "The 'War' Against Chinese Restaurants."
39. Chin and Ormonde, "The 'War' Against Chinese Restaurants."
40. Richard Auffrey, "The First Restaurants in Boston's Chinatown: The Tale of Ruby Foo," *Passionate Foodie*, March 17, 2020, accessed July 3, 2021, https://passionatefoodie.blogspot.com/2020/03/the-first-restaurants-in-bostons_17.html/.
41. "Chinese" in GlobalBoston, Department of History, Boston College, accessed July 5, 2021, https://globalboston.bc.edu/index.php/home/ethnic-groups/chinese/.
42. Wing-Kai To, "Restoring Chinese Heritage in Boston's History," *Bridgewater Review* (December 2008), 3–5; Auffrey, "The First Restaurants in Boston's Chinatown."
43. To, "Restoring Chinese Heritage in Boston's History"; Auffrey, "The First Restaurants in Boston's Chinatown."

CHAPTER 8

1. J. A. Rogers, "Jazz at Home," in Alain Locke, ed., *The New Negro*, 665–67; Jacqui Malone, *Steppin' on the Blues*, 27; Abigail Feely, "Dance, Performance" in James Ciment, ed., *Encyclopedia of the Jazz Age* (M. E. Sharpe Inc.), 158–59;

Ralph Ellison, "Juneteenth," *Quarterly Review of Literature* 13, no. 3–4 (1965): 274–76.

2. Sam Charters, *Jazz: A History of the New York Scene*, 32.
3. Sam Charters, *Jazz, 33;* Lars Bjorn, Before Motown: A History of Jazz in Detroit, 7–8.
4. Maud Cuney Hare, *Negro Music*, 135–36.
5. Hare, *Negro Music*, 135–36.
6. Feely, "Dance, Performance;" "A 1920s Charleston," uploaded to YouTube by Vintage Swing Dance, April 19, 2016, accessed June 11, 2022, https://www.youtube.com/watch?v=2npKAlQnDJY/.
7. Richard Powers, "Dances of the Jazz Age," webpage for class in Social Dance at Stanford University, accessed May 31, 2021, https://socialdance.stanford.edu/Syllabi/jazz_age.htm; "No Jazz Dances at Saugus High Prom," *Boston Globe*, February 11, 1922 (via ProQuest archive).
8. Richard Gazarik and Karen Anthony Cole, *A History of Pittsburgh Jazz*, 77–78.
9. "Pastor Jolts the Jazz Generation," *Boston Daily Globe*, May 2, 1922 (via ProQuest archive).
10. "Back to the Polka and Schottische," *Boston Daily Globe*, December 24, 1922; "Folk Dances Rout Jazz and Pa and Ma are Dancing Again," *Boston Daily Globe*, November 20, 1929 (via ProQuest archive).
11. Stroller, "When Grandma Danced," *Boston Daily Globe*, December 17, 1925 (via ProQuest archive).
12. Corinne Danforth, "How Ford Found a Dancing Master in Hudson to Conduct Revival," *Boston Daily Globe*, December 20, 1925 (via ProQuest archive).
13. "Leaping of Dancers Caused the Collapse, View of Survivor," *Boston Daily Globe*, July 6, 1925; Jerome Sullivan, "Late-Night Merrymaking Ended in Tragedy 50 Years Ago Today," *Boston Globe*, July 4, 1975 (via ProQuest archive).
14. Uncle Dudley, "Rhythmic Response," *Boston Daily Globe*, August 21, 1925 (via ProQuest archive).
15. "In the News: Mildred Davenport 'a real joy,'" *Bay State Banner*, July 5, 1973 (via ProQuest archive).
16. "Guide to Mildred Davenport Dance Programs," Special Collections and Archives, UCI Libraries (University of California Irvine); "In the News: Mildred Davenport 'a real joy,'" *Bay State Banner*, July 5, 1973 (via ProQuest archive); "Mildred Davenport, 89; was dancer and member of antibias agency," *Boston Globe*, October 17, 1990 (via ProQuest archive).
17. "Mildred Davenport Dance Programs," UCI Libraries; "Mildred Davenport 'a real joy,'" *Bay State Banner*; "Mildred Davenport, 89," *Boston Globe*.

18. Malone, *Steppin' on the Blues*, 28; Kay Bourne, "Stanley E. Brown," *Bay State Banner*, September 15, 1977.
19. Margo Miller, "A Look Back, Forward: Jazz Dancing's Great Days," *Boston Globe*, July 20, 1969; Bourne, "Stanley E. Brown."
20. Preston Sandiford, "Through the Years with Preston Sandiford," interview by Dan Kochakian, *Whiskey, Women and . . .* (December 1985).
21. Dean Earl, interviewed February 12, 1999, Boston Musicians Association oral history transcript.
22. Miller, "A Look Back, Forward"; Bourne, "Stanley E. Brown."
23. "The Shepard Company" [landmarks study], *Rhode Island Historical Preservation Commission*, 1975, www.preservation.ri.gov/.
24. "The Shepard Company" [landmarks study].
25. Richard Vacca, "Perley Breed's Department Store Dance Band," *Troy Street Observer*, April 30, 2013, accessed July 5, 2021, https://www.richardvacca.com/on-april-25-1925/; Lloyd Greene, "Radio Broadcasts: Radio Program Schedule for Today," *Boston Daily Globe*, October 19, 1927 (via ProQuest Archive).
26. "Cocoanut Grove to Open Thursday," *Boston Daily Globe*, October 27, 1927 (via ProQuest archive).
27. "Cocoanut Grove to Open Thursday," *Boston Daily Globe*.
28. "New Supper Club Will Open Tonight," *Boston Daily Globe*, September 17, 1931 (via ProQuest archive).
29. "New Supper Club Will Open Tonight," *Boston Daily Globe*.
30. "Aimee Goes to Night Clubs After Service," *Boston Daily Globe*, October 13, 1931 (via ProQuest archive).
31. "Celebrators Pack Hotels, Theatres," *Boston Daily Globe*, November 20, 1927; "Hotels Enjoy Best Thanksgiving Day: Biggest Dinner Patronage Ever," *Boston Daily Globe*, November 25, 1927 (via ProQuest archive).
32. "'Knock out' and 'Sellout' for Hotels in Boston," *Boston Daily Globe*, January 1, 1929 (via ProQuest archive).
33. "New Egyptian Room Opens at Brunswick," *Boston Daily Globe*, September 16, 1927; advertisement for Egyptian Room, *Boston Daily Globe*, September 9, 1926.
34. Richard Vacca, *Boston Jazz Chronicles*, 39; Max Kaminsky, *Life in Jazz*, 64–65.
35. Kaminsky, *Life in Jazz*, 64–65.
36. "Leo Reisman RHYTHMS," uploaded to YouTube by Ugaccio, November 12, 2013, accessed June 11, 2022, https://www.youtube.com/watch?v=6GGA9uK93m8/.
37. "Governor at Dedication of Herald Station WBZ," *Boston Daily Globe*, February 26, 1924 (via ProQuest archive); Kaminsky, *Life in Jazz*, 64–65.

CHAPTER 9

1. Sam Charters, *Jazz: A History of the New York Scene*, 240.
2. Court Carney, *Cuttin' Up*, 93; Lars Bjorn, *Before Motown*, 37.
3. Teddy Wilson, *Teddy Wilson Talks Jazz*, 51.
4. Carney, *Cuttin' Up*, 139–40.
5. Burton Peretti, *Creation of Jazz*, 189.
6. "Paul Whiteman—Mississippi Mud 1928 Bix Beiderbecke (Bing Crosby & Irene Taylor)," uploaded to YouTube by Warholsoup 100, February 23, 2020, accessed June 11, 2022, https://www.youtube.com/watch?v=_NoQaQ5aP5M/.
7. Edward "Duke" Ellington, *Music Is My Mistress*, 103.
8. Paul Whiteman, "In Defense of Jazz," *New York Times*, March 13, 1927 (via ProQuest archive).
9. Whiteman, "In Defense of Jazz."
10. Max Kaminsky, *A Life in Jazz*, 64.
11. "Paul Whiteman at the Metropolitan," *Boston Daily Globe*, September 26, 1927 (via ProQuest archive).
12. Ellington, *Music Is My Mistress*," 98–99; "Harry Carney Talks to Valerie Wilmer," *Ellingtonia*, April 1964, http://www.ellingtonia.com/articles/jazz-monthly/harry-carney-talks-to-valer.html/; Carney, *Cuttin' Up*, 94–95.
13. Tom Reney, "Duke Ellington's Boston," New England Public Radio, April 29, 2014, accessed July 6, 2021, https://digital.nepr.net/music/2014/04/29/duke-ellingtons-boston/.
14. "Harry Carney Talks to Valerie Wilmer," *Ellingtonia*.
15. DeMichael, "Interview with Johnny Hodges and Harry Carney."
16. "Harry Carney Talks to Valerie Wilmer," *Ellingtonia*; DeMichael, "Interview with Johnny Hodges and Harry Carney."
17. Ellington, *Music Is My Mistress*, 98–99.
18. "Harry Carney Talks to Valerie Wilmer," *Ellingtonia*.
19. Reney, "Duke Ellington's Boston."
20. "'Once a Sinner' at Metropolitan/Duke Ellington's Cotton Club Orchestra on Bill," *Boston Daily Globe*, February 6, 1931 (via ProQuest archive).
21. "Boston Turns Out to Greet Duke, Charlie," *Chicago Defender*, February 13, 1931 (via ProQuest archive).
22. "Metropolitan—'Girls About Town,'" *Boston Daily Globe*, November 7, 1931 (via ProQuest archive).
23. "Flask-Toting Football Rooters Denounced at Dartmouth Dinner," Boston Daily Globe, January 31, 1926 (via ProQuest archive).
24. "Yale Crowds Hold Carnival: Thousands Celebrate in Biggest Night Ever,"

Boston Daily Globe, November 25, 1923 (via ProQuest archive); Lars Bjorn, Before Motown, 25–26.

25. "Rival Dances Held Without Outbreaks/Duke Ellington and Band Escorted by Police," *Boston Daily Globe*, November 7, 1931 (via ProQuest archive).
26. "Rival Dances Held Without Outbreaks," *Boston Daily Globe*.
27. "Rival Dances Held Without Outbreaks," *Boston Daily Globe*.
28. "Rival Dances Held Without Outbreaks," *Boston Daily Globe*.
29. "From the Great Migration to Boston's Charlestown Navy Yard," Boston National Park Service, accessed June 6, 2022, https://www.nps.gov/articles/great-migration-to-charlestown-navy-yard.htm.
30. Con Chapman, *Rabbit's Blues*, 18–19.
31. Chapman, *Rabbit's Blues*, 18.
32. DeMichael, "Interview with Johnny Hodges and Harry Carney."
33. Max Kaminsky, *Jazz Band* (Da Capo Press, 1963), 26.
34. "George Tynes" under "History—Major Contributors" of *Boston Jazz Scene*, https://bostonjazzscene.blogspot.com/.
35. "Eddie Deas," *Discography of American Historical Recordings*, UC Santa Barbara library, accessed July 6, 2021, https://adp.library.ucsb.edu/index.php/mastertalent/detail/101111/Deas_Eddie/; "Jes Shufflin' by Eddie Deas and His Boston Brownies 1932 Victor," uploaded to YouTube by SMARBA100, August 25, 2019, accessed June 11, 2022, https://www.youtube.com/watch?v=E-tDNpqsXpg/.
36. Preston Sandiford, "Through the Years with Preston Sandiford," interview by Dan Kochakian, *Whiskey, Women and . . .* (December 1985).
37. "George Latimer" under Stu Vandermark. "History—Major Contributors" of *Boston Jazz Scene*, https://bostonjazzscene.blogspot.com/.
38. Carney, "Cuttin' Up," 139; Stephanie Schorow, *Drinking Boston: A History of the City and its Spirits*, 132–35; Dean Earl, interviewed February 12, 1999, Boston Musicians Association oral history transcript.

CODA

1. "Boston Bounce—the Sabby Lewis Orchestra and Sextet," Phoenix Jazz Records, 1975; Richard Vacca, *Boston Jazz Chronicles*, 65–67; "Tasker Crosson" under "History—Major Contributors" of *Boston Jazz Scene*, https://bostonjazzscene.blogspot.com (accessed June 24, 2021).
2. Vacca, *Boston Jazz Chronicles*, 65–66.
3. "Sabby Lewis Orchestra—Bottoms Up," uploaded to YouTube by Richard Vacca, December 17, 2013, accessed June 11, 2022. https://www.youtube.com/watch?v=btB1zQlgqyk/.

4. Vacca, *Boston Jazz Chronicles*, 179–86.
5. Bo White, "Sonny Stitt is the Lone Wolf," January 27, 2013, accessed July 7, 2021, https://whitesbarnews.blogspot.com/2013/01/sonny-stitt-is-lone-wolf-saginaw-jazz.html/; Gordon Jack, "Sonny Stitt—The Early Years, 1941-1952," June 9, 2020, accessed July 7, 2021, https://jazzprofiles.blogspot.com/2020/06/sonny-stitt-early-years-1941-1952-by.html/; Tim Brooks, *Lost Sounds* [liner notes]; "Broome Specialty Phonograph Records," *78RPM Club*, https://78rpm.club/record-labels/broome-special-phonograph-records/.
6. White, "Sonny Stitt"; Jack, "Sonny Stitt"; Vacca, *Boston Jazz Chronicles*, 71.
7. Jack, "Sonny Stitt"; Sonny Stitt Quartet, *In Boston '54 Live at the Hi-Hat*, recorded February 11, 1954, Fresh Sound Records FSCD 1002, released 1991, CD, https://www.discogs.com/Sonny-Stitt-Quartet-In-Boston-54-Live-at-the-Hi-Hat/release/10908615/.
8. "Sonny Stitt—Jazz at the Hi-Hat Volume 1," uploaded to YouTube by Stitt-MoSh!t, August 17, 2020, accessed July 7, 2021, https://www.youtube.com/watch?v=SPfCdbGNiHk/.
9. Vacca, *Boston Jazz Chronicles*, 242–43.
10. Richard Vacca, "Fat Man Robinson: There's Life Here!," November 18, 2020, https://www.richardvacca.com/fat-man-robinson-theres-life-here/.
11. "My Bucket's Got a Hole in It—Fat Man Robinson Quintet," uploaded to YouTube by Richard Vacca, November 17, 2020, accessed June 11, 2022, https://www.youtube.com/watch?v=okWxdqzWBac/.
12. Mabel Simms Robinson, interviewed March 30, 1999, Boston Musicians Association oral history transcript.
13. Vacca, *Boston Jazz Chronicles*, 147.
14. Robert Hayden, *African-Americans in Boston: More than 350 Years* (Boston Public Library: 1991), 26; Mae Arnette, interview for Berklee College oral history project, February 9, 2007.
15. Mae Arnette, interview for Berklee College oral history project, February 9, 2007.
16. Guscott, Lower Roxbury Black History Project.
17. Guscott, Lower Roxbury Black History Project.
18. Vacca, *Boston Jazz Chronicles*, 149–55.
19. Nat Hentoff, *Boston Boy*, 162.
20. Hentoff, *Boston Boy*, 132.
21. Hentoff, *Boston Boy*, 148.
22. Hentoff, *Boston Boy*, 136.
23. Teddy Wilson, *Teddy Wilson Talks Jazz*, 75–78; Liner notes to *The Frankie Newton Collection 1929–1946*, Acrobat Licensing LTD, released 2019, 3-CD box set.

24. Thomas Cunniffe, "Frankie Newton: The Forgotten Trumpeter" (parts I and II), March 9, 2019, https://jazzhistoryonline.com/frankie-newton-1a/; Hentoff, *Boston Boy*, 136.
25. George Wein, *Myself Among Others*, 82.
26. Wein, *Myself Among Others*, 88–89.
27. Dean Anderson, "Alan Dawson," entry in Drummerworld.com, accessed June 10, 2022, https://www.drummerworld.com/drummers/Alan_Dawson.html; Con Chapman, "Alan Dawson," entry in Music Museum of New England, accessed June 10, 2022, https://www.mmone.org/alan-dawson/; "George Alan Dawson," BerkleePress.com, accessed June 10, 2022, https://berkleepress.com/berklee-authors/alan-dawson/.
28. Dean Anderson, "Alan Dawson," Drummerworld.com.
29. "Anthony Williams," entry in MusicianGuide.com, accessed June 11, 2022, https://musicianguide.com/biographies/1608001719/Tony-Williams.html.
30. Rick Mattingly, "Tony Williams," PercussiveArtsSociety.org, accessed June 11, 2022, https://www.pas.org/about/hall-of-fame/alan-dawson.
31. Rick Mattingly, "Tony Williams."
32. Rick Mattingly, "Tony Williams."
33. Malcolm X, *Autobiography of Malcolm X*, 51–52.
34. Malcolm X, *Autobiography*, 51–53.
35. Malcolm X, *By Any Means Necessary (Speeches and Writings)*, 117; "The Malcolm X—Ella Little-Collins House," Boston Landmarks Commission, August 21, 1998; Tobias Ehrenbold, et al., "Malcolm X in the Norfolk Debating Society," States of Incarceration, accessed June 11, 2022, https://statesofincarceration.org/story/malcolm-x-norfolk-debating-society.

Bibliography

ORAL HISTORY COLLECTIONS AND BOSTON LANDMARKS REPORTS

The memories of longtime residents and personalities have been preserved in the oral history archives of the Northeastern University Library's Lower Roxbury Black History Project, the University of Massachusetts–Boston's Archives & Special Collections in the Joseph P. Healey Library, the Berklee College of Music's Oral History Project, and the Boston Musicians Union's Oral History Project. Finally, the Landmarks Commission of the City of Boston maintains an archive of reports on historic buildings, places, and neighborhoods.

"A. Philip Randolph and Boston's African American Railroad Worker: A Public History Commemoration." Richard C. Hayden and James R. Green. Massachusetts Bay Transportation Authority. February 24, 1991.

"Berklee Oral History Project." Stan Getz Library, Berklee College of Music. Interviews conducted with musicians active in the Boston jazz scene and associated with the college between 1998 and 2005.

Boston Musicians' Union. "The Oral History Project." Archive of about fifty musicians active in the early years of the union. Conducted in 2000.

"Connolly's Bar 1184 Tremont Street, Roxbury." Boston Landmarks Commission, Environment Department, City of Boston. July 11, 1997.

"Frederick Douglass Square Historic District." National Register of Historic Places, National Park Service, US Department of the Interior. August 27, 1996.

"Gaiety Theater Study Report." Boston Landmarks Commission, Environment Department, City of Boston. July 16, 2015.

"Lower Roxbury Black History Project." Snell Library, Northeastern University, Boston, MA. Archive of forty-seven interviews conducted with longtime residents, made available online in 2017.

"Robert C. Hayden interviews with Boston African American railroad workers, 1977–1991." University Archives & Special Collections, Joseph P. Healey Library, University of Massachusetts–Boston. Collection of interviews conducted for MBTA history and donated by James R. Green.
"The Malcolm X–Ella Little-Collins House." Boston Landmarks Commission, Environment Department, City of Boston. August 21, 1998.

HISTORICAL NEWSPAPER COLLECTIONS

The *Guardian* of Boston Collection in the Howard Gotlieb Archival Research Center at Boston University consists of printed materials and microfilm copies of the newspaper. Articles cited in the text are listed below in chronological order.

Harry Hicks Jazz Band concert announcement. *Boston Guardian*, April 12, 1919, p. 3.
Fraternal order concert announcement. *Boston Guardian*, April 12, 1919, p. 8.
Harry Hicks Jazz Band concert announcement. *Boston Guardian*, May 16, 1919, p. 8.
Ladies auxiliary and fraternal concert announcements. *Boston Guardian*, May 16, 1919, p. 8.
"Colored American Made Lasting Record," *Boston Guardian*, May 16, 1919.
Women's club concert announcement. *Boston Guardian*, June 14, 1919, p. 8.
Musicians Union concert announcement. *Boston Guardian*, January 10, 1920, p. 8.
Ad for Mary E. Moore Co. *Boston Guardian*, January 10, 1920, p. 8.
Ad for Star Lunch. *Boston Guardian*, January 10, 1920, p. 5.
Ad for Douglass Square barber. *Boston Guardian*, January 10, 1920, p. 5.
Ad for Farm Outlet. *Boston Guardian*, January 10, 1920, p. 5.
Ad for Hotel Melbourne. *Boston Guardian*, January 24, 1920, p. 7.
Ads for David Crawford, attorney, and John O'Brien, undertaker. *Boston Guardian*, January 24, 1920, p. 7.
Ad for Modern Hair. *Boston Guardian*, January 24, 1920, p. 7.
Ad for Bay State Pharmacy. *Boston Guardian*, March 31, 1923, p. 1.
Fraternal order concert announcement. *Boston Guardian*, March 31, 1923, p. 8.
Ad for Gamer's Music. *Boston Guardian*, April 7, 1923, p. 7.
Boston Tigers concert announcement, *Boston Guardian*, April 7, 1923, p. 8.
Editorial. *Boston Guardian*, July 28, 1923.
"Shuffle Along" advertisement in *Boston Guardian*, March 31, 1923 p. 5.
"Runnin' Wild" advertisement in *Boston Guardian*, April 28, 1923, p. 2.

"The King of Jazz is Coming," *Boston Guardian*, July 28, 1923.

"In Bamville" advertisement in *Boston Guardian*, July 13, 1924, p. 2.

The ProQuest Historical Newspaper database of the Iwasaki Library of Emerson College was a valuable resource for discovering articles in the *Boston Daily Globe*, *New York Times*, and other assorted newspapers. The *Boston Daily Globe* articles that were contemporary to the interwar years and cited in the text are listed below in chronological order.

"Attractions at the Theatres." *Boston Daily Globe*, September 13, 1908, p. 39.

"Would Name Square After Douglass." *Boston Daily Globe*, January 30, 1917, p. 11.

"Boston Honors Douglass Today." *Boston Daily Globe*, February 14, 1917, p. 14.

"Concerts by the Famous 369th U.S. Infantry Band," under "Attractions at the Theatres." Boston Daily *Globe*, March 23, 1919, p. 62.

"Boston Opera House." *Boston Daily Globe*, March 27, 1919, p. 7.

"All Set for the Great Parade." *Boston Daily Globe*, April 25, 1919, p. 1.

"How Yankee 26th Fought Its Way to Fame." *Boston Daily Globe*, April 25, 1919, p. 13.

"J.R. Europe, Band Leader, Murdered." *Boston Daily Globe*, May 10, 1919, p. 1.

"Welcome I.B.P.O.E in Faneuil Hall." *Boston Daily Globe*, August 23, 1921, p. 7.

"No Jazz Dances at Saugus High Prom." *Boston Daily Globe*, February 11, 1922, p. 7.

"Pastor Jolts the Jazz Generation." *Boston Daily Globe*, May 2, 1922, p. 20.

"Back to the Polka and Schottische." *Boston Daily Globe*, December 24, 1922, p. 16.

"Colored Knights of Pythias Parade." *Boston Daily Globe*, May 21, 1923, p. 6.

"Music Notes and Comment." *Boston Daily Globe*, November 4, 1923, p. 68.

"Yale Crowds Hold Carnival: Thousands Celebrate in Biggest Night Ever." *Boston Daily Globe*, November 25, 1923, p. 22.

"Notes About the Players." *Boston Daily Globe*, September 2, 1923, p. 52.

"Governor at Dedication of Herald Station WBZ." *Boston Daily Globe*, February 26, 1924, p. 15.

"Music and Musicians: Musicians' Views on Jazz." *Boston Daily Globe*, August 24, 1924, p. 58.

"Leaping of Dancers Caused the Collapse, View of Survivor." *Boston Daily Globe*, July 6, 1925, p. 1.

Uncle Dudley. "Rhythmic Response." *Boston Daily Globe*, August 21, 1925, p. 14.

Stroller. "When Grandma Danced." *Boston Daily Globe*, December 17, 1925, p. 18.

Danforth, Corinne. "How Ford Found a Dancing Master in Hudson to Conduct Revival." *Boston Daily Globe*, December 20, 1925, p. B1.

Advertisement for Egyptian Room. *Boston Daily Globe*, September 9, 1926, p. A1.

"George Gershwin at Symphony Hall." *Boston Daily Globe*, January 17, 1927, p. 7.
Whiteman, Paul. "In Defense of Jazz." *New York Times*, March 13, 1927, p. SM4.
"German Coming to Seek." *New York Times*, April 8, 1927, p. 4.
Somervell, Stephen. "Public Never Wrong." *Boston Daily Globe*, May 5, 1927, p. 60.
"Jazz is Not Music." *New York Times*, June 12, 1927, p. 19.
"New Egyptian Room Opens at Brunswick." *Boston Daily Globe*, September 16, 1927, p. 20.
"Paul Whiteman at the Metropolitan." *Boston Daily Globe*, September 26, 1927, p. 5.
Greene, Lloyd. "Radio Broadcasts: Radio Program Schedule for Today." *Boston Daily Globe,* Oct. 19, 1927; p. 26.
"Cocoanut Grove to Open Thursday." *Boston Daily Globe*, October 27, 1927, p. 10.
"Celebrators Pack Hotels, Theatres." *Boston Daily Globe*, November 20, 1927, p. A32.
"Hotels Enjoy Best Thanksgiving Day: Biggest Dinner Patronage Ever." *Boston Daily Globe*, November 25, 1927, p. 17.
"Music Notes and Comment." *Boston Daily Globe*, December 9, 1928, p. A51.
"Whiteman's Band at Symphony Hall." *Boston Daily Globe*, December 10, 1928, p. 5.
"'Knock out' and 'Sellout' for Hotels in Boston." *Boston Daily Globe*, January 1, 1929, p. 24.
"Folk Dances Rout Jazz and Pa and Ma Are Dancing Again." *Boston Daily Globe*, November 20, 1929, p. 28.
"'Once a Sinner' at Metropolitan/Duke Ellington's Cotton Club Orchestra on Bill." *Boston Daily Globe*, February 6, 1931, p. 21.
"Boston Turns Out to Greet Duke, Charlie." *Chicago Defender*, February 13, 1931, p. 6.
"New Supper Club Will Open Tonight." *Boston Daily Globe*, September 17, 1931, p. 10.
"Aimee Goes to Night Clubs After Service." *Boston Daily Globe*, October 13, 1931, p. 1.
"Metropolitan—'Girls About Town.'" *Boston Daily Globe*, November 7, 1931, p. 4.
"Rival Dances Held Without Outbreaks/Duke Ellington and Band Escorted by Police." *Boston Daily Globe*, November 7, 1931, p. 15.

Finally, the Boston Public Library has archived historic copies of the *Boston Post* on microfilm. The Arthur Schomburg Center for Research in Black Culture at the New York Public Library houses a collection of the *New York Age*. A few historical articles were discovered through searches on Google. Two articles contemporary to the interwar years and cited in the text are listed in chronological order.

"Jim Europe Wears Jazz Garb." *New York Sun*, May 14 1919, p. 18.
"Drummer Who Killed Europe." *Baltimore Afro-American*, April 9, 1927.

BOOKS AND ARTICLES

Alexander, Caroline. "The Shock of War." *Smithsonian Magazine* (September 2010). https://www.smithsonianmag.com/history/the-shock-of-war-55376701/.

Anderson, Dean. "Alan Dawson." Drummerworld.com, accessed June 10, 2022, https://www.drummerworld.com/drummers/Alan_Dawson.html.

Ater, Renee. *Remaking Race and History: The Sculpture of Meta Warrick Fuller*. Berkeley and Los Angeles: University of California Press, 2011.

Auffrey, Richard. "The First Restaurants in Boston's Chinatown: The Tale of Ruby Foo." *Passionate Foodie*. March 17, 2020. Accessed July 3, 2021. https://passionatefoodie.blogspot.com/2020/03/the-first-restaurants-in-bostons_17.html/.

"Automatic Radio Mfg. Co." Accessed July 11, 2021. https://www.radiomuseum.org/dsp_hersteller_detail.cfm?company_id=1932/.

Badger, Reid. *A Life in Ragtime: A Biography of James Reese Europe*. Oxford: Oxford University Press, 1995.

Bahne, Charles. *Chronicles of Old Boston: Exploring New England's Historic Capital*. New York: Museyon Inc., 2012.

Bailey, Ronald, Diane Turner, and Robert Hayden. *Lower Roxbury: A Community of Treasures in the City of Boston*. Roxbury: The Lower Roxbury Community Corporation and the Afro Scholar Press, 1993.

Bayne, Bijan C. "Black baseball in Boston: recovering a lost legacy." *Bay State Banner*, April 27, 2006. Accessed June 3, 2022. http://www.baystate-banner.com/archives/stories/2006/04/042706-03.htm

Benjamin, Tritobia Hayes. *The Life and Art of Lois Mailou Jones*. San Francisco: Pomegranate Artbooks, 1994.

Bjerstedt, Sven. "Stealing Knowledge in a Landscape of Learning: Conceptualizations of Jazz Education." *British Journal of Music Education* 33, no. 3 (November 2016). Accessed June 12, 2022. https://www.cambridge.org/core/journals/british-journal-of-music-education/article/stealing-knowledge-in-a-landscape-of-learning-conceptualizations-of-jazz-education/.

Bjorn, Lars with Jim Gallert. *Before Motown: A History of Jazz in Detroit, 1920–1960*. Ann Arbor: The University of Michigan Press, 2001.

"Black and White Revue." Public domain posters available at https://picryl.com. Accessed May 2021.

Bourne, Kay. "Stanley E. Brown." *Bay State Banner*, September 15, 1977.
Boston, MA City Council. *City Documents,* volume 3, issues 33–49. City Council Printing Section, 1922. Accessed July 8, 2021. https://play.google.com/store/books/details/Boston_Mass_City_Council_City_Documents?id=1rJEAQAAMAAJ/.
"Broome Specialty Phonograph Records." *78RPM Club*. Accessed July 2, 2021. https://78rpm.club/record-labels/broome-special-phonograph-records/.
Brooks, Tim. *Lost Sounds: Blacks and the Birth of the Recording Industry, 1891–1922* [liner notes included with CD set]. Archeophone Records 1005. Released 2005.
Butcher, Philip, ed. *The William Stanley Braithwaite Reader*. Ann Arbor: University of Michigan Press, 1972.
Celenza, Anna. "Our jazz is culturally black, but its global dissemination owes a lot to Italians." *The Lens*, May 17, 2017. Accessed June 6, 2022. https://thelensnola.org/2017/05/01/our-jazz-is-culturally-black-but-its-global-dissemination-owes-a-lot-to-italians.
Carney, Court. *Cuttin' Up: How Early Jazz Got America's Ear*. Lawrence: University of Kansas Press, 2009.
"Castle Square Theater." *Cinema Treasures*. Accessed May 30, 2021. http://cinematreasures.org.
Chapman, Con. "Alan Dawson." Music Museum of New England. Accessed June 10, 2022. https://www.mmone.org/alan-dawson/.
Chapman, Con. *Rabbit's Blues: The Life and Music of Johnny Hodges*. Oxford: Oxford University Press, 2019.
Charters, Samuel B. and Leonard Kunstadt. *Jazz: A History of the New York Scene*. New York: Da Capo, 1981.
Chen, Jialu. "Back Where He Started." *Boston.com*. July 26, 2011.
"Chick Corea, Jazz Keyboardist born." Accessed June 12, 2022. https://aaregistry.org/story/chick-corea-jazz-keybordist-born/.
Chin, Gabriel, and John Ormonde. "The 'War' Against Chinese Restaurants." *Regulation* (Summer 2017): 32–38.
Church of God and Saints of Christ. "Leaders." Accessed July 8, 2021. https://www.cogasoc.org/leaders/.
Ciment, James. *Encyclopedia of the Jazz Age: From the End of World War I to the Great Crash,* volume one. Armonk: M. E. Sharpe Inc., 2008.
"Clarence Cameron White Papers, 1910–1940." Arthur Schomburg Center for Research in Black Culture, New York Public Library. Processed 1977.
Clarke, John Henrik, ed. *Marcus Garvey and the Vision of Africa.* Baltimore: Black Classic Press, 1974.

Condon, Eddie, and Thomas Sugrue. *We Called It Music: A Generation of Jazz*. New York: Da Capo Press, 1992.

Coffin, Sarah D., and Stephen Harrison. *The Jazz Age: American Style in the 1920s*. Cleveland Museum of Art, 2017.

Cohen, Aaron. *Move on Up: Chicago Soul Music and Black Cultural Power*. University of Chicago Press, 2019.

Concord Music Group. "Johnny Hodges." Accessed June 24, 2018. www.concordmusicgroup.com/.

Conway, Lorie. *Boston the Way It Was: Pictures and Memories from the '30s and '40s*. Boston: WGBH Educational Foundation, 1996.

Corio, Ann, and Joseph DiMona. *This Was Burlesque*. New York: Grosset & Dunlap, 1968.

Cromwell, Adelaide M. "Afterword." In *The Living is Easy,* by Dorothy West. New York: The Feminist Press at the City University of New York, 1982.

Cuddy, G. A. *Where Hash Rules: The Love Story of Charlie's Sandwich Shoppe in Boston,* 2nd edition. Self-published, 2015.

Cunniffe, Thomas. "Frankie Newton: The Forgotten Trumpeter," parts I and II. *Jazz History Online.* March 9, 2019. Accessed July 8, 2021. https://jazzhistoryonline.com/frankie-newton-1a/.

Curry, Leonard P. *The Free Black in Urban America, 1800–1850: The Shadow of the Dream*. Chicago: University of Chicago Press, 1981.

"CV Black History Makers – Paul Gonsalves (1920–1974)." The Creola Genealogist, March 4, 2018, accessed June 13, 2022. https://thecreolagenealogist.com/2018/03/04/cv-black-history-makers-paul-gonsalves-1920-1974/.

Dance, Stanley. *The World of Duke Ellington*. New York: Da Capo Press, 1970.

Dance, Stanley. *The World of Swing: An Oral History of Big Band Jazz*. New York: Da Capo Press, 1974.

Daniels, John. *In Freedom's Birthplace: A Study of the Boston Negroes.* New York: Negro Universities Press, 1968.

DeMichael, Don. "Double Play: Carney to Hodges to Ellington." *Downbeat* (June 1962). Accessed June 29, 2021. Reproduced at confabwithrab.blogspot.com.

Deffaa, Chip. *Voices of the Jazz Age.* Urbana: University of Illinois Press, 1992.

"Eddie Deas." *Discography of American Historical Recordings*. UC Santa Barbara library. Accessed July 6, 2021. https://adp.library.ucsb.edu/index.php/mastertalent/detail/101111/Deas_Eddie/.

Ehrenbold, Tobias, Jacqueline Gertner, Jessica Muttitt, and Maureen Tannetta. "Malcolm X in the Norfolk Debating Society." States of Incarceration. Accessed June 11, 2022, https://statesofincarceration.org/story/malcolm-x-norfolk-debating-society.

Eichler, Jeremy. "Ghost Opera: The Rise and Fall of the Original Boston Opera House—and the Void it Left Behind." *Boston Globe*, November 8, 2009.

Ellington, Edward Kennedy. *Music Is My Mistress*. New York: Da Capo Press, 1976.

Ellison, Ralph. "Juneteenth." *Quarterly Review of Literature* 13, no. 3–4 (1965): 274–76.

Esposito, John C. *Fire in the Grove: The Cocoanut Grove Tragedy and its Aftermath*. New York: Da Capo Press, 2005.

Feely, Abigail. "Dance, Performance." In *Encyclopedia of the Jazz Age: From the End of World War I to the Great Crash*, edited by James Ciment, 158–59. Armonk: M. E. Sharpe, Inc., 2008.

Floyd, Samuel A. Jr. *The Power of Black Music: Interpreting Its History from African to the United States*. Oxford: Oxford University Press, 1995.

"Free African American Population in the U.S.: 1790–1860," University of Virginia Library, http://fisher.lib.virginia.edu/collections/stats/histcensus/.

"From the Great Migration to Boston's Charlestown Navy Yard." Boston National Park Service. Accessed June 6, 2022. https://www.nps.gov/articles/great-migration-to-charlestown-navy-yard.htm.

Fox, Stephen R. *The Guardian of Boston: William Monroe Trotter*. New York: Atheneum, 1970.

The Frankie Newton Collection, 1929–46. Acrobat Licensing LTD. AcrobatCD9081. 2019.

Gamm, Gerald. *Urban Exodus: Why the Jews Left Boston and the Catholics Stayed*. Cambridge: Harvard University Press, 1999.

Gates, Henry Louis Jr., and Evelyn Brooks Higginbotham, eds. "Blake, Eubie," "Hall, Adelaide," and "Mack, Cecil." In *Harlem Renaissance Lives*. New York and Oxford: Oxford University Press, 2009.

Gazarik, Richard and Karen Anthony Cole. *A History of Pittsburgh Jazz*. Charleston, SC: The History Press, 2021.

"George Alan Dawson." BerkleePress.com. Accessed June 10, 2022. https://berkleepress.com/berklee-authors/alan-dawson/.

Goldberg, Jacob. "Black and White United: African American musicians and the formation of Local 802." *Allegro* CX, no. 2 (February 2010). Accessed May 29, 2022. https://www.local802afm.org/allegro/articles/black-and-white-united/.

Green, James R., and Hugh Carter Donahue. *Boston's Workers: A Labor History*. Boston: Trustees of the Public Library of the City of Boston, 1979.

Green, Martin. *The Problem of Boston: Some Readings in Cultural History*. London: Longmans, Green and Co., 1966.

Greenidge, Kerri. *Boston's Abolitionists*. Beverly, MA: Commonwealth Editions, 2006.

Greenidge, Kerri. *Black Radical: The Life and Times of William Monroe Trotter*. New York: Liveright Publishing Corporation, 2020.

Grimes, William. "Eric J. Hobsbawn." *New York Times*, October 9, 2012.

"Guide to Mildred Davenport Dance Programs." Special Collections and Archives. UCI Libraries, University of California Irvine.

Hajdu, David. "Who's Got the Blues?" *Mother Jones*, September/October 2003.

Halper, Donna L. *Boston Radio: 1920–2010*. Charleston, SC: Arcadia Publishing, 2011.

Halper, Donna. "Boston Radio in the Early 1920s." Accessed May 2021. https://www.oocities.org/.

Handlin, Oscar. *Boston's Immigrants: A Study in Acculturation*. Cambridge: The Belknap Press of Harvard University Press, 1979.

Hare, Maude Cuney. *Negro Musicians and Their Music*. New York: G. K. Hall & Co., 1996.

Harlan, Louis R. "Booker T. Washington and the Politics of Accommodation." In *Black Leaders of the Twentieth Century*, edited by John Hope Franklin and August Meier. Urbana and Chicago: University of Illinois Press, 1982.

"Harry Carney Talks to Valerie Wilmer." *Ellingtonia*, April 1964. http://www.ellingtonia.com/articles/jazz-monthly/harry-carney-talks-to-valer.html/.

Hatch, James V., and Leo Hamalian, eds. *Lost Plays of the Harlem Renaissance, 1920–1940*. Detroit: Wayne State University Press, 1996.

Hayden, Robert C. *African-Americans in Boston: More Than 350 Years*. Boston: Trustees of the Public Library of the City of Boston, 1991.

Hayden, Robert C. "Not to Be Forgotten: A Rationale." *The Art of Roland Hayes* [liner notes]. Smithsonian Collection of Recordings. CD RD041. 1990.

Heller, Michael C. *Loft Jazz: Improvising New York in the 1970s*. Oakland: University of California Press, 2017.

Hentoff, Nat. *Boston Boy*. Philadelphia: Paul Dry Books, Inc., 1986.

"History of Symphony Hall" entry in "History/Archives" of Symphony Hall. Accessed May 30, 2021. https://www.bso.org/.

Horton, James Oliver. *Free People of Color: Inside the African American Community*. Washington, DC: Smithsonian, 1993.

Horton, James Oliver, and Lois E. Horton. *Black Bostonians: Family Life and Community Struggle in the Antebellum North*. Teaneck: Holmes & Meier Publishers, 2000.

Horton, James Oliver, and Lois E. Horton. *In Hope of Liberty: Culture, Community and Protest Among Northern Free Blacks, 1700–1860*. New York: Oxford University Press, 1997.

Horton, Lois, and James Oliver Horton. "Power and Social Responsibility: Entrepreneurs and the Black Community in Antebellum Boston." In *Boston's Histories: Essays in Honor of Thomas H. O'Connor*, edited by James M. O'Toole and David Quigley, 37–51. Boston: Northeastern University Press, 2004.

Hubbert, Julie. "Jenkins Orphanage." University of South Carolina library film archive. Accessed May 30, 2021. http://www.sc.edu/orphanfilm/.

Huggins, Nathan Irvin. *Harlem Renaissance.* New York and Oxford: Oxford University Press, 1971.

Hudson, David, Marvin Bergman, and Loren Horten, eds. "Beiderbecke, Leon Bismarck 'Bix.'" In *Biographical Dictionary of Iowa.* University of Iowa Press Digital Editions. Accessed July 3, 2021. http://uipress.lib.uiowa.edu/bdi/DetailsPage.aspx?id=22/.

Hutchisson, James. "The Cradle of Jazz." *Charleston Magazine*, April 2005. Reprinted by the Jenkins Institute. Accessed July 8, 2021. https://jenkinsinstitute.org/index.php/our-history/.

"In the News: Mildred Davenport 'A Real Joy.'" *Bay State Banner*, July 5, 1973.

Jack, Gordon. "Sonny Stitt—The Early Years, 1941–1952." June 9, 2020. Accessed July 7, 2021. https://jazzprofiles.blogspot.com/2020/06/sonny-stitt-early-years-1941-1952-by.html/.

Jackson, Eric. "Riff Tide." *Boston Magazine*, May 15, 2006. https://www.bostonmagazine.com/2006/05/15/riff-tide/.

Jackson, Travis A. *Blowin' the Blues Away: Performance and Meaning on the New York Jazz Scene*. Berkeley: University of California Press, 2012.

"Jean Goldkette Orchestra." *Discography of American Historical Recordings*. UC Santa Barbara library. Accessed July 3, 2021. https://adp.library.ucsb.edu/index.php/mastertalent/detail/323277/Jean_Goldkette_Orchestra/.

Johnson, Violet Showers. *The Other Black Bostonians: West Indians in Boston, 1900–1950*. Bloomington and Indianapolis: Indiana University Press, 2006.

Kaminsky, Max. *My Life in Jazz*. New York: Harper & Row, 1965.

Kay, Jane Holtz. *Lost Boston*. Boston: Houghton Mifflin Company, 1980.

Kennedy, Lawrence W. *Planning the City upon a Hill: Boston since 1630*. Amherst: University of Massachusetts Press, 1992.

Kenney, William Howland. *Chicago Jazz: A Cultural History, 1904–1930*. New York: Oxford University Press, 1993.

Kruh, David. *Always Somethings Doing: Boston's Infamous Scollay Square*. Boston: Northeastern University Press, 1999.

Kyvig, David E. *Daily Life in the United States, 1920–1940: How Americans Lived Through the "Roaring Twenties" and the Great Depression*. Lanham: Rowman & Littlefield, 2004.

Lamb, Gregory. "Drama Unfolds." *Christian Science Monitor*, March 7, 2003.

Lasseter, M. E. *Jonkonnu, Jankunu, Junkanoo, John Canoe: Reorienting North Carolina's Practice in the American Mediterranean*. 2014. Accessed May 29, 2021. https://docsouth.unc.edu.

Lerner, Gerda. "Early Community Work of Black Club Women." *Journal of Negro History* 59, no. 2 (April 1974): 158–67.

Lewis, David Levering, ed. *The Portable Harlem Renaissance Reader*. New York: Penguin Books, 1994.

Liu, Haiming. "Chop Suey as Imagined Authentic Chinese Food." *Journal of Trans-Atlantic American Studies* (February 2009).

Locke, Alain. *The New Negro: Voices of the Harlem Renaissance*. New York: Touchstone, 1997.

"Lois Deppe: First African American Swing Band in Pittsburgh." Accessed May 2021. pittsburghmusichistory.com/.

Lopez, Cintia. "Berklee Announces End of Beantown Jazz Festival." *WBUR*, April 2, 2019.

Lugt, Mason Vander. "The *Other* Sub-Companies." *Association for Recorded Sound Collections*. Accessed May 2021. https://arsc-audio.org/.

Lyndon, Donlyn. *The City Observed: Boston, A Guide to the Architecture of the Hub*. New York: Random House, 1982.

Malcolm X. *Autobiography of Malcolm X: As Told to Alex Haley*. New York: Ballantine Books, 1992.

Malcolm X. *By Any Means Necessary (Speeches and Writings)*. New York: Pathfinder Press, 1992.

Malone, Jacqui. *Steppin' on the Blues: The Visible Rhythms of African American Dance*. Urbana and Chicago: University of Illinois Press, 1996.

Maultsby, Portia K. "Africanisms in African American Music." In *Africanisms in American Culture*, edited by Joseph Holloway, 326–49. Bloomington: Indiana University Press, 2005.

McKee, Margaret, and Fred Chisenhall. *Beale Black and Blue: Life and Music on Black America's Main Street*. Baton Rouge: Louisiana State University Press, 1981.

McNally, Owen. "Jazz In Connecticut — The Early Years." Reprinted from *The Hartford Courant* by the Hartford Jazz Society. Accessed May 31, 2022. https://hartfordjazzsociety.com/history.

McNatt, Kevin and Andrew Todesco. "Boston Tigers, New England's top African-American baseball team, met Mansfield team on diamond in 1927." WickedLocal.com, February 22, 2022. Accessed June 3, 2022. https://www.wickedlocal.com/story/journal-news-independent/2022/02/22/mansfield-took-n-e-s-top-african-american-baseball-team-1920-s/6880358001/

"Mildred Davenport, 89; Was Dancer and Member of Antibias Agency." *Boston Globe*, October 17, 1990.

Miller, Margo. "A Look Back, Forward: Jazz Dancing's Great Days." *Boston Globe*, July 20, 1969.

Miller, Neil. *Banned in Boston: The Watch and Ward Society's Crusade against Books, Burlesque, and the Social Evil.* Boston: Beacon Press, 2010.

Moonoogian, George A. "Boston Bandstand: A Musical Odyssey." *Whiskey, Women and. . .*, no. 15 (December 1985).

Morton, Patricia Hoskins. "National Negro Business League." *Encyclopedia of Alabama*. May 6, 2009. Accessed May 29, 2021. http://encyclopediaofalabama.org/.

Nash, Gary. "Forging Freedom: The Emancipation Experience in the Northern Seaport Cities, 1775–1820." In *Slavery and Freedom in the Age of the American Revolution*, edited by Ira Berlin and Ronald Hoffman. Urbana and Chicago: University of Illinois Press, 1986.

"Nuncio 'Toots' Mondello Papers." New England Conservatory Archives. Accessed July 3, 2021. https://necmusic.edu/archives/nuncio-toots-mondello/.

O'Connor, Thomas H. *The Hub: Boston Past and Present*. Boston: Northeastern University Press, 2001.

Okocha, Victor. "W. C. Handy (1873–1958)." *Blackpast*, March 19, 2007. Accessed July 2, 2021. https://www.blackpast.org/african-american-history/handy-w-c-1873-1958/.

O'Toole, James M. "Portrait of a Parish: Race, Ethnicity and Class in Boston's Cathedral of the Holy Cross, 1865–1880." In *Boston's Histories: Essays in Honor of Thomas H. O'Connor*, edited by James M. O'Toole and David Quigley, 92–112. Boston: Northeastern University Press, 2004.

Peretti, Burton W. *The Creation of Jazz: Music, Race, and Culture in Urban America.* Urbana: University of Illinois Press, 1992.

Perry, Jeffrey B. *Hubert Harrison: The Voice of Harlem Radicalism, 1883–1918*. New York: Columbia University Press, 2009.

Pleck, Elizabeth H. *Black Migration and Poverty: Boston 1865–1900*. New York: Academic Press, 1979.

Powell, Richard J., and Virginia M. Mecklenburg. *African-American Art: Harlem Renaissance Civil Rights Era and Beyond*. New York: Skira Rizzoli Publications, 2012.

Powers, Richard. "Dances of the Jazz Age." Webpage for class in Social Dance at Stanford University. Accessed May 31, 2021. https://socialdance.stanford.edu/.

Reney, Tom. "Duke Ellington's Boston." New England Public Radio. April 29, 2014. Accessed July 6, 2021. https://digital.nepr.net/music/2014/04/29/duke-ellingtons-boston/.

Richmond, Clint. *Political Places of Boston*. Brookline, MA: Muddy River Press, 2004.

Robinson, Stephen. "Basketball in 1920s Harlem," Digital Harlem Blog, June 3, 2011, accessed June 12, 2022. https://drstephenrobertson.com/digitalharlemblog/maps/basketball-in-1920s-harlem/.

Rogers, J. A. "Jazz at Home." In *The New Negro: Voices of the Harlem Renaissance*, edited by Alain Locke, 665–67. New York: Touchstone, 1997.

Roses, Lorraine Elena. *Black Bostonians and the Politics of Culture, 1920–1940*. Amherst and Boston: University of Massachusetts Press, 2017.

Rust, Brian. *The American Dance Band Discography, 1917–1942*. New York: Arlington House Publishers, 1975.

"Sacco and Vanzetti: Justice on Trial." Commonwealth of Massachusetts website. Accessed June 6, 2022. https://www.mass.gov/info-details/sacco-vanzetti-justice-on-trial.

Sammarco, Anthony Mitchell. *Boston's South End*. Charleston, SC: Arcadia Publishing, 2005.

Sandiford, Preston. "Through the Years with Preston Sandiford." Interview by Dan Kochakian. *Whiskey, Women and . . .* (December 1985).

Schneider, Mark R. *Boston Confronts Jim Crow, 1890–1920*. Boston: Northeastern University Press, 1997.

Schorow, Stephanie. *Drinking Boston: A History of the City and Its Spirits*. Wellesley, MA: Union Park Press, 2012.

Scott, Carole. "The History of the Radio Industry in the United States to 1940." Accessed May 2021. https://eh.net/encyclopedia.org/.

Shand-Tucci, Douglass. *Built in Boston: City and Suburb, 1800–1950*. Amherst: University of Massachusetts Press, 1988.

Simas, Art. *Boston's Blues*. Boston: 1st Book Library, 2002.

Singer, Arthur, and Ron Goodman. *Boston's Downtown Movie Palaces*. Charleston, SC: Arcadia Publishing, 2011.

Southern, Eileen. *The Music of Black Americans: A History*. New York: W. W. Norton and Company, 1983.

Spencer, Frederick Jr. *Jazz and Death: Medical Profiles of Jazz Greats*, 63–70. Jackson: University of Mississippi Press, 2002.

Stewart, Rex. *Boy Meets Horn*. Ann Arbor: University of Michigan Press, 1991.

Stryker, Mark. *Jazz from Detroit*. Ann Arbor: The University of Michigan Press, 2019.

Stuckey, Sterling. *Slave Culture: Nationalist Theory & the Foundations of Black America*. New York and Oxford: Oxford University Press, 1987.

"The Shepard Company" [landmarks study]. *Rhode Island Historical Preservation Commission*. 1975. www.preservation.ri.gov/.

Suisman, David. "Co-Workers in the Kingdom of Culture." *Journal of American Music* (March 2004): 1296.

Sullivan, Jerome. "Late-Night Merrymaking Ended in Tragedy 50 Years Ago Today." *Boston Globe*, July 4, 1975.

Sutton, Allan. "Boston Talking Machine Company and the Little Wonder Phonograph (1910–1913)." Mainspring Press, November 28, 2017. Accessed May 2021. https://78records.wordpress.com/.

Tamarkin, Jeff. "Boston Pianist Al Vega." *Jazztimes*, April 25, 2019.

Temin, Peter, ed. *Engines of Enterprise: An Economic History of New England*. Cambridge: Harvard University Press, 2000.

Thernstrom, Stephan. *The Other Bostonians: Poverty and Progress in the American Metropolis, 1880–1970*. Cambridge: Harvard University Press, 1999.

Thompson, John. "Fraternal Orders." Oklahoma Historical Society. Accessed May 30, 2021. https://www.okhistory.org/.

Thompson, Robert Farris. *Flash of the Spirit: African & Afro-American Art & Philosophy*. New York: Vintage Books, 1984.

To, Wing-Kai. "Restoring Chinese Heritage in Boston's History." *Bridgewater Review* (December 2008): 3–5.

"Tremont Theater." African American Trail Project. Tufts University, 2021. Accessed July 2, 2021. https://africanamericantrailproject.tufts.edu/.

Ulanov, Barry. *Duke Ellington*. New York: Da Capo Press, 1975.

Vacca, Richard. *The Boston Jazz Chronicles: Faces, Places, and Nightlife, 1937–1962*. Belmont, MA: Troy Street Publishing, 2012.

Vacca, Richard. "Perley Breed's Department Store Dance Band." *Troy Street Observer*, April 30, 2013. Accessed July 5, 2021. https://www.richardvacca.com/on-april-25-1925/.

Vandermark, Stu. "History—Major Contributors." *Boston Jazz Scene*. Accessed July 8, 2021. https://bostonjazzscene.blogspot.com.

"The Victor-Victrola Page." Accessed May 2021. http://www.victor-victrola.com/.

Vincent, Ted. "The Window of Opportunity." *The Black Scholar* 22, no. 4, Black Culture 1992 (Fall 1992): 6–16.

Vinylmint [username]. "History of the Record Industry, 1877–1920s." *Medium*. Accessed June 29, 2021. https://medium.com/@Vinylmint/history-of-the-record-industry-1920-1950s-6d491d7cb606/.

Warner, Sam Bass Jr. *Streetcar Suburbs: The Process of Growth in Boston, 1870–1900*. Cambridge: Harvard University Press, 1978.

Wein, George. *Myself Among Others: A Life in Music*. New York: Da Capo Press, 2003.

West, Dorothy. *The Living is Easy*. New York: The Feminist Press at the City University of New York, 1982.

White, Bo. "Sonny Stitt is the Lone Wolf: Saginaw Jazz Icon Up Close and Personal." January 22, 2013. Accessed July 7, 2021. https://whitesbarnews.blogspot.com/2013/01/sonny-stitt-is-lone-wolf-saginaw-jazz.html/.

Wilson, Teddy with Arie Ligthart and Humphrey van Loo. *Teddy Wilson Talks Jazz.* New York: Continuum, 1996.

Wolfe, Albert Benedict. *The Lodging House Problem in Boston*. London: Forgotten Books, 2012.

Woods, Robert A., ed. *Americans in Process: A Settlement Study (North and West Ends Boston).* New York: Arno Press and The New York Times, 1970.

Woods, Robert A., ed. *The City Wilderness: A Settlement Study (South End Boston).* New York: Garrett Press, 1970.

"Worth Reading and Hearing: "The Blue Sky Boys" and "Black Swans."" Mainspring Press, December 11, 2019. Accessed June 12, 2022. https://78records.wordpress.com/tag/broome-special-phonograph-records/.

Yanow, Scott. "Jean Goldkette—Artist Biography." *Allmusic.com*. Accessed July 3, 2021. https://www.allmusic.com/artist/jean-goldkette-mn0000224739/biography/.

MULTIMEDIA

The YouTube web addresses to jazz recordings and video clips relevant to Boston's history are listed below in their order of inclusion.

"I'm Shoutin' Again—Count Basie." Uploaded to YouTube by "johnnystaccata," May 22, 2018. Accessed July 11, 2021. https://www.youtube.com/watch?v=8LQe5JG70mk/.

Bert Williams. "Nobody," recorded May 22, 1905. Uploaded by "Remember Our Music." Accessed July 8, 2021. https://www.youtube.com/watch?v=LGnlmWTNBbk/.

Clarence Cameron White. "Chant." *The Bandanna Sketches*, recorded 1921. Performed by The Paragon Ragtime Orchestra, Rick Benjamin, director, *Black Manhattan* vol. 3 (2019). Accessed July 8, 2021. https://www.youtube.com/watch?v=u8H1A7wkDkl/.

James Reese Europe's 369th U.S. Infantry "Hell Fighters" Band. "The Darktown Strutters' Ball." The Orchard Enterprises (January 2015). Accessed June 20, 2021. https://www.youtube.com/watch?v=HwkisCEOndo/.

"James Reese Europe." Alabama Public Television (2019). Accessed June 20, 2021. https://www.youtube.com/watch?v=sjYHrsD-oZU/.

Ron Herd, producer. "Jazz Great Roy Haynes" [podcast]. *W.E. A.L.L. B.E. News*, March 20, 2016.

"1928—Jenkins Orphanage band—outtakes." Moving Image Research Collections, producer. April 2020. Accessed June 24, 2021. https://www.youtube.com/watch?v=W7QUH_1D4Ys/.

Georgia Cotton Pickers (led by George Tynes). "Louisiana Bo Bo." Recorded 1930, Harmony 1127-H. Uploaded to YouTube by Tim Gracyk, August 17, 2019. https://www.youtube.com/watch?v=8fWXV3uQ6pU/.

"1936 Mal Hallett: In The Chapel In The Moonlight (Jerry Perkins & chorus, vocal)." Uploaded to YouTube by the78profto, May 3, 2019. https://www.youtube.com/watch?v=qdy3WUDdo4E/.

"Teddy Grace w/ Mal Hallett & His Orchestra." Uploaded to YouTube by derekbjenkins, October 3, 2007. https://www.youtube.com/watch?v=ehqGJ3I3ra4/.

"Eubie Blake and his 'Shuffle Along' Orchestra—Bandana Days (1921)." Uploaded to YouTube by ASACurator, January 2021. Accessed July 2, 2021. https://www.youtube.com/watch?v=SmsTrhxQTGI/.

"Jan. 5, 1923 recording 'Aunt Hagar's Blues' W C Handy's Orchestra." Uploaded to YouTube by Remember Our Music, January 5, 2017. Accessed July 2, 2021. https://www.youtube.com/watch?v=AiAV7ogRujw/.

"American Tenor Roland Hayes: Two Songs (1942)." Uploaded to YouTube by CurzonRoad, July 30, 2013. Accessed July 2, 2021. https://www.youtube.com/watch?v=qWqkb4alznI/.

"Nobody's Sweetheart—Eddie Condon's Chicagoans." Uploaded to YouTube by Godfrey Daniels, April 26, 2014. Accessed July 3, 2021. https://www.youtube.com/watch?v=DALWy2H5VTg.

"A 1920s Charleston." Uploaded to YouTube by Vintage Swing Dance, April 19, 2016. Accessed July 5, 2021. https://www.youtube.com/watch?v=2npKAlQnDJY/.

"Leo Reisman RHYTHMS." Uploaded to YouTube by Ugaccio, November 12, 2013. Accessed July 5, 2021. https://www.youtube.com/watch?v=6GGA9uK93m8/.

"Paul Whiteman—Mississippi Mud 1928 Bix Beiderbecke (Bing Crosby & Irene Taylor)." Uploaded to YouTube by Warholsoup 100, February 23, 2020. Accessed July 6, 2021. https://www.youtube.com/watch?v=_NoQaQ5aP5M/.

"Jes Shufflin' by Eddie Deas and His Boston Brownies 1932 Victor." Uploaded to YouTube by SMARBA100, August 25, 2019. Accessed July 6, 2021. https://www.youtube.com/watch?v=E-tDNpqsXpg/.

"Sabby Lewis Orchestra—Bottoms Up." Uploaded to YouTube by Richard Vacca, December 17, 2013. Accessed July 7, 2021. https://www.youtube.com/watch?v=btB1zQlgqyk/.

"Sonny Stitt—Jazz at the Hi-Hat Volume 1." Uploaded to YouTube by StittMoSh!t, August 17, 2020. Accessed July 7, 2021. https://www.youtube.com/watch?v=SPfCdbGNiHk/.

"My Bucket's Got a Hole in It—Fat Man Robinson Quintet." Uploaded to YouTube by Richard Vacca, November 17, 2020. Accessed July 7, 2021. https://www.youtube.com/watch?v=okWxdqzWBac/.

DISCOGRAPHY

Representative albums on the jazz and cultural history of Boston are included below.

"The Art of Roland Hayes," with Reginald Boardman (piano). Smithsonian Collection of Recordings B0000017SF, 2007.

"Boston Bounce." Sabby Lewis Orchestra and Sextet. Phoenix Jazz B0023VXIEO, 1975.

"The Boston Bust-Out." Nat Pierce and His Orchestra. HEP Records HEP CD 13, 1995.

"Sonny Stitt—Jazz at the Hi-Hat." Roulette Jazz CD. Original recording 1954.

"Scandalous Mayor." Thomas Lennon, producer. *The American Experience*. Boston: WGBH and PBS Video, 1991.